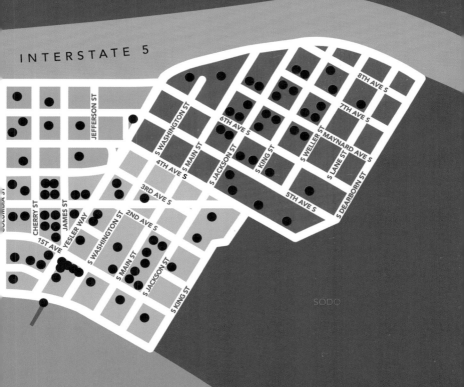

SEATTLE ARCHITECTURE
A WALKING GUIDE TO DOWNTOWN

AUTHOR
Maureen R. Elenga

EDITORIAL BOARD
Sydney W. Dobson, MNPL
Dan Fernandez
Victoria Gless
Chris King
Ted Sive, FSMPS

PHOTOGRAPHY EDITOR
Roger Williams, FAIA

BOOK DESIGNER
Christina E. Merkelbach

SEATTLE ARCHITECTURE
A WALKING GUIDE TO DOWNTOWN

ADVISORY COMMITTEE
Sydney W. Dobson, MNPL
Dan Fernandez
Sonja Sokol Fürész
Victoria Gless
Heather Hargesheimer, AIA
Chris King
Emily Li
Allen R. Sandico
Mimi Sheridan, AICP
Ted Sive, FSMPS
Cary M. Stitt
Robert Tindall, AIA
Roger Williams, FAIA

AND FOR THEIR EARLY SUPPORT
Joseph Balachowksi
Gary Fuller
Kitty Wong

SEATTLE ARCHITECTURE FOUNDATION
DESIGN SHAPES PEOPLE + PEOPLE SHAPE DESIGN

© 2007, Seattle Architecture Foundation, Seattle WA
Printed in Canada
Designed by Christina Merkelbach

Second Printing, 2008

Library of Congress Control Number: 2007901443

ISBN 978-0-615-14129-9

Printed in Canada

Distributed by University of Washington Press
P.O. Box 50096
Seattle, WA 98145-5096
www.washington.edu/uwpress

Seattle Architecture Foundation
1333 Fifth Avenue, Suite 300
Seattle, WA 98101
206-667-9184
www.seattlearchitecture.org

CONTENTS

ACKNOWLEDGEMENTS

Seattle Architecture Foundation (SAF) is a nonprofit organization dedicated to connecting people to the profound influence of design and inspiring them to engage in shaping their communities. SAF is grateful to Maureen Elenga for selecting this project for her University of Washington Department of Art History Master's practicum and to Cary Stitt for selecting this project as a way to honor the memory of his partner, Keith M. Pegorsch, AIA. This guidebook would not have been possible without their commitments.

SEATTLE ARCHITECTURE FOUNDATION

Many dedicated and generous individuals contributed to the production of this guidebook. The Guidebook Advisory Committee and Editorial Board were a continuing source of support, offering their time, energy and constructive criticism over the course of two years. Special thanks to SAF Director Sydney Dobson for planning this project and bringing this dynamic group together.

Jeffrey Karl Ochsner and Mimi Sheridan provided guidance throughout the production of the text; their contributions and insight were invaluable.

Roger Williams and Dennis Haskell donated hours behind the camera to complete the inventory of images for this book. Many thanks as well to the architecture firms, property owners and managers that donated images from their private collections; they are acknowledged individually in the photo credits.

Christina Merkelbach is not only a very patient and talented book designer, but she generously provided consultation on the process of producing this book. I am also very grateful to Dan Fernandez, who donated time copyediting and proofreading the final text.

For much of the information provided in this book I am indebted to previous scholarship by historians and critics, including: Dennis Andersen; Mildred Tanner Andrews; Walt Crowley; Paul Dorpat; Lawrence Kreisman; Roger Montgomery; Jeffrey Karl Ochsner; Roger Sale; Caroline Tobin; Sally Woodbridge; the Seattle Department of Neighborhoods; and through research carried out by Seattle Architecture Foundation volunteers, who have contributed to the production of the downtown tours series. Among them are: Joseph Balachowski; Marlene Chen; Steve Erickson; Randy Everett; Gary Fuller; Elaine Gagnon; Richard Jost; Chris King; Lawrence Kreisman; Clarence Kwan; Guy Michaelsen; Julie Montgomery; Jason Morse; Robert S. Purser; David Rash; Aaron Raymond; Mimi Sheridan; Sybrina Soga; William Strong; and Wendi Walsh.

And finally, a very big thank you to the Seattle Architecture Foundation's Emeritus Directors for their efforts in raising the funds to cover the production costs of this book.

MAUREEN R. ELENGA

DONORS

NESHOLM FAMILY FOUNDATION

SCLATER PARTNERS ARCHITECTS

**KEITH M. PEGORSCH AIA
MEMORIAL FUND**
AIA Seattle
Donald J. Best, Jr.
Harley Buyert and Thomas R. Foley
Callison Architecture
Keith's Team at Callison
Lynne Carroll
Martha Clarkson and Jim Carpenter
Katrina and Chris Cooper
Craft Architects, PLLC
Karen S. Dickinson
John R. Dilges
Sydney W. Dobson
Maureen R. Elenga
Louise W. Foley
Gena and Dennis Grelis
Christopher Hamilton
George Hein & Don Barr
V. Pauline Hodges
Dysa Kafoury
Sarah Kirk
Chris and Patti Kopcsak
Joe and Ilse Kosobucki
Kathleen Conway Maurel
Christina Merkelbach
Tom and Carol Meyer
Peggy H. Meyer
Susan Palermo
Sherry Paulsen
Kent, Bernadette, Charles, and Joe
  Pegorsch
Allen R. Sandico
Anthony Sano and Terry Vechazone
Ted Sive & Ted Kennedy Watson
Kathy Stanaway
Cary M. Stitt
Valerie and John Switzer
F. Steven Trevallee

Gary J. Wakatsuki
Wells Fargo Bank, Corporate
  Properties Group
Wells Fargo Team: Joe Weber,
  Peggi Hawes, Gary Gerard, Liz
  Newhouse, Chris Morrison,
  John Glover and Tom Dawes
Eugene Zavala and Elizabeth Zavala

**SEATTLE ARCHITECTURE
FOUNDATION EMERITUS
DIRECTORS FUND**
James R. Duncan & Sparling
Thom Emrich
Susan and Frank Finneran
Bill, Lindy and Louisa Gaylord
Robert Hull FAIA
Phillip L. Jacobson FAIA
Judsen Marquardt FAIA
Mary Kae McCullough
Alan Sclater FAIA
Michael Scott AIA
Mitchell C. Smith
Unico Properties LLC
Roger B. Williams FAIA

**EXTRAORDINARY IN-KIND
CONTRIBUTIONS**
Maureen R. Elenga
Dan Fernandez
Dennis Haskell FAIA
Christina Merkelbach
Mimi Sheridan
Roger B. Williams FAIA

DEDICATION

This book is dedicated to the memory of **KEITH M. PEGORSCH, AIA**.

A child and product of the heartland, Keith lived in and loved Seattle for the last two decades of his life. Keith was a guy of little pretense, an architect who loved his profession because it combines beauty and practicality, style and substance. He was quiet and disciplined, and when you got him talking, a man of opinion and articulate feeling. He was a model seen less and less these days: a renaissance architect, one who worked a project from the very beginning to the very end, in detail, with a rare calm, thoroughness, and responsibility. He loved the complexity of architecture, the puzzle of finding the solution to a complex program, of making all the parts and pieces work. And he loved looking at the results.

Keith also enjoyed giving tours of Seattle architecture. Part civic booster, part teacher, part impassioned lover of design, he would take folk to his favorite buildings, like the Rainier Tower with its intriguing base or the Exchange Building and its deco glory.

As that tour guide, as that architect, and as a citizen in a democratic society, Keith was engaged. This book—about engaging residents and visitors in the buildings and design of Seattle—celebrates that spirit. We hope you, the reader, will look around a bit differently walking down the street or speak up about a proposed project in your city. Keith would definitely applaud that.

Keith would have loved the grass-roots manner in which this book has come to be. It has been the effort of a diverse and energetic group, individuals who share love for our city, see it in a variety of ways, and want to engage with others in learning and talking about the built environment.

On Keith's behalf, I thank those many people who worked and gave time to this effort. And on their behalf—and my own—thanks, Keith, for being our inspiration.

TED SIVE
SEATTLE, WA
SEPTEMBER 2006

FOREWORD

Athens, the Parthenon...Beijing, the Forbidden City...Rome, the Coliseum...Paris, the Eiffel Tower...New York, Central Park...dramatic illustrations of the connection between architecture and place. Cities and even entire cultures are defined by their architecture.

The design of a city can tell us of its founding, growth, commerce and the culture of its people. This perspective into the soul of a city tells of its past and can provide the opportunity to glimpse its future. The decisions we make today about the built environment will shape our lives for decades. Thoughtful architecture and design improves quality of life and becomes a catalyst around which a city can affirm its course for the future.

We're often not fully aware of the design that surrounds our daily lives. Places we regularly experience have new meaning when we learn the forces that shaped them, and how the resulting design influences our mind-set and behavior. Without appreciation for the design that shapes our lives, how can we make good decisions about places and issues that will shape our city's future? Therein lies the mission of the Seattle Architecture Foundation (SAF).

Through volunteer-orchestrated Architecture Tours, Youth Programs, Exhibits, a wide variety of Special Events, and this Guidebook, SAF educates and inspires people to engage in shaping their communities. We encourage you to visit our website to learn more about our programs (www.seattlearchitecture.org) and to get involved with SAF as a participant, volunteer or supporter.

Seattle's quality of life depends on people like you getting involved in community design decisions, both big and seemingly small. Involvement takes many forms, from participation in a design review process, to actively advocating sound financial and planning priorities from our leaders. Your participation helps ensure that our city is a reflection of our community's culture and values.

As you read this book, and walk our city, we hope you gain insight into Seattle's soul, both where we started and how we've matured. More importantly, we hope you'll be asking questions about Seattle's future. What might projects like Seattle's Central Library and the SAM's Olympic Sculpture Park say about where the city is heading? What type of civic quality and character will emerge as our waterfront undergoes inevitable change? Whether a resident of our city or a visitor, we hope you'll find yourself inspired to engage in shaping your community for the better.

So...read on, enjoy, and take a walk downtown....

GUY MICHAELSEN
PRESIDENT,
SEATTLE ARCHITECTURE FOUNDATION BOARD OF DIRECTORS

HOW TO USE THIS BOOK

ORGANIZATION

Seattle Architecture: A Walking Guide to Downtown opens with a historical overview and timeline featuring the people and events that have shaped the Seattle that we know today. The guidebook is divided into nine tours beginning where Seattle did, at Pioneer Square, and ending at Seattle Center, the location of the futuristic-themed Century 21, 1962 World's Fair. To help you navigate the book, each tour is color coded:

1. Pioneer Square
2. International District
3. Civic & Financial District
4. Retail District
5. West Edge
6. Pike Place Market
7. Waterfront
8. Belltown
9. Seattle Center

The front flap folds out, providing a comprehensive map of all nine tours.

Each tour is accompanied by an introduction and area map with points of interest identified by numbers that correspond to that of the individual entries. Tour routes are not explicitly provided, but are suggested by the ordering of the points of interest. These suggested routes, for the most part, follow a north-south direction to ease traversing Seattle's steep slopes.

Each entry in this guidebook is organized with a heading, photograph, and a paragraph or more of text. The heading provides name, date, name of designer, historic landmark designation, where applicable, and address. The name listed first is the current building name; the historical name of the building (where applicable) is provided in parentheses. The date given is the date of the completion of construction. Some dates may disagree with those found in previous guidebooks reflecting new research. Every effort was made to achieve a very high level of accuracy; dates are generally based on evidence found in primary sources. Dates that could not be precisely confirmed are preceded by "ca." The date of completion is followed by the name of the architect (or firm) as known at the time of the project. If the architect is not local, the city in which the architect was based is provided in parentheses. If the name of the architect or designer could not be determined, the listing indicates that the name is unknown (however, future research may uncover these architects' names). Some buildings have complex histories, so more than one architect may be listed; where this occurs, the names of the architects are presented in chronological order—the earliest appears first, and those responsible for later renovations or additions follow. In some cases, other consultants such as engineers and/or landscape architects are included as well. The addresses provided are current street names. The body of each entry generally provides the following information in the order listed below, where applicable:

Physical description
Materials
Structural information
Historical significance or significance to pattern of development
Other information connected with a building may be provided as well.

This book does not aim to make critical evaluations of the buildings presented, but rather to give accurate descriptions and information about them and their relationship to the development of Seattle's built environment. Although architecturally significant buildings are included, points of interests have also been selected for their historical significance or significance to the development of Seattle or their neighborhood in particular, or as examples of a particular period style or architectural trend.

LANDMARK DESIGNATION, NATIONAL REGISTER LISTING, HISTORIC DISTRICT LISTING, AND NATIONAL HISTORIC LANDMARK DESIGNATION

If a building has been designated a "Landmark" by the City of Seattle, the ¶ icon appears at the end of its heading. If a building is listed in the National Register of Historic Places, a **¶** icon is used.

Three historic districts are described in this book: the Pioneer Square Historic District; the International Special Review District; and the Pike Place Market. The appearance and/or historical integrity of structures and public spaces within each district are regulated locally by a citizen's board in accordance with processes and criteria established by the city.

Although the three historic districts in this book are designated as local historic districts and included as historic districts in the National Register, the boundaries recognized by the local designation and National Register differ. Therefore the chapters in this book are not arranged strictly according to district boundaries. In the rare instance that a building is inside a historic district but not within the district chapter, its inclusion within the boundaries of a historic district is noted in the text.

"National Historic Landmarks" are nationally significant historic places designated by the Secretary of Interior because they possess exceptional value or quality in illustrating or interpreting the heritage of the United States. While there are over 80,000 sites on the National Register, fewer than 2,500 historic places are designated as National Historic Landmarks. As noted in the text, four National Historic Landmarks are included in this book–the Panama Hotel in the International District and the Pioneer Building, pergola and totem pole in Pioneer Square.

GETTING AROUND DOWNTOWN SEATTLE

Downtown Seattle's Streets are named and run east-west; Avenues are numbered and run north-south, with the exception of Western Avenue; Elliott Avenue; and in the International District and Pioneer Square Historic Districts, which have some named Avenues.

King County Metro Transit offers free bus rides within downtown Seattle between 6 a.m. and 7 p.m., daily. The Ride Free Area extends north to Battery Street; south to S. Jackson Street; and east at 6th Avenue to the waterfront (routes 116, 118 and 119 are not included in the Ride Free Area).

Although there are plenty of coffee shops and restaurants along the way, it would be quite a feat to cover all the tours on a one-day excursion. We suggest taking this book along while exploring downtown Seattle over the course of a visit, or at leisure if you are lucky enough to live here.

Please note that many of the buildings in this guidebook are privately owned. Inclusion of buildings in this guidebook does not indicate any right of access to any property.

SAF offers many guided architectural tours of downtown Seattle and neighborhoods, as well as other programs. Check them out at www.seattlearchitecture.org.

We hope you enjoy these tours and our wonderful city.

SEATTLE ARCHITECTURE FOUNDATION

HISTORICAL OVERVIEW

Since the 1980s Seattle has been touted as one of the nation's most livable cities. The 3.5 million people who live in the greater Seattle area (580,000 in the Seattle metropolitan area) enjoy a mild climate, outstanding natural beauty and recreational activities offered by mountain ranges, the waters of Puget Sound and several lakes and rivers. But to the settlers who established Seattle, many of its physical features were obstacles to the growth of their city. It took a great deal of hard work, engineering, civic and business leadership, perseverance and more than a little luck to build the city we know today.

The earliest inhabitants of the Seattle area were members of the Coastal Salish tribes, who over thousands of years developed a rich and complex culture. They lived in villages and encampments along Elliott Bay, Lake Union and the Duwamish River, fishing, hunting and gathering, and leaving little imprint on their physical environment. Their villages consisted of one or more small cedar plank houses with bare earth floors, as well as longhouses, some measuring up to 640 feet long and 60 feet wide. These longhouses were used for important community events and potlatches, but were also lived in by up to 200 people. None of their structures has survived the region's damp climate and subsequent Euro-American settlement.

The first European to navigate the waters of Puget Sound was Captain George Vancouver, who anchored off Bainbridge Island in 1792. He named the body of water for his Second Lieutenant, Peter Puget. They conducted a survey of the waterways but did not make ground at the future site of Seattle. In 1824 a group of Hudson's Bay Company explorers passed through mapping trade routes. Lieutenant George Wilkes surveyed the waters of Puget Sound for the U.S. Navy in 1841, naming Elliott Bay for his onboard chaplain, Reverend J.L. Elliott.

By the mid-1840s the Oregon Territory south of the Columbia River was attracting wagon train pioneers who established farms in the Willamette Valley. Several early towns competed to become the preeminent city of the Pacific Northwest, including Portland, Astoria and Oregon City. Euro-American settlement north of the Columbia River was delayed by the northern border dispute between the United States and Britain, from which emerged the rallying cry "54-40 or fight!" When the issue was resolved in 1846, and the border was established at the 49th parallel, the Puget Sound region was open for settlement.

Small communities were established along the Sound by people attracted to the vast stands of old-growth timber, but more settlers were drawn to the southeastern area of the Washington Territory for the transportation link provided by the Columbia River and its rich, flat farmland. The first settlers in the area of Elliott Bay were drawn to the area of the Duwamish and White rivers for farming in September 1851. But the party that arrived

Yesler's cookhouse located at his mill was Seattle's first public gathering space.

in November 1851, led by Arthur Denny, was not looking for farm land; they aimed to build a city.

There were a dozen adults and ten children aboard the schooner *Exact* when it landed at what is now West Seattle on November 13, 1851. Among them were people whose names are attached to many Seattle streets, schools and parks today: Denny, Boren, Bell, Terry, and others. They were joined by David Denny and Lee Terry, who had preceded them by two months, and had summoned them to settle here. The Denny party quickly established relations with the native people, who helped them through that damp and difficult first winter. The party named their settlement New York Alki, which in Chinook trade jargon means, "New York By and By." They had every hope that theirs would be the "Queen City" of the Pacific Northwest.

In February 1852, Arthur Denny, Carson Boren and William Bell plumbed Elliott Bay with a horseshoe tied to a laundry line and found deep, protected waters near its eastern shore, a location more suited to their ambitions. They landed at what is now the base of Washington Street and beheld the site of tideflats to the south and steep hills to the north and east and a grassy marsh separated from the bay by a narrow peninsula. They had only a small area of flat, dry land on which to build, but they eagerly set about staking their claims and promoting their town, which they called Duwamps. David "Doc" Maynard relocated his store from the Olympia area to the settlement when the settlers moved from Alki to their claims in April 1852, and was fortunately able to convince them to change the name to Seattle, a variation on the name of his friend, Chief Sealth, leader of the Duwamish and Suquamish people.

Seattle's first major boost came in October 1852, when the settlers convinced Henry Yesler to make their village the location of the region's first steam-powered sawmill, initiating exportation of lumber, Seattle's first industry. Henry Yesler constructed a cookhouse at his mill, which became Seattle's first public gathering place and the center of all village activity. Construction of wharves soon followed and a "mosquito fleet" of small boats based in Seattle began transporting mail, goods and people to the settlements along the inland waters of Puget Sound and the San Juan Islands.

Relations with local native people were generally good; however, settlers in Thurston and south King Counties were attacked in October 1855 by Native Americans who were angered by the treaties forced upon them by the territorial government. After a number of skirmishes over the following months, friendly tribes warned the settlers of Seattle that a raid was coming their way. The warning gave them time to take shelter when the attack came on January 25, 1856. The village was protected by cannon fire from the Navy gunship Decatur and the "Battle of Seattle," as it came to be known, ended after one day.

The remoteness of Puget Sound and the lack of both road and railroad connections as well as fear of further Native American attacks stunted Seattle's growth in the 1850s. In the 1860s, the Civil War slowed western expansion and by 1862, Seattle's population had reached only 182. The economy was sustained by maritime trade in lumber and salmon during the early decades of slow growth.

The early built form of Seattle consisted of simple wood frame vernacular structures, including one- and two-story gabled houses and false-front businesses lining Front Street (now First Avenue). The one exception was the Territorial University Building, a two-story Classical Revival building with a large portico supported by four ionic columns, which was constructed northeast of the center of town on "Denny's Knoll" in 1861.

In 1864, President Abraham Lincoln signed a bill that granted a charter to the Northern Pacific to build a railroad along a northern route from Lake Superior to Puget Sound. Seattle, Olympia, Tacoma and virtually every other town along the Sound competed for selection as the terminus of the line. Seattle, with its location due east of the lowest pass through the Cascade Mountains and on the central Sound, firmly believed that it would be chosen. The announcement in 1873 that the Northern Pacific had selected Tacoma as their terminus was a major setback.

Rather than waste their energy on disappointment and anger, the settlers decided in 1875 to build their own line, the Seattle & Walla Walla. But instead of reaching Walla Walla, the line went only as far as the recently discovered coal fields 16 miles south, near Renton. Coal exportation provided another important boost to Seattle's economy, which was soon further diversified by the ship-building industry. The population grew from 1,170 in 1870 to 3,533 in 1880.

Financial troubles plagued the Northern Pacific and completion of the transcontinental line was delayed. Finally, in 1884, after Henry Villard had taken over the railroad, Tacoma became the terminus of a line that ran from Minnesota to Portland, then north to Tacoma and Seattle. Speculation had precipitated Seattle's first real estate boom beginning in 1882, which lasted until Villard's railroad empire crashed in 1884. After 1884,

Northern Pacific interests favored Tacoma and rail service to Seattle was so inconvenient and intermittent and the track so poorly maintained that the line was thereafter nicknamed the "Orphan Road."

An earmark of culture among pioneer cities, the arrival of professional architects (who then often emerged from the building trade rather than academic training), came with the first real estate boom. Downtown Seattle took on a grander scale and appearance with elaborate wood and brick Victorian buildings up to four stories in height. In 1884, George Frye constructed an opulent opera house, designed by John Nestor, on Front and Marion Streets, a testament to Seattle's early cultural development. Cable car and streetcar lines were also introduced, facilitating the development of neighborhoods along their routes outside of downtown.

In 1885, Seattle business leaders John Leary, Daniel Gilman and Judge Thomas Burke incorporated the Seattle, Lake Shore & Eastern Railway to once again attempt to establish a line over the Cascades to Spokane and Walla Walla. Meanwhile, by 1887, the Northern Pacific line was completed across Stampede Pass, further boosting Puget Sound ports and initiating a second real estate boom.

Although the Seattle, Lake Shore & Eastern Railway failed to cross the mountains, the little line did provide additional transportation links for Seattle industries between the waterfront and locations along lakes Union and Washington and east to Snoqualmie Falls. Judge Burke's tenacity in building the Seattle, Lake Shore & Eastern Railway caught the attention of James J. Hill, who had consolidated control of several railroads to create the Great Northern. Hill retained Burke as his attorney in 1889 to assist him in securing a right-of-way and making Seattle the West Coast terminus of his line. By 1893, Seattle would finally gain competitive transcontinental railroad service.

But Hill's selection of Seattle was not the only event that would shape the city and spark growth in 1889. At 2:45 p.m., on June 6, a glue pot boiled over in a cabinet maker's shop located on the southwest corner of what are now First Avenue and Madison Street, igniting wood shavings and sawdust. The fire destroyed the building and, pushed by winds from the northwest, quickly consumed the entire block before jumping across the street to the Frye Opera House. From there the conflagration moved south into the commercial core. By the time the fire was out, it had consumed over thirty blocks and destroyed downtown Seattle.

Fortunately, Seattle was enjoying a prosperous time when the fire struck and the citizens resolved to rebuild. Banker Jacob Furth proclaimed that the disaster would in short time be viewed as a benefit to the city, which he was confident could be rebuilt to a higher standard within 18 months. Indeed, construction began in less than a month under a new building ordinance that mandated buildings of brick, stone, iron and heavy timber in the commercial core. Merchants operated out of tents during reconstruction, announcing optimism with the pun, "our business is in-tents!"

The fire brought on an unprecedented construction boom, as well as improvements to infrastructure, including sewer and water systems and street widening, realignment and regrading. The new downtown that emerged boasted buildings of up to seven stories that reflected architectural trends emerging from the East Coast and Midwest.

Reconstruction from the fire as well as Seattle's victory in its hard-fought battle to gain transcontinental railroad service was reflected in a population jump from 3,533 in 1880 to 42,800 in 1890.

Onlookers watch the start of Seattle's Great Fire on Front Street (First Avenue) on June 6, 1889.

Seattle's dependence on investments by eastern banks made it particularly vulnerable to national economic trends. The city was thrust into depression by the Panic of 1893, halting growth and construction for nearly five years. Many architects left Seattle during the depression. Those who remained promoted their profession by establish-

Seattle merchants constructed platforms for tents amidst the ruins of the Great Fire.

ing the Washington Society of Architects in 1894, which soon became the Washington State Chapter of the American Institute of Architects.

It was the Klondike Gold Rush that finally pulled Seattle out of its slump and pushed the city toward economic independence. Gold had been discovered along the banks of the Klondike River in Canada's Yukon Territory. On July 17, 1897, the S.S. *Portland* steamed into Seattle from Alaska holding two tons of gold and 68 wealthy miners. "Klondike fever" spread throughout the city and across the nation. Thousands of people quit their jobs to head to Alaska (including Seattle's mayor, William Wood, who telegraphed his resignation from a conference in San Francisco).

The Seattle Chamber of Commerce established the Bureau of Information in August 1897 to promote Seattle as the jumping off point to Alaska and the Klondike. Press-Times editor Erastus Brainerd, who was appointed to head up the bureau, launched an aggressive and successful marketing campaign. Seattle merchants, such as Schwabacher Brothers and Cooper & Levy, made millions outfitting every prospector who came through town with the full-year's-worth of supplies that was required by the Canadian government for entry into the Yukon. Local banks

Cooper & Levy Outfitters stacked with Gold Rush provisions.

The 1909 Alaska-Yukon-Pacific Exposition Fair Grounds.

prospered as well, making Seattle the financial center of the Pacific Northwest.

The sudden emergence of Seattle as the premier city of the region was naturally a source of civic pride, and community leaders wished to cultivate an urban environment befitting their sophisticated city. A park and boulevard plan that had been proposed in the early 1890s failed due to lack of funds. In 1903, with its Gold Rush affluence, the city turned to the Olmsted Brothers of Brookline, Massachusetts for the development of a city-wide park and boulevard plan. Implementation began immediately and was expanded over the next several decades.

The Olmsted Brothers returned to Seattle in 1907 to plan the site for the Alaska-Yukon-Pacific Exposition of 1909. The Exposition, a showcase of Seattle's prosperity and importance as a gateway to Alaska and the Pacific Rim nations of Asia, was held on the University of Washington's new campus on Portage Bay. The Olmsted plan reflected the City Beautiful movement with its unified Beaux-Arts buildings and axial orientation toward Mount Rainier. The popular and financially successful exhibition served as Seattle's official "coming-out" party and provided landscaped grounds for the University. The fair also prompted the construction of several hotels downtown, such as the Moore Hotel, to accommodate visitors to the city.

Gold Rush prosperity continued for over a decade, pushing Seattle's population from 80,671 in 1900 to 237,194 in 1910. This growth sparked rapid northward expansion of downtown. Reclaiming of the tideflats was completed by 1910, expanding warehouse and industrial areas along the waterfront and south of downtown. By 1911, the hills that had concentrated the city around Pioneer Square and along the waterfront to the north were being leveled in a massive regrading campaign that was initiated in 1897 by City Engineer R.H. Thompson.

Seattle's growing political progressiveness brought about the establishment of Pike Place Market in 1907 and a vote to create the Port of Seattle in 1911 to combat the corrupt business practices of produce brokers and railroad and shipping monopolies. However, the Bogue Plan, which included a rapid transit system, port and infrastructure improvements, as well as the development of a civic center in the Denny Regrade area and reserving all of Mercer Island as a public park, was rejected by voters in 1912.

1898 image of partially filled tideflats taken from Beacon Hill.

Seattle's maturity drew academically-trained architects to the city after 1900 and the University of Washington established its own Department of Architecture in 1914. Advances in building technology increased the scale of downtown with steel frame structures, such as the 14-story Alaska building, completed in 1904, and most dramatically with the 1914 completion of the 522-foot-tall Smith Tower.

World War I slowed development, as financing became more difficult. However, military contracts for ships and airplanes gave local industry a significant boost. At the same time, Seattle became an epicenter of labor reform, led by activists like Anna Louise Strong whose impassioned editorials in The Seattle Union Record inspired the nation's first city-wide general strike in 1919.

The Smith Tower under construction, 1913.

By the mid-1920s, the strong local and national economy helped transform both Seattle's downtown and its neighborhoods. The financial and business center had shifted north from the older post-fire city center to the area of Second Avenue and Cherry Street by 1910. Steel and concrete frame buildings clad in terra-cotta characterized the new downtown, while the old downtown south of Yesler Way entered a period of decline.

The Metropolitan Tract, on the former site of the University of Washington, was well under development and was attracting some early office construction north of the business center at Second Avenue and Cherry Street. The retail district was also shifting to its present location along Pine Street from its earlier center along Second Avenue by the 1920s.

The Great Depression halted significant construction downtown other than federally-funded projects, including the 1933 Federal Office Building and the 1940 Federal Courthouse. Projects to accommodate the region's growing number of automobiles provided jobs during the Depression and would facilitate post-war suburbanization. The George Washington Memorial Bridge (Aurora Bridge) created a direct connection between downtown and areas to the north in 1932. The Lacey V. Murrow Bridge, the world's first concrete floating bridge, directly connected drivers to Mercer Island and areas east of Lake Washington in 1940. The Seattle streetcar and cable car system was phased out at this time, and replaced by electric trolley buses in 1941.

The Seattle Housing Authority approved the Yesler Terrace Housing Project in 1939, a 43-acre slum-clearance development. The project, completed in 1942, provided defense worker housing during World War II. Subsequent defense housing and war industry projects occupied architects throughout the war. Boeing boomed during the war, and afterwards emerged as an aerospace giant and the region's largest employer in the years from 1945 to the 1980s.

The post-war years saw increasing suburbanization and Seattle's historic areas and retail district suffered as a result. Construction was slow to resume in downtown Seattle. The first major post-war downtown building was the 1950 Federal Reserve Bank; this and the Public Safety Building, completed in 1951, were among a series of Modern buildings that were constructed downtown through the 1960s.

Urban renewal proposals and highway construction were threatening to dramatically impact Seattle's built environment. In 1953, the Alaskan Way Viaduct opened, creating a physical barrier to the historic link between downtown and the central waterfront. Plans to construct Interstate-5 adjacent to downtown meant clearance of inner-city homes and apartments as well as severing the city's connection to First Hill and Capitol Hill. Proposals to lid a 12-block downtown section of the freeway did not find adequate funding. In the midst of all this automobile-fueled "progress," a concerned group of architects, artists, planners and intellectuals formed Allied Arts in 1954. Allied Arts would play an increasingly important role in the coming preservation and urban design years of the 1960s and 70s.

In 1962, Seattle hosted a second World's Fair. "Century 21" fully embraced post-war optimism with its focus on modernity, science, technology and a prosperous World of Tomorrow. "Futuristic" modern architecture and structural innovation characterized the buildings designed for the fair and gave Seattle a striking new symbol, the Space Needle. After the fair's run, the grounds provided the city with a 74-acre urban park and cultural center.

The utopia of modernization showcased at the 1962 World's Fair was not an accurate reflection of its local impact. In the 1960s, proposals to raze Pioneer Square and Pike Place Market for office buildings, parking structures and improved freeway access generated significant opposition. The post-war attitude that changes in the name of progress and modernity are a good thing was beginning to lose ground, particularly after the passage of the National Historic Preservation Act in 1966. People were becoming aware of the loss of Seattle's historic fabric and they aimed to preserve a sense of the essential character of the city.

Allied Arts and a group of concerned citizens, including Victor Stein-

The 1962 Century 21 fair grounds.

brueck, Ralph Anderson, Richard White and Alan Black, led efforts to save the historic districts from demolition. The group promoted adaptive reuse of old structures to revitalize historic neighborhoods and encourage downtown living. As a result of these efforts Pioneer Square was given protection by the city as an historic district in 1970, with Pike Place Market following in 1971. Both districts and the International District were subsequently listed on the National Register of Historic Places. Seattle's Landmarks Preservation Ordinance was adopted and its Office of Historic Preservation established in 1973, and several other historic districts were designated. Seattle soon emerged as a leader in historic preservation in the western United States.

The general quality of Seattle's urban fabric and investment in the future was also a priority at this time. In 1968, voters approved a package of bond measures called Forward Thrust to fund improvements to infrastructure, sewers and neighborhoods, and to create more parks and construct a domed stadium, the Kingdome. As a result, Interstate-5 was partially lidded with the construction of Freeway Park in 1976; it was spanned again in the 1980s by the Washington State Convention & Trade Center, which was linked to Freeway Park. The central waterfront was improved with the development of Waterfront Park in 1974 and the Seattle Aquarium in 1976.

In 1973, the Seattle City Council approved the 1% for Art ordinance, which mandates that one percent of most municipal capital improvement project budgets be allocated for public art. The art ordinance and the Washington State Art in Public Places program have contributed to the wide variety of artwork that can be found throughout the city.

The improvement projects of the 1970s came when Seattle's economy was suffering badly from the 1971 aerospace depression known locally as the "Boeing Bust." The addition of parks and artwork to the cityscape marked a high point in a bleak time for the city.

With the return of prosperous times and a pro-development climate in the 1980s came a flurry of downtown construction that dramatically changed Seattle's skyline. Tall buildings, such as the 76-story Columbia Center and the 55-story Washington Mutual Tower, characterized the new developments. In 1989, Seattleites startled by the rapidly increasing scale of downtown, voted in favor of the Citizen's Alternative Plan (CAP), which imposed height restrictions of 450 feet (about 30 stories) on office buildings.

The way in which high-rises relate to the street was of increasing concern in the 1970s and 80s. Many buildings of the 1950s and 60s were indifferent to the pedestrian environment, offering little more than desolate, windswept plazas as respite from the street. This was particularly evident in Seattle where several buildings were constructed on massive podiums to accommodate the steep grades.

The negative effects of such planning and development on the vitality of cities were studied by author and urbanologist William H. Whyte. His 1980 book, *The Social Life of Small Urban Spaces,* emphasized the importance of attracting people to city living and fostering safe, pedestrian-friendly urban environments by offering street-level amenities and creating landscaped, smaller-scale open spaces to facilitate human interaction. This publication and others influenced urban design ordinances implemented in Seattle and elsewhere in the early 1980s to address these issues. The ordinances are reflected in the various forms of steps and landings and retail uses that define the base of such buildings as the 48-story Wells Fargo Center.

The bulk of new construction in the 1980s was concentrated between Third and Sixth Avenues, as the business and financial centers had steadily moved away from the waterfront since the post-war era. However, efforts by Cornerstone Development Company to revitalize the blocks immediately east of Alaskan Way in the early 1980s began to pay off in the 1990s.

In the early 1990s the Seattle Art Museum selected First Avenue and University Street as the location for its new building, providing a major boost to the neighborhood now known as "West Edge." The Harbor Steps development brought a large residential community to First Avenue and a pedestrian link between the waterfront, the Seattle Art Museum and later, Benaroya Hall.

The revitalization of downtown neighborhoods was also bolstered by the technology boom of the 1990s, which brought Seattle to the forefront of the international business world and drew an increasing number of young professionals attracted to urban living. The city established Design Review Boards in 1998 to encourage development in Seattle neighborhoods that is sensitive to its surroundings and the pedestrian environment.

Sensitivity to the natural environment has been a major focus in recent years. In 2000, Seattle became the first municipality in the nation to adopt the U.S. Green Building Council's Leadership in Energy and Environmental Design (LEED) silver target for city construction projects over 5,000 square feet and has subsequently established programs to encourage sustainable architecture in the private sector.

The revitalization of downtown neighborhoods and the adoption of programs to encourage environmental design are making downtown living an attractive option for people who enjoy proximity to cultural institutions, shopping and employers and who wish to avoid the taxing commute to suburban areas. However, the challenge of maintaining affordable housing options in an increasingly upscale downtown remains. In 2006, the Seattle City Council approved lifting height restrictions imposed by CAP to encourage taller, thinner buildings downtown and to allow loftier towers in exchange for providing low- to moderate-income units or paying into a fund for other affordable housing developments downtown. The hope is to make downtown living an attractive and viable option to a diverse population and to continue to develop a "24-hour downtown." With the lifting of height restrictions, however, the viability of small-scale historic buildings on increasingly valuable land may face further threats.

Thanks to the efforts of preservation activists in the critical years of the 1960s and 70s, private development inspired by the appeal of the historic districts, and votes to fund improvements, Seattle has managed to escape the urban decay that many cities have suffered due to suburbanization and urban renewal projects. Cultural activities, shopping and urban parks such as Seattle Center and the Olympic Sculpture Park contribute to a vibrant downtown with something for everyone to enjoy.

Seattle's natural beauty of course cannot be ignored as part of its appeal. Efforts to improve the health of Puget Sound and restore salmon habitat are underway. If the citizens and government of Seattle remain committed to the health of Puget Sound, thoughtful urban planning, environmentally conscious construction, effective transit alternatives and affordable housing options, Seattle of the next century will continue to be a most livable city.

TIMELINE

	Native Americans settle throughout Puget Sound.
1792	British explorers survey Puget Sound.
1846	Great Britain cedes control of the Oregon Territory, opening up Puget Sound to American settlers.
1851	The Collins, Van Asselt and Maple families establish farms in the Duwamish Valley. The Denny Party arrives at Alki Point, just in time to spend a rainy winter.
1852	The settlers move from Alki to the peninsula to the east, a better location to build a port city. Henry Yesler begins building a sawmill and cookhouse, the area's first industry and public gathering place.
1853	Henry Yesler opens first steam-powered sawmill on Puget Sound in Seattle.
1855	January 22, Point Elliott Treaty cedes most of Native American land in Western Washington to the U.S. government, and relocates the tribes to reservations.
1856	The Battle of Seattle occurs between Native Americans and white settlers.
1860	The Military Road to Fort Vancouver connects Seattle to other towns for the first time.
1861	The Washington Territorial University is established.
1869	Seattle incorporates.
1870	Seattle's population grows to 1,170 people.
1873	Tacoma is chosen as terminus of the Northern Pacific's transcontinental railroad.
1875	Seattle's first railroad is completed between the waterfront and coal fields near Renton.
1880	Seattle's population nearly triples to 3,533.

1884	The first horse-drawn streetcar line is established along Second Avenue.
	Transcontinental railroad to Puget Sound completed via Columbia Gorge and Portland.
1886	Anti-Chinese riots force the evacuation of 350 Chinese residents.
	The Seattle, Lake Shore & Eastern Railroad connects Seattle, around Lake Washington, to Snoqualmie.
1887	The first cable car line is established on Yesler Way.
1889	The first electric streetcar line is established along Second Avenue.
	The Great Fire of June 6 destroys 32 blocks of downtown Seattle.
	Washington becomes the 42nd state.
1890	Seattle's population explodes from 3,533 in 1880 to 42,800.
1893	The Great Northern Railroad comes to Seattle.
	The Panic of 1893 sends Seattle into an economic depression, halting construction for five years.
1894	Washington State Chapter of the American Institute of Architects is established.
1895	The University of Washington moves to a new campus north of Lake Union, but retains ownership of its downtown property.
1897	The Klondike Gold Rush sparks economic turnaround and an unprecedented era of growth for Seattle.
	City Engineer R.H. Thompson initiates regrading projects that continue through 1930.
1900	With the Gold Rush, Seattle's population nearly doubles to 80,671.
1903	The Olmsted Brothers develop a park and boulevard plan for Seattle.
1904	Seattle's first skyscraper, the 14-story, steel-framed Alaska Building, is completed.
1906	A new Seattle Central Library opens on the site of the present Central Library.

1905	The railroad tunnel under downtown Seattle is completed.
1906	King Street Station opens serving the Great Northern and Northern Pacific railroads.
1907	Pike Place Market opens.
1909	The Alaska-Yukon-Pacific Exposition opens on the grounds of the University of Washington.
1910	Continued prosperity pushes Seattle's population to 237,194. Filling of the tideflats south of downtown is completed.
1911	Port of Seattle is established. Union Station opens, serving the Union Pacific Railroad, and Chicago, Milwaukee, St. Paul & Pacific Railroad ("Milwaukee Road").
1912	Bogue Plan is defeated.
1914	The University of Washington School of Architecture is established. The 522-foot Smith Tower is completed, the tallest building west of Chicago for nearly fifty years.
1917	Lake Washington Ship Canal and Hiram Chittenden Locks are completed, connecting Shilshole Bay, Lake Union and Lake Washington. Boeing Airplane Company is established. United States involvement in World War I begins.
1918	World War I ended by armistice on November 11.
1919	Nation's first city-wide general strike takes place in Seattle, February 6-11.
1920	Seattle's population reaches 315,312.
1923	Seattle's first zoning ordinance is established, controlling building scale and land-use location, and requiring setbacks on tall buildings.
1928	Boeing Field, the area's first major airport, opens.
1929	Stock Market crash precipitates the Great Depression; downtown high-rise construction halts for 30 years.

1930	Seattle's population is 365,583. The Denny Regrade is completed; the last in a series of major regrading projects began in 1897.
1932	The George Washington Memorial Bridge (Aurora Bridge) is completed, Seattle's first major highway bridge.
1936	An innovative seawall system is completed along Seattle's central waterfront.
1939	Yesler Terrace project is approved, the first racially-integrated housing project in the nation.
1940	Seattle's population levels off, with an increase of only 2,719 during the depression years, to reach 368,302. The Lacey V. Murrow Floating Bridge to Mercer Island opens.
1941	Pearl Harbor is attacked, drawing the United States into World War II and initiating booming war-time industry in Seattle, including airplane production and ship building.
1942	Internment of West Coast Japanese Americans, over 12,000 from King County.
1945	World War II ends.
1948	Seattle-Tacoma airport opens.
1949	A 7.1 magnitude earthquake strikes Seattle; cornices are removed from many historic buildings as a pedestrian safety precaution.
1950	Seattle's population is 467,591. Northgate Shopping Center, a harbinger of the suburban malls that would challenge the retail district for the next forty years, opens north of downtown.
1953	The Alaskan Way Viaduct opens.
1954	Boeing launches the first successful passenger jet, the 707. Allied Arts is formed.
1960	Seattle's population is 557,087. The Port of Seattle is among the first major U.S. ports to convert to containerization.
1962	Seattle hosts "Century 21" World's Fair; the Space Needle surpasses the Smith Tower in height.

1963	Evergreen Point (Governor Albert D. Rosellini Bridge) across Lake Washington, the world's longest floating bridge, opens. "Sinking ship garage" replaces the historic Seattle Hotel in Pioneer Square.
1964	"Underground Seattle" tours begin.
1965	A 6.5- to 7-magnitude earthquake strikes Seattle.
1966	National Historic Preservation Act is passed; efforts to preserve Pioneer Square are underway.
1967	Interstate-5 is completed from Tacoma to Everett.
1968	Seattle voters approve $40 million "Forward Thrust" bond package.
1969	Seattle First National Bank Building is completed; it remains the tallest building downtown until 1985.
1970	Suburbanization contributes to Seattle's first decade of declining population to 530,831. Pioneer Square is designated Seattle's first historic district. An arson Fire at the Ozark Hotel kills 20 people and leads to more stringent fire codes requiring sprinklers, causing the closure of many single-room-occupancy hotels (also called workingmen's hotels).
1971	Pike Place Market is saved by voters and designated an historic district. Washington State Shoreline Management Act is passed.
1973	Seattle Landmarks Ordinance is established. City Council approves Seattle's 1 % for Art initiative.
1976	Freeway Park opens.
1978	Microsoft relocates from Albuquerque, NM to Bellevue, WA.
1980	Seattle's population declines to 493,846.
1985	Seattle's tallest building, the 76-story Columbia Center, is completed.
1988	Metro Transit tunnel is completed under downtown Seattle.
1989	Seattle voters approve CAP—the Citizen's Alternative Plan—restricting heights on downtown buildings to 450 feet.

1990   Seattle's population is on the rise again to 516,259. Washington's Growth Management Act is approved to curb urban sprawl and encourage close-in living.

1998   Seattle's downtown Design Review Board is established.

2000   Seattle's population surpasses 1960 peak to reach 563,374. Seattle becomes first major U.S. city to adopt the U.S. Green Building Council's Leadership in Energy and Environmental Design (LEED) silver target for city construction projects over 5,000 square feet.

2001   The 6.8-magnitude Nisqually earthquake strikes Seattle, damaging several historic buildings and the Alaskan Way Viaduct.

2006   City Council lifts height restrictions on downtown buildings to encourage taller, slimmer buildings and encourage development of low- and middle-income housing downtown.

SEATTLE ARCHITECTURE
A WALKING GUIDE TO DOWNTOWN

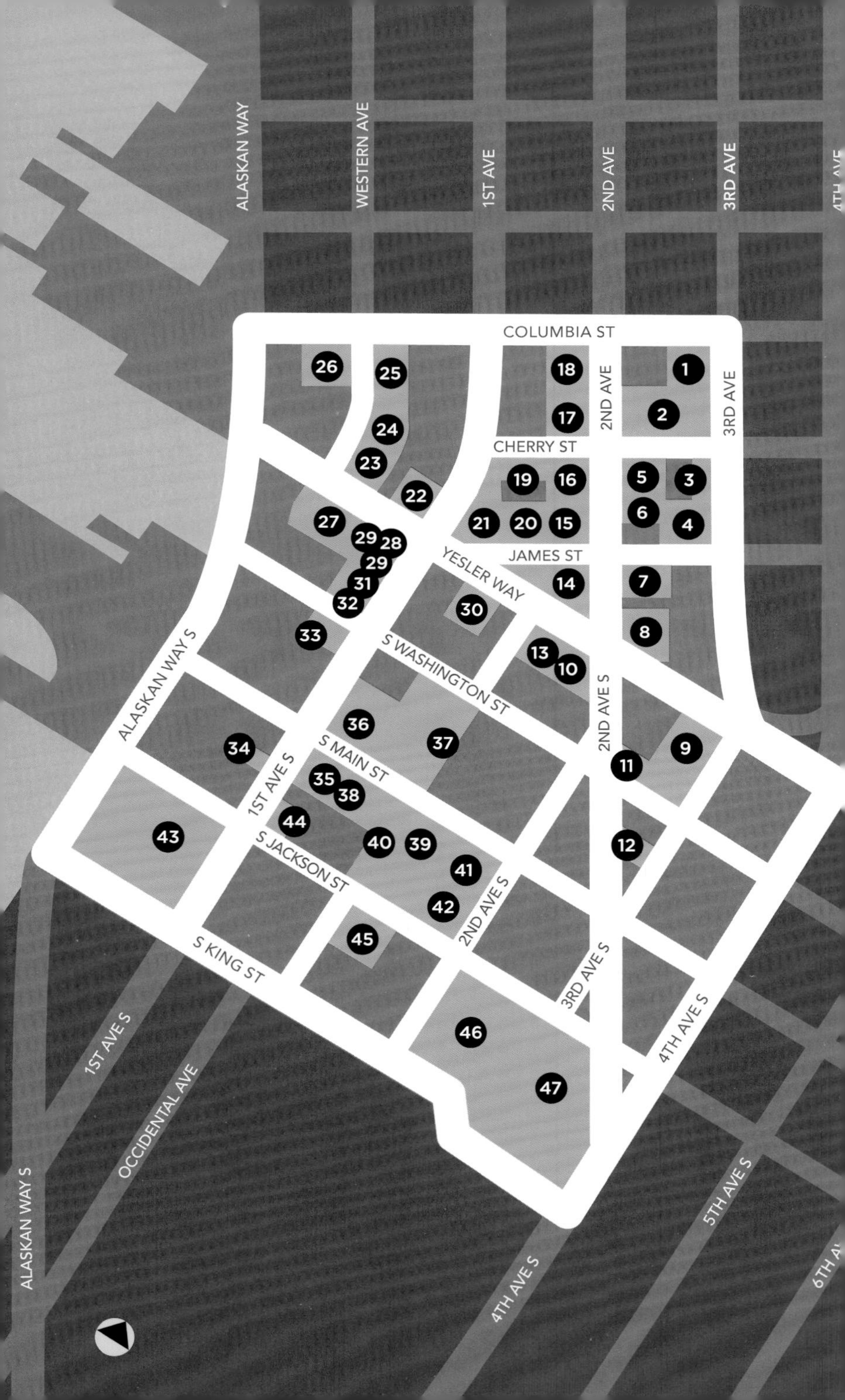
ALASKAN WAY
WESTERN AVE
1ST AVE
2ND AVE
3RD AVE
COLUMBIA ST
CHERRY ST
JAMES ST
YESLER WAY
S WASHINGTON ST
S MAIN ST
S JACKSON ST
S KING ST
ALASKAN WAY S
1ST AVE S
2ND AVE S
3RD AVE S
4TH AVE S
5TH AVE S
OCCIDENTAL AVE
1
2
3
4
5
6
7
8
9
10
11
12
13
14
15
16
17
18
19
20
21
22
23
24
25
26
27
28
29
29
31
32
33
34
35
36
37
38
39
40
41
42
43
44
45
46
47

CHAPTER 1
PIONEER SQUARE

Pioneer Square is the birthplace of Seattle and the city's oldest neighborhood. It consists of a collection of late nineteenth-century masonry buildings, many of which date from the first three years after the Great Fire of 1889. Benign neglect of the area during the middle years of the twentieth century left Seattle with a remarkably intact and well-preserved historic district. However, Seattle would likely have lost this treasure trove of historic buildings if not for the dedication of a group of preservation activists who fought to save the Pioneer Square neighborhood.

The environment in which the Duwamish people lived in today's Pioneer Square area was bordered by Elliot Bay to the west, tideflats to the south and steep forested slopes to the north and east. Their built environment here was a winter village that consisted of eight longhouses constructed of split cedars, near what is now the intersection of Yesler Way and First Avenue.

In April 1852, after spending their first winter at Alki, in present-day West Seattle, most of the Denny Party relocated to their claims on the east side of Elliott Bay, near the foot of Washington Street. The land on which Seattle began was divided among William Bell, who claimed land to the north; Carson Boren, who claimed land to the south; and Arthur Denny, who claimed the land in between.

The settlement's first industry was established by luring Henry Yesler to locate his steam-powered saw mill on property donated by the three men, including a strip of land that ran from the wooded hillside to the waterfront. The strip, generally paralleling Mill Street, today's Yesler Way, was known as "skid road" for the logs that were skidded down the muddy path to Yesler's mill. The nickname came to be adopted nationally during the Great Depression as "skid row" to describe blighted urban areas. The completion of the mill and wharf in 1853 allowed the export of lumber to San Francisco.

The newcomers were welcomed by Chief Seattle who had established trading relations with settlers in the Fort Nisqually area, near Olympia. Among his acquaintances was David "Doc" Maynard, a physician who operated a store in the settlement to the south. The Chief urged Maynard to relocate his store to the newly established village, informally known as "Duwamps." Maynard relocated his store, "Seattle Exchange," to what is now First Avenue South and Main Street, and convinced the settlers to change the settlement's name to honor his friend, Chief Seattle.

Early street platting reflected a disagreement with a lasting legacy in Pioneer Square. Doc Maynard platted the grid south of skid road, which was named Mill Street (now Yesler Way), in a north-south direction parallel to the shoreline. Arthur Denny platted the land north of Yesler Way parallel to the shoreline, which veered northwest. The result was the misalignment of streets at Yesler Way that is still evident in the triangular lots resulting from the irregularity.

The built environment of early Seattle consisted of frame structures constructed of milled lumber from Yesler's mill and other steam mills that were established around Puget Sound. The slowly-growing town was made up of one- and two-story frame buildings with clapboard siding, typically painted white. They were mostly gabled structures, although some commercial structures had the false fronts that one associates with western pioneer towns.

Seattle's growth was stunted in the 1850s and 1860s by its remoteness, the lack of railroad connections to the east or south, skirmishes with Native Americans and a slow-down in western settlement caused by the Civil War. By the 1870s, however, buildings with modest Victorian detailing began to appear. The expansion of industry to include coal exportation and regional shipping, as well as the addition of more saw mills and a brick yard, facilitated the construction of more substantial buildings.

By the 1880s Seattle was booming due to the coming transcontinental railroad connection. Victorian buildings up to four stories were being built to the designs of architects such as William Boone and Donald MacKay. These early architects had emerged from the building trades, as would most Seattle architects prior to the turn of the century. Many arrived from San Francisco and Portland and drew upon the eclectic Victorian modes popular in those areas. Protrusions such as bay windows and turrets characterized these buildings, as did elaborate ornamentation inspired by Gothic, Italianate and Second Empire styles. Some of these buildings were a combination of wood and masonry, such as William Boone's ornate 1884 Yesler-Leary Building; however, most were of wood frame construction. Boone oversaw the construction of the four-story Boston Block in 1888, which was equipped with Seattle's first passenger elevator.

Almost nothing remains of the first downtown Seattle. The Great Fire of June 6, 1889, destroyed nearly all of it. Post-fire Seattle would rise from the ashes of the burnt district, which extended north of the area now known as Pioneer Square. The form of the buildings, many of which still stand today, would be dictated by the newly adopted Ordinance 1147, which was among Seattle's first building codes, and by architects, builders and developers who saw opportunity in the rebuilding of the city. This began the first significant period of construction in the present Pioneer Square area.

Architects such as Elmer Fisher, who is said to have received more than 50 post-fire commissions, Charles Saunders, Edwin Houghton and John Parkinson were responsible for many of the immediate post-fire buildings. They drew on their familiarity with Victorian design convention and on examples in the newly-established national architectural journals, which featured the work of Chicago School architects such as Burnham and Root; and Richardsonian-Romanesque design, which had been touted as an ideal form for American architecture after the death of H.H. Richardson in 1886.

Ordinance 1147 mandated that all buildings in the "burnt district" have exterior walls constructed of brick or stone. The thickness of the exterior walls depended on their height. For masonry load-bearing walls of a four-story building, the basement walls could be no less than 21 inches thick; first, second and third-story walls could be no less than 16 inches; and fourth floor walls no less than 12 inches. Similar, yet slightly beefier requirements applied to buildings of five and six stories. Foundations were required to be at least four feet below grade. Wood cornices were prohibited and protrusions such as bay windows and turrets were limited in size. In

The Yesler-Leary Building, 1883, designed by William Boone of Boone & Meeker.

Post-fire reconstruction is well underway in this image taken in September 1889.

large buildings, masonry division walls were to be spaced no more than 66 feet apart, with restricted allowances for arched openings. Interiors were to use "slow-burning" construction utilizing heavy timber, steel or iron columns for spans greater than 27 feet. The ordinance also required metal anchors between floor beams and exterior walls, although some believed that if unattached timbers were allowed to burn freely, they would not pull down exterior walls.

The building code is reflected in the form of post-fire Pioneer Square buildings, most obviously in the lack of protrusions and in the graduating thickness of exterior walls, often expressed by horizontal banding. The short period in which most of the burnt district was rebuilt and the small group of architects responsible for most of the designs accounts for the relative architectural harmony that characterized the new downtown.

Seeing the fire as an opportunity to fix problems that had plagued early Seattle, the City Council voted to elevate several streets, some as much as 32 feet, for better drainage and sanitation. Front Street (now First Avenue) was significantly widened, as were Second and Third Streets (now Second and Third Avenues); and a few sections of streets were re-platted to address the misalignment at Mill Street (now Yesler Way).

Because reconstruction began prior to the elevating of the streets, buildings along the yet-to-be-raised routes were constructed with street-levels on two floors, with the knowledge that the ground floors would soon become basements. Businesses struggled and inevitably closed in these underground locations, and most of the stairs leading to them were paved over. Evidence remains above ground in the tops of window arches that peek up where the sidewalk meets the buildings and in the glass prism blocks that were set into the sidewalk to allow light into the underground passages.

The post-fire building boom began to slow by 1891 and construction halted completely with the Panic of 1893; it was not to resume for five years and many architects left town. The Klondike Gold Rush, spurred by the arrival of a "ton of gold" in 1897, prompted another wave of construction in the Pioneer Square area, an influx of new architects as well as the return of some who had left after the Panic of 1893.

Several well-appointed hotels were constructed north of Yesler Way, while many post-fire hotels south of Yesler gained a reputation for housing illicit activity. The Gold Rush-era developments were the earliest signs that the business district was spreading north of its historic center. Advances in building technology brought more sophisticated architecture of a grander scale to the expanding commercial core with the 1904 completion of the 14-story, steel-frame Alaska building, Seattle's first skyscraper, and the 1911 completion of the 18-story Hoge Building.

Filling of the tideflats to the west and south began in 1895 with soil from regrade projects and from the boring of the Northern Pacific tunnel in 1905. Filling was mostly complete by 1910 and several warehouses, such as the Polson Building, were constructed on the reclaimed land west of the commercial center.

Between 1900 and World War I, there were attempts by landholders in the south end of town to curb the northern spread of the business district. Most notable was the construction of the Smith Tower in 1914, which for decades dwarfed all other downtown buildings. But the area of Second Avenue and Cherry Street was firmly established as the commercial core, having large, "modern" office buildings such as the Dexter Horton, the Alaska and Hoge buildings. Developments on the University's Metropolitan Tract and on regraded blocks several blocks north also pulled the center further from the historic center.

The Second Avenue Extension, which was constructed between 1928 and 1931, cleared a huge swath of buildings along Second Avenue from Yesler Way to Fourth Avenue South and destroyed what was previously the location of Chinatown. The extension, which was to provide easier access to the King Street and Union train stations, resulted in the removal and replacement of the façades of many of the buildings that remained on the edge of its path. This public works project was the last major construction (or destruction in the case of Chinatown) in the historic Pioneer Square neighborhood for over 40 years.

The Great Depression stopped any subsequent development and the area fell into disrepair. Many buildings became flophouses for transients who made up much of the area's population. However, in the post-World War II years, a thriving Jazz scene began to develop in Pioneer Square and several buildings were transformed into lively late-night hot spots and beatnik poetry joints. The emergence of Pioneer Square as a location with an active night life and alternative culture in the 1940s and 1950s started a trend that continues to this day.

The 7.1-magnitude earthquake that struck Seattle on April 13, 1949, damaged many already run-down buildings in Pioneer Square and resulted in the removal of most of the surviving cornices as a pedestrian safety precaution.

The lack of development in the area and steady expansion of the business district to the north and east did have the unintentional effect of preserving the collection of nineteenth-century buildings. By the early 1960s, however, the area was threatened with total destruction in the name of urban renewal. In 1963, plans were proposed for the wholesale demolition of Pioneer Square to make way for parking garages and freeway access. A 1966 proposal called for the preservation of one block of Pioneer Square and massive clearance of the area for new office buildings and parking lots.

While these plans were being drawn up, however, the preservation movement was gaining ground in Seattle. In 1962, the architect and preservation activist Victor Steinbrueck published his sketches in the University of Washington Press book, *Seattle Cityscape*, which captured the unique character of Pioneer Square and raised public awareness about its potential loss. That potential became tangible in 1963 when the 1889 Seattle Hotel, designed by Stephen Meany, was destroyed and replaced by a parking garage. Public interest was also aroused by the "Underground Seattle" tours, begun in 1964 by journalist and local historian Bill Speidel. These tours, which continue today, took people through the underground areas beneath sidewalks, spaces left from the early days of post-fire reconstruction.

A car crushed by falling bricks in Pioneer Square during the earthquake of 1949.

The efforts to save Pioneer Square were led by Allied Arts, an activist group of artists, architects and urban planners who recognized the value and potential of the area. Architect Ralph Anderson and gallery owner Richard White began purchasing and sensitively rehabilitating some of the old structures, such as the Capitol Brewing/Jackson Building, for use by small businesses and artists. In 1968, the city, led by newly-elected Mayor Wes Uhlman, conducted a survey of the neighborhood. It was listed on the National Register of Historic Places in 1970, creating the 30-acre Pioneer Square-Skid Road National Historic District. In 1973, Seattle adopted its own landmarks preservation ordinance, establishing a landmarks preservation board. Several historic districts were established, including the Pioneer Square Preservation District (slightly larger than the national district), with its own board to oversee alterations and new construction. The district boundaries have been expanded twice since it was first established, in 1978 and 1988.

Although the success of the preservation movement saved several historic buildings, a tragic fire at the Ozark Hotel in 1970, which prompted the City Council to enact stricter fire codes, resulted in the loss of many historic single-room-occupancy hotels in Pioneer Square and throughout the city. Although some were converted, a great deal of low-income housing was lost because building owners could not afford to update the buildings to meet the new fire codes and were forced to abandon or sell them. Fortunately some of the buildings, like the St. Charles Hotel, have been rehabilitated by housing advocacy groups and now provide low-income housing, although more is still needed.

Public funding to make street improvements and develop pedestrian areas, such as Occidental Park and Occidental Mall, was supplemented with private investments by developers who rehabilitated many of the historic buildings. Some of the buildings now contain high-end condominiums or apartments, such as the Terry-Denny Building. Small businesses, art galleries, restaurants, social service agencies and retail establishments have moved into the ground floors of these buildings in the decades since Pioneer Square's preservation, resulting in the lively and diverse neighborhood that we know today. Thanks to the hard work and foresight of early preservation activists, Seattle boasts a large and well-preserved collection of nineteenth-century commercial buildings.

In recent years, Pioneer Square has been impacted by the replacement of the Kingdome with Safeco and Qwest fields. The activity around these arenas and new development south of Pioneer Square has raised concerns about the impact of traffic on the historic district. The restructuring of freeway access in the coming years will hopefully mitigate some of the potentially long-term negative affects that increased vehicular traffic could have on the district.

The uncontrollable and mighty force of nature will continue to threaten Pioneer Square's historic masonry structures. The 6.8-magnitude Nisqually earthquake that struck Seattle in 2001 damaged several buildings in the district and necessitated a large number of seismic retrofits. The Cadillac Hotel was so severely damaged that the owners sought to tear it down based on an inspection by an engineer. Fortunately, the preservation organization Historic Seattle was able to obtain a second opinion and subsequently purchased and restored the building. With any luck, the surviving historic buildings will be retrofitted before the next quake shakes Seattle.

The buildings listed here are all within Seattle's Pioneer Square Historic District. Some of them are also listed in the National Register, as noted in the text.

1) 215 COLUMBIA BUILDING
(Chamber of Commerce)
1925, Harlan Thomas and Schack Young & Meyers
215 Columbia Street

Formerly home to the Seattle Chamber of Commerce, the design of the 215 Columbia Building was inspired by Roman basilica form. The façade features decorative friezes along its base and peaked roofline. The ground-level frieze, flanking the arched entrance, depicts Native American hunters and gatherers on one side and images of early local industry on the other. The upper frieze depicts a parading menagerie including horses, cougars and rams, among other powerful beasts. Arches are a consistent element, extending the full height of the bays and at the window and door openings. The central bay features a rose window and the main entrance is flanked by winged lions emerging from the flush stone surface.

2) DEXTER HORTON BUILDING 🏛
1924, John Graham, Sr.
710 Second Avenue

The terra-cotta-clad Dexter Horton building is made up of a four-story base supporting an E-shaped, 10-story office block, with light wells facing south along the Cherry Street elevation to maximize natural light to the many offices within. The Second Avenue façade features columns rising three stories from the base, which appear to be granite but are actually the terra-cotta product, "granitex" encasing the steel frame. A Roman coffered barrel vault lobby and banking hall provide a grand entrance from Second Avenue. The Dexter Horton Building exemplifies the large-scale commercial projects typically undertaken by the office of John Graham, Sr.

3) ST. CHARLES HOTEL ㅠ ㅠ
(Rector Hotel)
1913, John Graham, Sr.; rehabilitation, 2004, Stickney Murphy Romine Architects
619-621 Third Avenue

When construction began on the Rector Hotel in 1911, a nine-story building was planned but only six stories were built, resulting in the lack of a cornice or formal top. The terra-cotta and brick hotel was designed to serve the needs of its guests as well as the patrons and performers of the adjacent Grand Opera House, and it incorporated features such as an entrance from the stair landing in the lobby that opened to the balcony of the theater. The north elevation entrance originally led to a bank of doors that opened to the theater's mezzanine level. The hotel only briefly served the theater, which soon after was converted into a movie house. Today the building is owned and operated by Plymouth Housing Group and contains 64 low-income rooms.

The Grand Opera House (Edwin Houghton, 1900), which the Rector Hotel adjoined, was developed by John Cort, who ran the Northwestern Theatrical Association, a booking organization that controlled 37 theaters in seven states by 1904. The Grand Opera House opened as Seattle's premier theatrical venue in 1900. The building was damaged by fire in 1906, and its preeminence was surpassed in 1907 when Cort made the Moore Theatre his flagship venue in the burgeoning theatrical district to the north (see West Edge tour). Shortly after the completion of the Rector Hotel, the Grand was converted for use as a movie theater but was subsequently gutted by fire in 1917. What remains of the theater's structure now serves as a parking garage.

The Grand Opera House with an inset image of developer John Cort.

4) LYON BUILDING ⊓ ⊓
1910, Graham & Myers; rehabilitation, 1997, Mithun
607 Third Avenue

The Lyon Building marks an early effort to develop Third Avenue as part of Seattle's central business district. The avenue had been regraded in 1907 and the "Third Avenue Club" was formed by landowners to encourage development in the area. Although only six stories, the legible grid of its reinforced concrete frame, its unadorned brick piers and clearly articulated base, shaft and cornice reflect a move toward the aesthetic introduced with Seattle's first skyscraper, the 1904 Alaska Building. The building was rehabilitated in 1997 for special needs housing.

Prior to 1910, steel-frame office towers in Seattle were usually executed with terra-cotta bases and crowns with shafts faced in dark or light brick. With very few exceptions, buildings designed after 1910 until the 1940s were clad entirely in terra-cotta, due in part to local production of architectural terra cotta and rising brick prices and labor costs.

5) ALASKA BUILDING ⊓
1904, Eames & Young (St. Louis); Saunders & Lawton (superintending); rehabilitation, 1982, Stickney & Murphy; rehabilitation, 2007-2008, Clark Design Group
618 Second Avenue

The 14-story Alaska Building was Seattle's first steel-frame building and its first skyscraper. The building is made up of a two-story rectangular base surmounted by an L-shaped tower. This Beaux Arts style office tower features a terra-cotta-clad base with extensive ornamentation. Angel heads with wings, serpents wrapped around torches and interlocking geometric designs adorn the first two floors. Projecting belt courses separate the unadorned beige brick veneer shaft from the base, penthouse and cornice. Circular openings above the penthouse windows terminate the bays beneath the projecting cornice. The penthouse level was originally occupied by the Alaskan Club, founded to promote business between Alaska and the Pacific Northwest, which later merged with the Arctic Club (see Civic/Financial District tour, Arctic Building). The Alaska Building remained Seattle's tallest until 1911, when the 18-story Hoge Building was completed. The building was rehabilitated in 2008 and now contains ground-floor retail, a hotel and condominiums.

6) CORONA BUILDING
1903, Bebb & Mendel; rehabilitation, 2000, Stickney Murphy Romine Architects
606 Second Avenue

This six-story brick and terra-cotta building displays its architects' familiarity with Chicago School design principles and Sullivanesque ornamentation. The façade is divided into four vertical bays above the street-level storefronts and framed by piers with slightly recessed window openings and spandrels. The bays rise four stories and are divided from the top story by a belt course. Upper level windows corresponding to those below are separated by pilasters with stylized floral terra-cotta ornamentation. Similar ornamentation also occurs at the storefront level and second belt course, running the length of the façade, and covers most of the upper level. The design employs the Chicago School model of a clearly articulated base, shaft and cornice as well as Sullivan's approach to ornamentation, which is symmetrical and contained within the architectural elements. The building's upper floors sat vacant for over 50 years until rehabilitation in 2000 converted them to residential lofts with ground-floor commercial space.

Charles Bebb of Bebb & Mendel was employed in the offices of Adler and Sullivan in the 1880s. He was sent to Seattle in 1890 to superintend the construction of Adler and Sullivan's design for the Seattle Opera House; although the building was never built beyond the foundation, Bebb returned to Seattle in 1893 and worked with the Denny Clay Company producing architectural terra-cotta. Bebb's partner, Louis Mendel, also had experience working in Midwest firms.

7) COLLINS BUILDING
1894, Arthur B. Chamberlin; rehabilitation, 2001,
Emick Howard & Seibert
520 Second Avenue

This five-story brick masonry building features a rusticated sandstone base with a wood and cast iron glazed storefront on its main façade. An arcade of Romanesque round arched windows on the upper story springs from unadorned brick piers. Brickwork in the recessed spandrels creates a checkerboard pattern. Sandstone belt courses and window sills divide the façade on the top four floors. At the parapet level, corbelled bricks in the shape of inverted pyramids rest below an arched corbel table. The building is named for John Collins, a Seattle real estate and mining investor and civic leader. The Collins building was rehabilitated in 2001 and houses office space and ground-floor restaurants.

8) SMITH TOWER ⊤⊤
1914, Gaggin & Gaggin (Syracuse, NY); rehabilitation, 1999, NBBJ and Mithun
502-508 Second Avenue

At 522 feet, the Smith Tower was the fourth tallest building in the United States upon its completion. It remained the tallest structure in Seattle until 1962 when the 605-foot Space Needle was built (see Seattle Center tour). The terra-cotta-clad steel-frame structure is clearly articulated, and allows for expansive window openings. The building rises 24 floors and steps back to a tower centered over the western elevation, which rises to 35 floors; this form was advocated in the early twentieth cen-

L.C. Smith originally planned an eighteen-story building for this site, which his wife had purchased on an 1888 tour of the west. Smith's son, Burns L. Smith, encouraged him to build an outstanding office tower, similar to those he had seen rise in New York City. And in the spirit of friendly rivalry, a taller building would trump John Hoge's 18-story skyscraper, then the tallest in Seattle. L.C. Smith agreed, but not without first gaining assurance from Seattle city leaders that the municipal government offices would always remain within four blocks of his building, in hopes of anchoring the business center near his investment. Although the civic center does indeed remain within four blocks of the Smith Tower, the building was unable to prevent the core of the central business district from shifting north.

tury by New York architect Ernest Flagg to preserve light and air at the street level. Floor 36 and several loft and mezzanine levels that originally housed the building's water tank are contained within the pyramidal top, leading to the early claim that the building has 42 floors. The Smith Tower is framed in structural steel fireproofed in concrete and was advertised as "absolutely fireproof." The interior doors and trim are steel painted to simulate mahogany and the windows are framed in bronze. The 35th floor features an observation deck and the famous Chinese Room, named for its carved wood and porcelain ceiling and carved Blackwood furniture, given to the building's owner by the Empress of China. The lobby features Alaskan marble, Mexican onyx and polished brass trim on the elevators, which are the last manually operated elevators on the West Coast. The building is named for New York-based firearms and typewriter magnate L.C. Smith (Smith & Wesson, Smith Corona), who did not live to see his $1 million building completed. One of the building's two light wells was filled in with the 1999 rehabilitation. In February 2007, the owners of the Smith Tower, Chicago-based Walton Street Capital, announced that they are considering converting the building to condominiums.

9) FRYE APARTMENTS
(Frye Hotel)
1908, Bebb & Mendel; rehabilitation, 2001, Tonkin Hoyne Lokan Architects
223 Yesler Way

The eleven-story Frye Apartment building was originally built as a hotel and was among Seattle's finest upon its completion. Its Beaux Arts façade features cream terra-cotta cladding on the first two floors and cornice, with light brown brick facing the shaft. A rusticated concrete base makes up the first two floors of the Yesler Way façade. A small interior court along Third Avenue is created by the building's H-shaped plan. Staggered terra-cotta quoining divides the bays and terminates with elaborate cartouches at the ninth-floor belt course. The upper level is adorned with cartouches, circular openings and an elaborate cornice with ornamental brackets beneath. The building is named for Charles Frye, whose family's art collection is now housed in Seattle's Frye Art Museum. The building was rehabilitated for the Low Income Housing Institute in 2001.

10) METROPOLE BUILDING
1893, Elmer Fisher and Emil DeNeuf
421 Second Avenue Extension

This three-story trapezoidal building's street-facing façades are clad in rusticated sandstone. A round arch marks the main entrance on the Second Avenue Extension façade. Round arches pick up again on the third floor, interrupted at the central bay by rectangular openings. Subtle variation in the rustication of the sandstone adds interest to the otherwise unadorned surface. The Metropole Building was one of only two post-fire buildings with all-stone street façade. G.O. Guy's drugstore, which later grew to become a large chain, originally occupied the ground level. In 1898 a theater opened in the basement of the Metropole Building, which was the first in Seattle to display moving pictures.

11) CHIN GEE HEE BUILDING
1890, attributed to William Boone
400 Second Avenue Extension

This three-story stucco-faced building is the last vestige of Seattle's original Chinatown, which had gradually moved east of here by the early 1900s. What remained was almost entirely destroyed with the extension of Second Avenue in the mid-1920s. The third-story covered porch, although added slightly later, was a common feature in Chinatown. The building was built and owned by Chin Gee Hee, who operated the

Quon Tuck Company here, a successful Chinese labor contracting and import/export business.

12) UNION GOSPEL MISSION
(Ace Hotel)
1904 & 1930, unknown
318 Second Avenue Extension

Originally known as the Ace Hotel, this six-story building reflects the impact of the Second Avenue Extension project on buildings that remained on the edges of its path. The east façade, dating from 1904, features classically-inspired detailing including an ornamental cornice, a façade treatment typical of the period. The original western façade was destroyed with the Second Avenue Extension in 1928, and the replacement was executed in the Moderne style emerging at the time. Thin buff brick piers ascend the height of the building, terminating at a parapet with no cornice, resulting in a greater sense of verticality. Horizontal articulation is limited to light-colored, flush stone belt courses.

13) INTERURBAN BUILDING
(Seattle National Bank)
1892, John Parkinson
102 Occidental Avenue

Originally built as the Seattle National Bank Building, the Interurban Building displays the adaptation of the Richarsonian-Romanesque mode to commercial architecture in the late 1880s. It presents a stronger break with Victorian convention than many "Romanesque" Pioneer Square buildings exhibit in its overall

John Parkinson, the designer of the Interurban Building, left Seattle for Los Angeles during the Panic of 1893. He had a successful practice in California and was responsible for such landmark buildings as the Los Angeles Coliseum, Bullock's Wilshire department store and the Los Angeles City Hall.

coherence and lack of both grid composition and eclectic ornamentation. The building is arranged around a central light court and has two street-facing façades. The building's six floors are divided into four zones by horizontal banding, which at the second and fifth floors reflect changes in wall thickness dictated by the post-fire building ordinance. Double-height round arches divide the bays of the Colorado red sandstone base, meeting at the rounded corner, which served as the bank's entrance. A grouping of engaged Romanesque columns with elaborately carved capitals frames the recessed arched corner doorway, which features a carved lion head. Smaller round arches articulate the bays of the third through fifth floors with a corresponding arrangement of rectangular openings above. The offices of the Seattle-Tacoma Interurban railway were located in this building, from which it takes its current name. The architect's name is displayed on the Interurban Building's alley façade.

14) PIONEER SQUARE GARAGE/"SINKING SHIP GARAGE"
1963, Mandeville & Berge
James Street & Yesler Way

The rebuilt Occidental Hotel designed by Stephen Meany in 1889 was torn down and replaced by the "Sinking Ship Garage."

This unusual parking structure, which takes its nickname, "sinking ship garage," for obvious reasons, was instrumental in the preservation of Pioneer Square and its designation as an historic district. It stands on the site of the former Occidental Hotel (1884, Donald McKay), which was destroyed in the 1889 fire. The building's owner, John Collins, immediately replaced it with an even grander Occidental Hotel (1889, Stephen Meany), which later became known as the Seattle Hotel. The destruction of the Seattle Hotel in 1963 for the construction of this 240-space parking garage dismayed the community and contributed to the development of Seattle's historic preservation advocacy.

15) BUTLER GARAGE
(Butler Block)
1890, Parkinson & Evers; Butler Garage, 2001,
Hewitt Architects

The Butler Block, Parkinson & Evers 1890.

611 Second Avenue
This 12-story, 462-space parking garage incorporates the shell of the first two floors of the Butler Block into its façade (Parkinson & Evers, 1890). Originally built as the five-story Butler Block, it was converted to the Butler Hotel in 1894 and was, for a brief time, one of the finest hostelries in Seattle. The building had been stripped of its top three floors by the 1930's. The remaining two floors were gutted in 2001 for construction of the parking garage; but the rusticated sandstone and brick shell remains, with "Butler Block" in relief announcing the site's former occupant above the Romanesque arched entry on the Second Avenue façade.

16) BRODERICK BUILDING
(Bailey Building/Smith Tower Annex)
1892, Charles Saunders, Edwin Houghton; rehabilitation, 1975, Jones & Jones

A sketch of the Broderick Building rehabilitation by Jones & Jones.

615 Second Avenue
The six-story Broderick Building, also known as the Bailey Building, features street-facing façades faced entirely in Tenino sandstone. It was one of the few post-fire commercial block to be faced in stone. The building is divided into three zones by horizontal molding at the third and sixth floors, which correspond to changes in wall thickness required by the post-fire building ordinance. Beautifully carved acanthus leaves enliven the entrances to this minimally adorned building. The rectangular block, which the *Seattle Post Intelligencer* described in 1889 as displaying "Firmness, massiveness, elegance and architectural simplicity," reflects commercial architectural trends emerging from Chicago at the time.

17) HOGE BUILDING
1911, Bebb & Mendel
705 Second Avenue

The Hoge building was the tallest skyscraper in town upon its completion. Its 18-story steel frame was erected in just thirty days. The architects applied the results of studies of structures in the 1906 San Francisco earthquake to their design, reflecting an early concern for seismic events in Seattle architecture. The Hoge building's Beaux Arts façade features terra-cotta Corinthian pilasters dividing the structural bays at the first two floors of the three-story base with elaborate cartouches at the third floor. The shaft is clad in unadorned tan brick. Terra-cotta ornamentation at the crown includes cartouches, modillions, bracketry and a projecting cornice decorated with lion heads. The Hoge building held the title of Seattle's tallest for a brief three years, until friendly adversary L.C. Smith erected his namesake tower. These early twentieth-century steel-framed office towers reflect a change in the scale of downtown Seattle and, with the exception of the Smith Tower, a movement of the core of the central business district to the area of Second Avenue and Cherry Street.

18) MILLENNIUM TOWER
2001, Zimmer Gunsul Frasca Partnership
723 Second Avenue

This 20-story mixed-use tower, composed of a curving glazed volume intersecting a more solid, vertical L-shaped mass, includes condominiums on its upper floors and offices below. The building takes its name for being completed just as the new millennium began, January 1, 2001.

19) LOWMAN BUILDING
1903, Heide & DeNeuf; conversion, 2005, T.F. Borseth
Architects and BOLA Architecture+Planning
107 Cherry Street

The ten-story Lowman Building bears traces of French Renaissance eclecticism and chateaux design with its steep gabled roof forms and hipped dormers. Its steel frame is clad in steam-pressed gray brick on its two street-facing elevations, with buff terra-cotta coping and gray terra-cotta ornamentation. The building is named for Seattle civic and business leader James Lowman, who arrived in Seattle in 1877 at the urging of his uncle, Henry Yesler. Lowman was involved in the completion of the Pioneer Building and the Yesler Building (now Mutual Life Building) as the executor of Yesler's estate upon his death in 1892. The Lowman building was converted into apartments in 2005.

20) PIONEER BUILDING ⊓
1892, Elmer Fisher; rehabilitation, 1975,
Ralph Anderson
600 First Avenue

Commissioned by Henry Yesler in 1889, excavation for the Pioneer Building had already begun on the former site of his mill when the Great Fire leveled downtown Seattle. The subsequent construction boom, material shortages and Yesler's dispute with the City Council over widening the streets slowed construction and the building was finished after Yesler's death in 1892. Although cited by Fisher as being "Romanesque, after the great architect of

America, Mr. Richardson," the Pioneer Building employs the Victorian composition that marked much of Fisher's work. The six-story office block has brick exterior walls with a sandstone base and terra-cotta trim. The building's grid composition, with vertical bays divided at each floor by horizontal banding and decorated spandrels, its myriad window forms and sizes and projecting cast-iron bay windows are earmarks of Victorian convention; however, the grouping of windows under arches and the heavy masonry sandstone arches with clustered columns at the main and side entrances suggest the influence of Richardson. The stacked sandstone pilasters, which ascend the full height of the First Avenue façade, are a curious feature unique to this building. The Pioneer Building is widely considered Fisher's best extant work in Seattle. A one-story tower originally stood above the central bay, but was removed after the 1949 earthquake. The Pioneer Building is designated a National Historic Landmark.

21) PIONEER PLACE PARK
1893
Yesler Way & First Avenue

Pioneer Place Park began as a leftover triangle created by the post-fire street widening and re-platting projects; the park was developed in 1893. At the time, it was Seattle's primary public outdoor space. The Tlingit Indian Totem Pole was added to the park in 1899, after Chamber of Commerce members stole it from a native village in Alaska. The first Totem Pole was destroyed by fire in 1938, and the present replacement, carved by Tlingit Indians, was installed. It was restored in 1972 by Jones & Jones, with the help of Tsimshian tribe member John C. Hudson, Jr. and reinforced internally with a steel beam, which also anchors it to the ground. The Pergola was added to the park as a trolley station with an underground restroom in 1909 to greet visitors to the Alaska-Yukon-Pacific exposition of the same year. The ornate, filigreed and barrel-vaulted structure was designed by Seattle architect Julian Everett. Jones & Jones restored the pergola in 1972, utilizing original drawings. The pergola was knocked down in 2001 by a

The site of Pioneer Place Park was known by the Duwamish people as Djidjila'letch (djee-djee-lah-letch), meaning, "little crossing over place." The name referred to a path that connected a peninsula to the south with the higher land to the north. This was the site of one of their winter encampments, which had been abandoned by the time the Denny party arrived. Eight longhouses, which served as gathering spaces for a variety of purposes from potlatches to wedding ceremonies, are believed to have stood here. This park is the only site in Seattle that has continued to serve the purpose that it did when native people flourished here, as a public gathering space.

delivery truck and reconstructed by Seidelhuber Iron Works, who are believed to have been the original fabricators of the structure. The Chief Seattle fountain, sculpted by James Wehn, was also added in 1909. The "Day and Night" panels, by Edgar Heap of Birds, were added in 1989; they show native Lushootseed symbols and English translations. The Pergola and Totem pole are both designated National Historic Landmarks.

22) MUTUAL LIFE BUILDING
(Yesler Building)
1891, Elmer Fisher; 1892, Emil DeNeuf; ca. 1904, Robertson & Blackwell; rehabilitation, 1984, Olson/Walker
605 First Avenue

This six-story office block was begun by Elmer Fisher, but only the basement and rusticated red sandstone first floor were completed to his design. Fisher temporarily gave up architecture for real estate investment 1891, and the project was carried out by his former employee, Emil DeNeuf. DeNeuf completed the top five floors using light-colored brick and a more subtle articulation of the bays than Fisher's design, although he did retain the projecting end bays, which originally extended above the cornice. DeNeuf's use of unified, repeated arches is also a departure from Fisher's design, which called for a variety of openings and arch forms. The building was altered by Robertson & Blackwell around 1904, with an addition to the rear, redesign of the cornice and smoothing over of the rusticated base. The building was purchased by the Mutual Life Insurance Company in 1895, and has since gone by that name.

23) POST MEWS BUILDING
(Traveler's Hotel)
1913, Albert Wickersham; rehabilitation, 1979, Jones & Jones
80 Yesler Way/611 Post Avenue

This three-story brick masonry hotel was designed by the same architect who was responsible for the Yesler Hotel (now the Pioneer Square Hotel) across the street. The simple design of this building features well-proportioned, regularly organized window openings and an understated cornice. The building was rehabilitated by Jones & Jones, and was the first mixed-use condominium in Seattle.

24) SEATTLE STEAM
1902, Stone & Webster (utility company, Boston, MA)
620 Western Avenue/619 Post Avenue

This steam plant was built for the newly formed Mutual Light & Heat Company in 1902 to serve the area south of Madison Street. This facility was added to the adjoining Old Post Station, which is believed to have been built in 1890. The façade of this utilitarian building was given an elegant treatment with an arcade of double-height arched windows and a decorative bracketed intermediate cornice. Seattle Steam was formed in 1951 to take over operation of the plant, which now houses a back-up boiler that provides heat to many buildings in Pioneer Square to this day.

25) JOURNAL BUILDING
1898; addition, ca. 1914, unknown
83 Columbia Street

The Journal Building is a four-story masonry building believed to have been built only to the first floor in 1898, and the top three floors added around 1914. Large-cut sandstone faces the ground floor, which is punctuated by broad storefronts with clerestory windows. The upper floors are faced in brick and consist of regular bays of triple double-hung windows. A dentil band runs below the overhanging metal cornice at the parapet. The building has been occupied by the *Daily Journal of Commerce* since 1921.

26) POLSON BUILDING
1910, Saunders & Lawton; rehabilitation, 2000, Mahlum Architects
71 Columbia Street

This six-story warehouse building takes its name from its original owner, the Polson Realty Company. It was part of the industrial development of this area after the filling of the former tide flats and reflects an advance in building technology in its use of reinforced concrete. Warehouses built just a few years prior were constructed with brick masonry exterior walls and heavy timber interior structure. The Polson Building was twice damaged by fire, first in 1958, and again in a 1996 arson. The building was rehabilitated in 2000 based on historical photographs.

27) PIONEER SQUARE HOTEL
(Yesler Hotel)
1914, Albert Wickersham; rehabilitation, 1995,
Design Design (San Francisco)
77 Yesler Way

The façade of this simple, four-story brick hotel is enlivened by alternating large and small window groupings and a balanced arrangement of flat iron balconies. Built as a workingmen's hotel, the building had become a "flophouse" by the 1930's when much of this area was falling into disrepair. The Yesler Hotel was rehabilitated and renamed the Pioneer Square Hotel in 1995. The 75-room boutique-style hotel was the first tourist-oriented hotel to be developed in the Pioneer Square historic district.

28) YESLER BUILDING
(Bank of Commerce)
1891, Elmer Fisher; ca. 1895, Emil DeNeuf
91 Yesler Way

Henry Yesler once again turned to Elmer Fisher for the design of the four-story Yesler Building, constructed as the Bank of Commerce. The first three floors were built to Fisher's design and consist of an arcade of triple-height sandstone round arches springing from rusticated piers with elaborately carved capitals. His former draftsman, Emil DeNeuf, was responsible for the fourth floor, which is faced in brick with double-hung rectangular windows and a projecting cornice with decorative brackets.

29) SCHWABACHER BUILDING
1890, Elmer Fisher; 1893, Emil DeNeuf
105 First Avenue S.

The four-story, L-shaped brick masonry Schwabacher Building was badly damaged by a fire in 1892, which resulted in the need to replace the façade of the First Avenue elevation. The Yesler Way façade retains the original design by Fisher and suggests Romanesque influence with its sandstone base and fourth-floor arched arcade. The replacement façade by DeNeuf was executed in a Renaissance Revival mode in cream-colored brick with a fourth-floor arcade of small arches springing from short round columns with decorative capitals. The parapet is faced with a slightly projecting bracketed cornice. This building demonstrates the success of the post-fire building ordinance—as the 1892 fire was contained within the building—as well as a move away from Romanesque-inspired design after the first post-fire construction boom. The building was commissioned by the Schwabacher Brothers, grocery and hardware wholesalers who had operated from this site since 1869.

30) MERCHANTS CAFÉ
1890, William Boone; restoration, 1972,
Richard Lawson
109 Yesler Way

This three-story brick masonry building is home to Seattle's oldest standing restaurant, the Merchants Café, which has occupied the building since its founding in 1890. The grid composition of the façade consists of two floors above the glazed storefront level, which are divided into four narrow bays with horizontal banding and rectangular spandrel panels of cast stone. Most of the cornice was lost after the 1949 earthquake, and the original decorative parapet wall was replaced with the present concrete one. The interior of the café features its original pressed metal ceiling and a carved thirty-foot-long bar that was shipped around Cape Horn.

31) TERRY-DENNY BUILDING
1891, Saunders & Houghton; rehabilitation, 2000, Stickney Murphy Romine Architects
109-115 First Avenue S.

This five-story masonry building was commissioned by settlers Arthur Denny and Charles Terry in the immediate wake of the 1889 fire. Its façade shows residual Victorian convention with its grid composition, narrow window openings and eclectic ornamentation. A pediment that rose from the center of the cornice has been removed. The Northern Hotel originally occupied the upper floors, and was a popular stop for Klondike Gold Rush prospectors on their way to Alaska. After years of sitting vacant, the upper floors were rehabilitated into 48 residential units, eight of which are contained within a penthouse addition.

32) MAYNARD BUILDING
(Dexter Horton Bank)
1892, Albert Wickersham; rehabilitation, 1975, Olson/Walker
119 First Avenue S.

The five-story Maynard Building stands out among its neighbors, not only for its buff pressed brick and sandstone cladding, but also for its confident application of the design principles of Chicago School architects and their integration of Romanesque elements. The main entrance is situated beneath a squat round arch supported by columns with pink marble shafts and intricately carved capitals. The ground floor is punctuated by uniform round arched windows and divided by a belt course from the upper floors. Brick piers with rounded edges ascend the second through fourth floors beneath an arcade of round arches. The recessed spandrels feature a checkerboard motif, which is repeated above the arched arcade. The upper story consists of rectangular openings set beneath corbelling and a projecting cornice. The southeast corner is marked by a small engaged tower called a tourelle, which rises the full height of the building and originally terminated with a dome. A horizontal pediment over the slightly projecting main entrance bay has also been removed. The Maynard Building was constructed as the Dexter Horton Bank, which later became the Seattle First National Bank, now part of the Bank of America.

33) J & M HOTEL
(Marshall Block)
1889, Comstock & Troetsche, ca. 1902, unknown
201 First Avenue S.

 The first two floors of this brick masonry building sprang up immediately after the Great Fire and were executed in the mode of Victorian commercial architecture with its characteristic tall, narrow window openings topped by segmental arches. The third floor was added later, probably around 1902. Originally built as the Marshall Block, for Captain J.H. Marshall, the building is now known as the J & M Hotel for the ground-floor café, which has occupied the building since the Klondike Gold Rush years.

34) MAUD BUILDING
1890, Saunders & Houghton
311 First Avenue S.

Orange-red brick cladding contrasts with the light grey brick and stone trim, creating visual interest on this three-story brick masonry building. The ground-floor store fronts are divided by thin cast-iron columns and terminate at a narrow arched doorway. Irregular brick quoining marks the edges of the façade at the top two floors. The building was designed for William Maud and is believed to be the first commission completed by the partnership of Saunders & Houghton.

35) GLOBE BUILDING
(Marshall-Walker Building)
1891, William Boone; rehabilitation, 1982,
Jones & Jones
300 First Avenue S.

The four-story Globe Building provides another example of the combination of influences that characterizes many of the buildings during the first wave of construction after the fire. The grid-like façade with tall, narrow windows divided by flat pilasters betrays Victorian convention, while the rusticated sandstone arches and articulation of base, shaft and cornice (now lost) suggest the influence of Chicago School architects and the Romanesque revival. Constructed as the Marshall-Walker Building, it was developed by the two owners and divided down the center by a brick wall. The emphasis on the two corner bays marks the entrance to each owner's side. The building was occupied by a hotel and renamed the Globe Hotel in 1898. The Globe Building has been

The clock at the northwest corner of the Globe Building was placed here in 1984 in honor of Earl Layman, Seattle's first historic preservation officer. Originally known as the Young's Credit Jeweler's clock, it sat disassembled outdoors for years before being restored by Historic Seattle. Its original location was Fourth Avenue and Pike Street.

home to the Elliott Bay Book Company since its founding in 1973. The rehabilitation of the Globe Building involved breaking through the brick dividing wall, joining the two spaces and restoring the interior.

36) GRAND CENTRAL ON THE PARK
(Squire Latimer Building)
1890, Comstock & Troetsche; rehabilitation, 1972, Ralph Anderson
214 First Avenue S.

The four-story Squire Latimer Building was commissioned by former territorial governor Watson Squire and prominent businessman Norval Latimer. Ground level cast-iron and wood storefronts flank a round arched sandstone entrance on the main façade with a continuous frieze carved in a floral motif running above. The upper stories, which utilize a variety of window openings, are faced with red pressed brick and divided into equal bays by narrow piers. During the Klondike Gold Rush, the building housed the Grand Central Hotel, from which it takes its present name. The iron gates on the main façade and eastern façade facing Occidental Square were added with the 1972 rehabilitation, at which time the atrium was developed. The upper floors were reconverted to their original function as office space.

37) OCCIDENTAL SQUARE
(Occidental Park)
1972, Jones & Jones; redevelopment, 2006, Otak, Inc.
Occidental Avenue S. & S. Main Street

This .6-acre park was created on the site of a former parking lot as part of the early Pioneer Square preservation efforts. The site was developed as a pedestrian precinct connecting with Occidental Mall. The park was originally paved with cobblestones salvaged from other parts of Pioneer Square and its edges lined with London plane trees. The park recently underwent a major and controversial redevelopment, which resulted in the removal of seventeen trees. The trees had become overgrown, creating a dark and underused space. The cobblestone was replaced with ADA-accessible pavers and lighting was upgraded. Activity areas were added, including bocce ball courts, chess tables and a stage. The park's original Totem Poles, carved by Duane Pasco, were relocated to moss gardens north of the stage. The tallest Totem, titled "Sun and Raven," was created for the 1974 Spokane World's Fair. "Man Riding on the Tail of a Whale" was carved in 1971. The bear and Tsonoqua Totems were donated by Richard White, a developer who was involved in the early restoration of Pioneer Square. The Fallen Firefighter Memorial, by Hai Ying Wu, was added to the eastern edge of the park in 1998.

38) UNION TRUST BUILDING
1893, Skillings & Corner; rehabilitation, 1965, Ralph Anderson
117 S. Main Street

This four-story brick masonry building was one of the earliest Renaissance Revival buildings in Seattle and features a façade clad in light-beige brick, a move away from the red brick that characterizes much of the "burnt district." The Union Trust Building and its neighbor at 115 S. Main Street were among the earliest buildings to be rehabilitated by Ralph Anderson before the area was designated as an historic district. Anderson purchased the building and moved his offices there while incrementally restoring it.

39) STATE BUILDING
1891, Elmer Fisher
300 Occidental Avenue S.

This four-story warehouse building was designed to house the Schwabacher Brothers wholesale dry goods business, whose building at First Avenue South and Yesler Way, also designed by Fisher, did not have enough storage capacity. The warehouse was built with steel beams, cast-iron columns and heavy timber floor joists, said to be capable of supporting 500 pounds per square inch. Both street-facing façades are symmetrical, with a central bay dividing two flanking bays, having broad storefronts with double-height arched windows and four rectangular openings above. The State Building is one of very few in Pioneer Square that retains its original cornice.

40) OCCIDENTAL MALL
1972, Jones & Jones
Occidental Avenue between S. Main & S. Jackson Streets

Occidental Mall was developed along with Occidental Park and the rehabilitation of Pioneer Square. Occidental Avenue South from South Main Street to South Jackson Street was closed off to vehicle traffic and paved in red brick for use as a pedestrian thoroughfare. A single row of trees lines the open space.

41) FIRE STATION NO. 10/SEATTLE FIRE DEPARTMENT HEADQUARTERS
1929, Frank L. Baker
305 Second Avenue S.

This four-story concrete fire station was constructed to replace the previous fire department headquarters, which was destroyed in the Second Avenue Extension

Weinstein A/U rendering of new Seattle Fire Department Headquarters.

Sculpture at Fire Station #10 by Tom Askman, 1987.

Fire Station No. 10 is no longer sufficient to house the many operations of the modern fire department and a replacement headquarters, located on the block bordered by Fourth and Fifth avenues, Yesler Way and Washington Street, is scheduled to open in 2008. The 61,000 square-foot replacement facility, designed by Weinstein A/U, will house a fire station operations area, a fire alarm dispatch center and an emergency operations center.

project. The utilitarian structure features cast-stone trim and Renaissance Revival detailing, including an ornamental balustrade running along the north and east façades above the first floor. Rusticated pedestals are inset into the building's corners, creating niches that run the height of the building. The pedestals are topped by cut metal sculptures of firefighters by eastern Washington artist Tom Askman. The sculptures, added in 1987, depict one firefighter holding a rescued child, another holding a hose and a third wielding an axe. The sculptures are backlit at night, appearing as silhouettes in front of a fire.

42) CADILLAC HOTEL
1889, Hetherington Clements & Co.; rehabilitation, 2005, Stickney Murphy Romine Architects
319 Second Avenue S.

This three-story workingmen's hotel was one of only two brick structures to be constructed on South Jackson Street in the immediate aftermath of the 1889 fire; it was over a decade before the surrounding wooden structures were replaced by the more solid ones standing today. The façade, executed in the grid composition typical of Victorian commercial architecture, is largely in its original form except for the loss of a pediment that once rose from the center of the Second Avenue South façade. The building was badly damaged in the 2001 Nisqually earthquake, and its owners sought permission to tear it down. Historic Seattle intervened and purchased the hotel in 2002. The rehabilitation involved converting the upper floors into office spaces and developing the ground floor and basement as the new home of the Klondike Gold Rush National Historical Park.

43) MERRILL PLACE
1985, Olson/Walker and NBBJ
411 First Avenue S.

The Merrill Place mixed-use complex comprises an entire block and incorporates four historic buildings: the Schwabacher Hardware Co. Building (1905, Bebb & Mendel); the Seller Building (1906, A. Warren Gould); the Hambach Building (1913, Saunders & Lawton); and the Schwabacher Warehouse Annex (1909), located behind the Schwabacher Hardware Co. Building. The buildings were purchased by the R. D. Merrill Co. for redevelopment into retail, residential and office space. The alley façade of the Seller Building was replaced with a seven-story stepped curtain wall constructed of aluminum and green glass, which overlooks a promenade and reflecting pool, bringing natural light into the formerly dark office spaces. This development represents an important factor in revitalizing Seattle's historic districts, where government historic designation and funds help with the initial efforts, prompting private developers to step in to create inner-city neighborhoods with character and diversity.

44) JACKSON BUILDING
(Capitol Brewing Co.)
1900, Carl A. Breitung, rehabilitation, 1963,
Ralph Anderson
322 First Avenue S.

The three-story Jackson Building was originally constructed for the Capitol Brewing Co., which later became the Olympic Brewery. The main façade of this Renaissance Revival building runs along South Jackson Street. It is symmetrically composed and divided into three bays by two pilasters with floral capitals on each side of the central, pedimented bay. The stone-clad ground level features a central door with a decorative stone frame. The Jackson Building is very important to the history of Pioneer Square preservation as the first building to be rehabilitated in the area, seven years before its designation as an historic district.

45) WASHINGTON SHOE BUILDING
(Washington Iron Works Building)
1892, Boone & Willcox; 1912, Blackwell & Baker; ca. 1930, unknown; rehabilitation, 2001, Ron Wright & Associates
400 Occidental Avenue S

This six-story brick masonry building was originally built as the four-story Washington Iron Works Building. Two stories were added in 1912, reflecting the growing industrialization of the area. The addition was done compatibly, repeating the form of the window openings and carrying the theme of the arch on the upper level. The spandrels on the addition feature rusticated brick, similar to that on the top floor of the original structure, although the sandstone belt courses that divided the floors of the original building were not carried out on the addition, suggesting a desire to emphasize its verticality. The storefronts were altered in an Art Deco motif in the 1930s, by which time the building was primarily occupied by offices. The Washington Shoe Building was rehabilitated in 2001 for retail and office use.

46) KING STREET CENTER
1999, NBBJ
210 S. Jackson Street

This eight-story office building was intended to harmonize in scale, form and materials with the historic buildings that make up the Pioneer Square neighborhood. The building is shared by the King County Department of Natural Resources and Parks and the King County Department of Transportation. The tenants requested a building that would reflect the goals of their agencies by integrating progressive environmental design. Eighty percent of the construction waste was recycled; 32,000 square yards of used carpet were cleaned and re-dyed; recycled glass tiles and left over paint were used on the interior; and over 3,000 tons of soil were decontaminated during excavation and reused as top soil for landscaping. A rooftop rainwater collection system delivers water to storage tanks, which is recycled for flushing toilets. For these and many other features, King Street Center was awarded Gold LEED status.

47) KING STREET STATION ⊓
1906, Reed & Stem (St. Paul, MN); restoration, ongoing (2007), Otak, Inc.
301 S. Jackson Street

King Street Station was created in conjunction with the railroad tunnel that runs underneath downtown and marks an important era of growth for the city that helped establish Seattle as the primary shipping port of the Pacific Northwest. The ground floor of the station is faced in granite with upper walls of red pressed brick featuring stone and terra-cotta trim. The station is topped with a hipped tile roof. The 120-foot tower is modeled after the campanile on the Piazza San Marco in Venice and for many years, along with the Smith Tower, defined the skyline of Seattle. Its architects, Reed & Stem, designed many train stations throughout the United States, including Grand Central Station in New York City. The interior spaces were altered in the 1950s and 60s, resulting in the removal of the decorative plaster wall panels and covering of the plaster ceiling with a suspended acoustic tile roof. Restoration is underway to return the station to its original appearance.

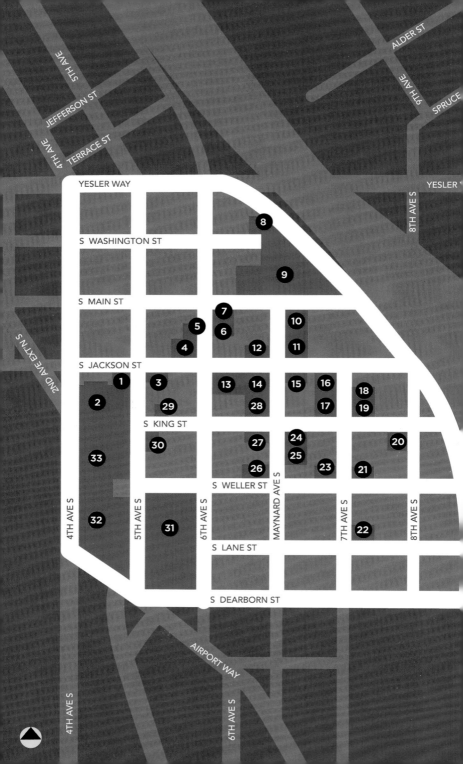

CHAPTER 2

INTERNATIONAL DISTRICT

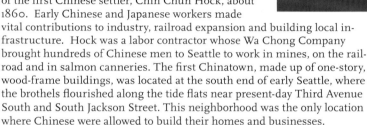

Seattle's International District is unusual in that Asians from many countries—Chinese, Japanese, Filipinos—have lived in close proximity in this area.   Although many of the buildings date to the first quarter of the twentieth century, the district continues to expand and incorporate more recent immigrant groups such as the Vietnamese.

Seattle's Asian population has played an important role in the city's development since the arrival of the first Chinese settler, Chin Chun Hock, about 1860. Early Chinese and Japanese workers made vital contributions to industry, railroad expansion and building local infrastructure. Hock was a labor contractor whose Wa Chong Company brought hundreds of Chinese men to Seattle to work in mines, on the railroad and in salmon canneries. The first Chinatown, made up of one-story, wood-frame buildings, was located at the south end of early Seattle, where the brothels flourished along the tide flats near present-day Third Avenue South and South Jackson Street. This neighborhood was the only location where Chinese were allowed to build their homes and businesses.

The first Japanese arrived in the late 1870s, not long after Japan opened to contacts with the West. The early population of both Chinese and Japanese immigrants was predominately male. Laws prohibiting Chinese from marrying non-Chinese kept their numbers relatively low.

Hard economic times in the early 1880s led to anti-Chinese sentiment among white laborers. The National Chinese Exclusion Act of 1882 prohibited further immigration of Chinese and fostered a climate of prejudice. The fear of Chinese labor erupted in violence in Seattle on February 7, 1886, when a mob of agitators called for the expulsion of all Chinese residents. The next day, 350 Chinese were led from their homes to the waterfront and forced aboard the *Queen of the Pacific*, bound for San Francisco. The ship could take only 200 passengers; the 150 Chinese who remained waited six

An illustration of the Anti-Chinese riot from West Shore, *March 1886*

days in a virtual pressure-cooker of intolerance for the next departure. When the police attempted to escort the Chinese back to their homes, the mob rioted in protest. Shots were fired into the crowd, killing one agitator. After the departure of the next ship, the original Chinatown was abandoned and only a dozen Chinese remained in Seattle.

Among the few Chinese who remained after the riot was Chin Gee Hee, a former associate of Chin Chun Hock in the Wa Chong Company who started his own business in labor contracting and importing, the Quon Tuck Company. His services brought vital Chinese labor back to Seattle in the building boom initiated by the Great Fire, just three years after the expulsion. The fire destroyed the buildings of old Chinatown, and a new Chinatown was soon developed near Second Avenue S. and S. Washington Street. Masonry structures such as the three-story Canton Building and the Chin Gee Hee Building (see Pioneer Square tour) brought a sense of economic independence and permanence to the new Chinatown. Chin Gee Hee left Seattle as a millionaire in 1905 and went on to finance China's Suning Railroad.

The Japanese were not covered by the Exclusion Act until 1924 and were permitted to bring in wives using the "picture bride" system, in which photographs were sent between the countries and marriages arranged. This system, which was also used by German and Scandinavian immigrants, facilitated growth of the Japanese population, making them the largest ethnic group in Seattle by the turn of the century.

The completion of the Jackson Street regrade in 1908 opened up land east of Chinatown to development, and the present-day International District quickly began to take shape, with Japanese population along the northern fringes and the Chinese expanding east and southeast on filled tide flats. A later infrastructure project, the construction of the Second Avenue Extension, begun in 1929, sliced through the second Chinatown (around Second Avenue S. and S. Washington Street), further reinforcing the eastward movement of the Asian communities.

After trade was established between Seattle and Japan with the 1896 landing of the *Miike Maru*, Seattle marketed itself as a gateway to Asian trade. This economic relationship was a major feature of the 1909 Alaska-Yukon-Pacific Exposition. However, the Japanese as individuals still faced discrimination, including relegation to balconies during theatrical performances. That same year they built their own theater, the Nippon Kan, in Nihonmachi, or Japantown, which had developed between Second and Twelfth avenues south along Yesler Way and Washington Street and centered at Sixth Avenue South and South Main Street.

Leaders in the Chinese community, such as Chinese Consul Goon Dip, began building impressive structures such as the Milwaukee Hotel, in the central part of the new Chinatown. Family associations and tongs—fraternal societies such as the Bing Kung Association that assisted immigrants—constructed buildings, many with upper-floor balconies in the tradition of southern China. Single-room-occupancy (SRO) hotel buildings with ground-floor retail were constructed throughout the district to provide housing for the mostly single male population.

Filipino immigrants began making up a significant number of the area's population around 1910, after the United States annexed the Philippine Islands from Spain in 1899 as American territory as a result of the Spanish-American War. Although not allowed citizenship at the time, hundreds of Filipino workers immigrated, mainly employed in canneries and agriculture. Because they were unable to join white labor unions, their only recourse against the corrupted labor contractors was to form unions of their own. Their efforts effectively ended the labor contracting system and gave them a powerful voice for labor reforms.

The Japanese, which by 1940 made up the largest minority population in Seattle, vanished virtually overnight. The attack on Pearl Harbor on

December 7, 1941, led to the devastating Executive Order 9066, issued on February 19, 1942, calling for the immediate relocation of all West Coast Japanese-Americans. Over 7,000 were hastily sent from Seattle to the internment camp in Minidoka, Idaho. Allowed to bring only what they could carry, they were forced to leave behind nearly all of their belongings, quickly stashing what they could at the homes of non-Japanese friends and other locations.

Bailey Gatzert School classroom after internment of Japanese Americans, 1942.

During the war, the Chinese and Filipino populations increased, as the 1943 repeal of the Exclusion Act allowed a larger number of Chinese to immigrate. They were able to develop an even stronger, more self-sufficient community.

Even before internment, the hilltop neighborhood where many Japanese and Filipinos lived had been demolished in 1939-40 for the Yesler Terrace housing project. This area of older houses near the county hospital ([1929-1931], now Harborview Medical Center) was considered a blight, and the Seattle Housing Authority selected it for its first slum clearance project. Although the project was built for low-income residents, it served as housing for defense workers and returning veterans until the 1950s.

The International District was also important to Seattle's African-American community. Defense industry jobs attracted African-Americans, whose numbers nearly tripled in only a few years, to 10,000. Some lived in Yesler Terrace, which was the country's first racially integrated housing project; however, most lived farther east, in the Central Area. The connecting South Jackson Street corridor became a lively hub of jazz, swing and rhythm-and-blues clubs.

Many of the Japanese who returned to Seattle after the war did not return to the International District, choosing instead to settle elsewhere.

Their population in the International District never returned to its pre-war peak, but the Japanese culture has remained an important part of the diverse fabric of the neighborhood.

The interests of Seattle's Asian population were given more political attention with the 1962 election of City Councilman Wing Luke, whose life was sadly cut short by a plane crash in 1965. The Wing Luke Asian Museum, a Pan-Asian-American museum, was named to honor his legacy. In 1965, national immigration restrictions were loosened, and significant numbers of Korean and Vietnamese immigrants joined the community in the 1960s and 70s. Newer buildings east of Interstate 5 house "Little Saigon" today.

The 1960s-70s brought hard times to the International District. Construction of Interstate 5 in the 1960s razed homes, hotels and churches, and destroyed neighborhood connections. Stronger fire codes, resulting from the 1970 Ozark Hotel fire, led the owners of many single-room-occupancy hotels to close their buildings rather than bear the expense of new sprinkler systems and other upgrades. As decay and abandonment spread, urban renewal plans threatened the area. However, the community organized to fight them. The International District Improvement Association (now known as Inter*im) was established in 1969 to promote revitalization. Concerns about impacts of the Kingdome prompted the establishment of a Special Review Board in 1973 to protect the buildings and public spaces in the community. The Seattle Chinatown-International District Public Development Authority was established in 1975 and completed one of the first building rehabilitations, the Bush Hotel, in 1978.

Commercial buildings and single-room-occupancy hotels in the neighborhood have been incrementally rehabilitated in the intervening decades, many to provide low-income and senior housing, as well as social services. Public improvement projects,

Anti-Kingdome demonstration, 197

including parks, Asian-inspired signage and street lights, have been added to underscore the ethnic character of the community. The historic core of the neighborhood, west of Interstate 5, was placed in the National Register of Historic Places in 1987.

Community members and organizations are now working with the city and surrounding neighborhoods to plan for continued revitalization. Efforts are underway to encourage renovation of those buildings that are still vacant or in disrepair, and infill compatible with the historic ethnic character is sought. Regional light rail service to nearby King Street Station (see Pioneer Square tour) is planned to begin in 2009, and will likely attract more residential development.

Proposals for changed freeway access and encroachment of office developments pose challenges. The key will be to enhance economic vitality while retaining small businesses, residential opportunities and ethnic character. Whatever decisions are made about the future development in and around the International District, Seattle is fortunate to have one of the most intact, self-sufficient and culturally diverse Asian-American communities on the West Coast.

The buildings listed in this section are all within a city historic district, the International Special Review District. Some of them are also local landmarks or are listed in the National Register, as noted in the text.

1) INTERNATIONAL DISTRICT STATION
Seattle Transit Tunnel, 1990, TRA Architects with Sonya Ishii and Alice Adams (artists)

This colorful steel structure marks the entrance to the International District Transit Tunnel Station, which is the southern terminus of the Metro Transit Tunnel that extends north to Ninth Avenue at Pine Street. Asian-inspired art is featured in the station area and below ground. The tunnel was closed between 2005 and 2007 while being upgraded and retrofitted for use by both busses and light rail. The completion of the project fulfills a long-time vision of the Union Station vicinity as a multi-modal transportation center, which was just beginning to be realized with the completion of this station in 1990.

2) UNION STATION 冊
1911, Daniel J. Patterson; rehabilitation, 1999, Ron Wright & Associates and NBBJ
401 S. Jackson Street

The three-story, neoclassical Union Station building opened as the Oregon and Washington Railroad Station to serve the Union Pacific Railroad and the Milwaukee Road. The reinforced concrete frame building features a symmetrical façade with brick veneer and white terra-cotta ornamentation. A monumental semicircular window spans the southern façade, allowing natural light to flood the 55-foot-high barrel vaulted Great Hall. Passenger service ceased here in 1971 when Amtrak consolidated service in the neighboring King Street Station. The station was rehabilitated in 1999 for use as the headquarters of Sound Transit, a regional transit authority serving King, Pierce and Snohomish counties. The rehabilitation was part of the larger development project by Union Station Associated, LLC, which was also responsible for the adjacent 505 Union Station and the Opus Center complex.

3) BUTY BUILDING
(Idaho Hotel)
1901, James Stephen; addition, 1910, James Stephen
501 S. Jackson Street

The three-story western portion of this building was constructed for Frank Buty in 1901. The 1907 regrade of Jackson Street required a new street-level floor and façade alterations. In 1910, the original turret was removed and a three-story east wing, the Idaho Hotel, was added. The Jackson Street façade features a cast-stone arched entrance with ionic columns and the building's name in relief. Sullivanesque ornamentation is contained within the window surrounds of the otherwise unadorned brick façade. Sullivanesque ornamentation, characterized by a weaving of linear and geometric forms with stylized foliage in a symmetrical pattern that is contained within the architectural elements, is unusual in Seattle.

4) GOVERNOR APARTMENTS
1926, J. L. McCauley
516-526 S. Jackson Street

This is the second of two finely executed terra-cotta-clad buildings on Jackson Street designed by J. L. McCauley. Both were built by the Rainier Heat and Power Company, which was a major landowner that produced heat and electricity at their plant at Fifth Avenue South and South Weller Street. Ornamentation on the two-story building includes a wave band above the first floor storefronts, dentils and brackets above the second story windows and a parapet with open niches forming a balustrade.

5) MAIN STREET SCHOOL ANNEX 🏯
1903, unknown; addition, 1910, James Stephen;
rehabilitation, 1989, Kovalenko Architects
307 Sixth Avenue S.

This wood frame structure was built as an annex to the 1873 Main Street School (destroyed), which stood at the corner of Sixth Avenue S. and S. Main Street. This annex was constructed to house Seattle's first kindergarten on land donated by the widow of Bailey Gatzert, Seattle's eighth mayor. The front porch, featuring ionic columns supporting a dentiled pediment, was added by Seattle School District architect James Stephen, in 1910. The building operated as a school until 1921. Threatened with demolition, the annex was purchased by Historic Seattle in 1974, the first transaction made by that organization. The building was later sold with protective covenants and now provides office space.

6) NP HOTEL
1914, John Graham, Sr.; rehabilitation, 1994,
Kovalenko Hale Architects
306 Sixth Avenue S.

This six-story brick building hosted Japanese dignitaries in its early years and continued to serve as a hotel until it closed in the 1970s. The building was purchased by the Inter*im Community Development Association and rehabilitated in 1994. The project included cleaning of the exterior brick and terra-cotta, restoration of the sheet metal cornice and remodeling of most of the rooms into low-income apartments. The historic configuration was retained on the second floor, which includes one bedroom units and shared bath facilities.

7) PANAMA HOTEL 🏨
1910, Sabro Ozasa
605-1/2 S. Main Street

This five-story brick hotel, featuring flat arch windows and corner quoining, was an important anchor to the Nihonmachi, or Japantown, that once flourished in the area of South Main Street. Its designer was the first Asian-American architect to practice in Seattle. The Panama Hotel houses within its basement the last remaining intact *sento*, a Japanese public bathhouse, in the United States. The bathhouse, an important community gathering spot, was in use until the 1950s. When the hotel's present owner purchased the building in 1986, she became the caretaker of dozens of suitcases and artifacts that had been stowed in the basement of the building by Japanese Americans who were forced to leave their homes and businesses for internment camps during World War II. Several of these unclaimed artifacts are visible in the hotel's tea and coffee house. One may call the hotel to arrange a tour of the basement and bathhouse. Because of its unique importance to American history and the story of Japanese-Americans, the Panama Hotel was designated a National Historic Landmark in 2006.

8) KOBE PARK BUILDING 🏨
(Astor Hotel/Nippon Kan)
1909, Thompson & Thompson; rehabilitation, 1981,
Edward M. Burke
628 S. Washington Street

This four-story red brick building features second-story arched windows and flat arch windows on the upper floors. Built as the Astor Hotel, the Kobe Park building contains the Nippon Kan, or Japanese Hall, an auditorium that was at the heart of Nihonmachi as the location of community events and theatrical performances until the internment of West Coast Japanese-Americans in 1942. Rehabilitation of the building began in 1978 and it reopened in 1981 for community and performance use until it was sold in 2005. It now serves as the offices and dispatch center of a messenger service. The building's hilltop location illustrates how the community was divided by the construction of the Yesler Terrace housing project and the construction of Interstate 5.

9) KOBE TERRACE PARK
1975, William Teufel
221 Sixth Avenue S.

This one-acre park, located on a terraced hillside on the northeast edge of the International district, was formerly part of the Yesler Terrace housing project (1941). After the 1965 construction of Interstate 5 divided this triangle of land from Yesler Terrace, it was redesigned with paths and benches and became known as Yesler Terrace Park. The site was redeveloped in 1975 as a "Forward Thrust" project and renamed Kobe Terrace Park, in honor of Seattle's Japanese sister city, Kobe. The park features Mt. Fuji and Yoshino flowering cherry trees and an 8,000 pound stone Yokimidoro ("view of the snow") lantern. Both the trees and the lantern were gifts from the citizens of Kobe. The lower path through Kobe Terrace Park leads to the one-acre Danny Woo Community Garden, named for the restaurant owner who donated the land. Structures and other improvements to the garden were built by University of Washington design/build classes.

The Yesler Terrace Housing Project, developed by the Seattle Housing Authority in 1939-1941, was the first public housing project in the Pacific Northwest and the first racially-integrated public housing in the country. Built on 43 acres overlooking Puget Sound, the project included 863 units in small buildings, allowing for generous amounts of green space. Although it was intended as a slum clearance project to provide low-income housing, it served as defense worker housing until the 1950s. Since then it has housed low-income residents who benefit from its convenient location near downtown and health care facilities. Yesler Terrace was humane and well-designed low-income housing. It was designed by a team of architects led by J. Lister Holmes including William Bain, William Aitken, John T. Jacobsen, George Stoddard and landscape architects Butler Sturtevant and E. Clair Heilman. About one-third of the units were removed to construct the freeway; the remaining units on the east side of Interstate 5 have been significantly altered. A planning process to replace the housing is now underway.

10) NIHONMACHI TERRACE
2006, Pyatok Architects
651 S. Main Street

Nihonmachi Terrace is a five-story, 50-unit development that provides affordable housing for seniors, families, disabled and low-income residents. The complex features an internal courtyard with children's play area and on-site parking. Nihonmachi Terrace was developed on a long-empty site that posed a safety risk to neighborhood residents. The name "Nihonmachi" was chosen to preserve the history of the Japantown that once thrived along South Main Street to 12th Avenue. The development of this complex is part of a larger effort to preserve and revitalize the Nihonmachi in Seattle and other West Coast cities.

11) RAINIER HEAT & POWER COMPANY
1917, J. L. McCauley
650-662 S. Jackson Street

The Rainier Heat & Power Company building is the second of two prominent terra-cotta-clad buildings designed by J.L. McCauley along Jackson Street. Classical ornamentation on this two-story commercial building includes shields, scroll brackets, swags and lion heads. The parapet is adorned with terra-cotta urns. The building was once home to the Japanese Chamber of Commerce and was, in 1930, the site of the founding of the Japanese American Citizen League, still an important national civil rights organization. In the 1940s and 50s, the second floor was the location of the local African American chapter of the Elk's Club, where, at age 17, musician Ray Charles first performed regularly.

12) FAR EAST BUILDING
(Havana Hotel)
ca. 1900, unknown; 1908, Thompson &Thompson;
rehabilitation, 1984, Kovalenko Architects
614-626 S. Jackson Street

The form of the Far East Building is a result of the Jackson Street regrade of 1907. The building's top two floors incorporate two of the only remaining ca.1900 wood-frame buildings in the area. The upper floors include the gabled Japanese Baptist Church and a neighboring workingmen's hotel. The two buildings were elevated in anticipation of the regrading and a brick retail building was constructed beneath to create 40 hotel rooms with seven retail store fronts. After sitting empty for over twenty years and suffering from neglect, the building was rehabilitated into 14 apartment units and ground-floor retail space in 1984.

13) WASHINGTON FEDERAL
(United Savings & Loan)
1972, Woo & Parker Architects
601 S. Jackson Street

Established on July 6, 1960, this bank was the first Asian American-owned savings and loan in the United States. The founders, Robert and Ruth J. Chinn, opened the bank to assist Asians who had difficulty acquiring loans elsewhere. The mural by the entrance, painted by Fay Chong, depicts "The Eight Immortals." United Savings & Loan merged with Washington Federal, Inc. in 2003.

14) BUSH-ASIA CENTER
(Bush Hotel)
1915, J. L. McCauley; rehabilitation, 1981,
Arai/Jackson; renovation, 1997, Kubota Kato
and Tonkin Hoyne Lokan Architects
621 S. Jackson Street

Originally built as the 225-room Bush Hotel, this simple six-story building was among the largest in the district. The building, which had become dilapidated, was rehabilitated in 1981 into 172 low-income housing units and spaces for community services. A 1997 renovation included mechanical and structural upgrades and improvements of all building systems and interiors on the residential floors. The building now includes office, retail, restaurant, and community service spaces in the basement and first two floors and 96 low-income apartments on the top four floors.

15) EVERGREEN APARTMENTS
(Tokiwa Hotel)
1916, Thompson & Thompson; rehabilitation, 1981,
Arai/Jackson Architects
655 S. Jackson Street

This three-story brick building features a terra-cotta central entrance adorned with swags. A raised, arched parapet corresponding to the entrance is treated as a pediment, an approach seen in other Thompson & Thompson buildings in the district. The parapet displays brickwork in a pattern of rectangles inset with diamonds marking the bays. Built as the Tokiwa Hotel, the building was rehabilitated into 16 apartments with ground floor commercial space in 1981.

Adjacent to the **Evergreen Apartments,** *on the southeast corner of South Jackson and Maynard Street South, stands George Tsutakawa's sculpture, Heaven, Man and Earth, which was installed in 1978. George Tsutakawa (1910-1997) moved to Seattle from Japan at the age of 16. He received a BFA from the University of Washington in 1937. During World War II, Tsutakawa taught Japanese language at a Military Intelligence school in Minnesota. He returned to Seattle, received his MFA and began a faculty position at the University of Washington where he taught in the School of Architecture, and later in the School of Art. He later received honorary doctorate degrees from Whitman College and Seattle University. Tsutakawa worked in paint, wood and bronze over his 60-year career, creating more than 75 bronze sculptures for public spaces in the United States, Japan and Canada.*

2 INTERNATIONAL DISTRICT

16) BUSH ASIA ANNEX
(T & C Garage)
1915, unknown
409 Seventh Avenue S.

This 10,000 square-foot former garage building is the location of the Theater Off Jackson, which is a venue for the Seattle performing arts community and the International District neighborhood, offering live performances, Asian film festivals and program viewing parties. The building was home to the Wing Luke Asian Museum from 1987 until 2007, when it relocated to new permanent headquarters in the East Kong Yick building.

17) MILWAUKEE HOTEL
(Goon Dip Building)
1911, Thompson & Thompson
668-1/2 S. King Street/415 Seventh Avenue S.

The five-story Milwaukee Hotel was developed by prominent businessman, labor contractor and Chinese community leader Goon Dip, whose name is inscribed above the main entrance on King Street. The entrance features an elaborate terra-cotta canopy supported by scroll brackets. Window openings on the central and end bays are marked with flat arches formed by radiating terra-cotta tiles; raised portions of the parapet further emphasize these bays. Goon Dip was appointed consul for Washington and Alaska during the 1909 Alaska-Yukon-Pacific Exposition and the building once housed the Chinese consulate. The building was an important anchor for the development of the "New Chinatown."

18) LYN YUEN APARTMENTS
(Republic Hotel)
1920, John Creutzer
410 Seventh Avenue S.

The four-story Lyn Yuen Apartment building features a wrought-iron second-story balcony, a common feature of family association meeting rooms, following the tradition of southern China to allow for fresh air and views down the street below. The building was constructed by a Chinese family association to house immigrants, many of whom were Alaskan cannery workers who resided here during the off season.

19) NEW AMERICAN HOTEL/BING KUNG ASSOCIATION
1916, Thompson & Thompson
708 S. King Street

This four-story brick hotel building features a fourth-floor tile-roof balcony. The building is the location of the Bing Kung Association, an early fraternal organization, known as a "tong," that provided assistance and protection to Chinese immigrants. The building also served as a Chinese Masonic meeting hall. The Masonic symbol is displayed on a cartouche above the balcony.

20) WING LUKE ASIAN MUSEUM
(East Kong Yick Building)
1910, Thompson & Thompson; rehabilitation, 2008, Olson Sundberg Kundig Allen Architects
719 S. King Street

This four-story brick hotel building was constructed with funds pooled by 170 Chinese settlers who formed the Kong Yick Investment Company. The building became an important business and social center for recently-arrived Chinese immigrants. The building's upper floors had been vacant since the 1970s, but family associations and a Chinese senior club continued to occupy the ground floor. In 2007, rehabilitation began to convert the building to the new home of the Wing Luke Asian Museum, the only pan-Asian-American Museum in the United States. The 60,000 square-foot facility includes historic immersion exhibits, exhibit halls, classrooms, meeting rooms, a museum store and a small theater. The facility also provides shared spaces for family associations. The museum is named for Seattle City Councilman Wing Luke, the first Asian-American to hold an elected office in the continental United States.

21) CHONG WA BENEVOLENT ASSOCIATION
1929, Max Van House and Sam Chinn
522 Seventh Avenue S.

This two-story brick building utilizes classical form and Chinese motifs, resulting in a structure that thoroughly combines Western and Chinese culture. The elaborate porch is supported by bamboo-like columns and its crown with upturned corners stands in for a traditional classical pediment. This hybrid style is particularly appropriate to the use of this building as the location of the Chong Wa Benevolent Association. The association is an important community resource that has worked for the rights of Chinese immigrants since its founding in 1915. It also functions as a school, offering language and citizenship courses among other services, including sponsorship of the Seattle Chinese Community Girl's Drill Team.

22) INTERNATIONAL DISTRICT CHILDREN'S PARK
1981, Joey Ing
Seventh Avenue S. & S. Lane Street

This quarter-acre park incorporates traditional and contemporary Asian design elements. It features a neon-lit pavilion, a bronze dragon play structure designed by George Tsutakawa, and plants indigenous to Asia.

23) GEE HOW OAK TIN BENEVOLENT SOCIETY
(Hotel Hudson)
1909, Charles Haynes; alterations, 1936, Bockerman & Chinn; rehabilitation, 1991, Kovalenko Architects
519 Seventh Avenue S.

The three-story Gee How Oak Tin Benevolent Society building operated as the Hotel Hudson, a workingmen's hotel, until being acquired by a Chinese family association. The building features radiating brickwork forming flat arches over the windows and brick quoining at its edges. The dramatic recessed tile-roof balcony was added to the building in 1936 and indicates the location of the association meeting hall. The building was rehabilitated and reconverted into apartments in 1991.

24) REX APARTMENTS
(Rex Hotel)
1909, F.H. Perkins; rehabilitation, 1995, Joey Ing
657 S. King Street

This four-story brick building is an early example of the typical workingmen's hotels that were constructed in the "New Chinatown" after the Jackson Street regrade, having ground level retail space and single-occupancy rooms on the upper floors. Like many buildings in the district, the window openings are topped with flat arches. The Rex Hotel façade is enlivened with white terra-cotta marking the arch crowns and dividing the base, shaft and top of the building. A continuous band running above the top floor openings echoes the fan shape of the flat arches. The overhanging cornice rests atop simple brackets and a dentil band. The Rex Hotel is the location of Tai Tung, the district's oldest continually operating restaurant, established in 1935. The building was rehabilitated for low-income housing in 1995.

〆 *At 511 Seventh Avenue South, on the façade of the Louisa Hotel, is the* **Chinese Community Bulletin Board.** *The use of bulletin boards by the Chinese to aid non-English-speaking immigrants dates back to 1890 in Seattle. The bulletin board was vital to the community prior to the establishment of Asian-language newspapers, but is still in use today. The present bulletin board was installed here in 1960.*

25) EASTERN HOTEL 〼
1911, David Dow; rehabilitation, 1998, Kovalenko Hale Architects
506 Maynard Avenue S.

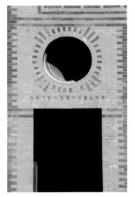

The Eastern Hotel building was constructed for the Wa Chong Company, Seattle's earliest and most successful Chinese mercantile and labor contracting business, which was founded in 1868 by Chin Chun Hock, who is thought to have been the first Chinese settler in King County. The building is distinguished by its fine decorative brickwork. At the storefront level along Maynard Avenue South, a round window above the hotel entrance is framed by an alternating pattern of black and red brick. A meander pattern executed in black brick divides the ground-floor retail from the upper floors. Recessed arch heads on the second story feature a tri-color trompe l'oeil stepped pattern. The third-floor arch heads were given a simpler checker motif. A similar treatment occurs above flat arched fourth-story windows below the bracketed copper cornice. The building was rehabilitated in 1998 and now contains 46 low-income apartment units and renovated retail space. A lobby museum honors Filipino writer Carlos Bulosan, who lived here while working in a cannery.

26) FREEDMAN BUILDING
(Adams Hotel)
1910, unknown; rehabilitation, 1983, Arai/Jackson
513 Maynard Avenue S.

The distinctive façade of this four-story beige brick apartment building displays eclectic Renaissance Revival styling. The façade is divided into six bays on the upper floors, marked by a hierarchy of windows including round arched second-story windows, flat arched third-story windows and double rectangular window openings on the top floor. The second-story arched windows are topped with scrolled crowns that also serve as brackets for the third-story window balconettes. The Freedman Building was rehabilitated in 1983 and now contains 20 apartments and ground-level commercial space.

27) ALPS HOTEL
1910, Graham & Myers
621 S. King Street

This six-story Renaissance Revival building is clad in beige pressed brick on the first two floors with red brick on the upper floors. Radiating brickwork on the third through fifth floors forms flat arches above the window openings with terra-cotta crowns. A belt course divides the shaft from the upper level, which is ornamented with a dentil band and sheet metal cornice featuring a diamond pattern. The Alps Hotel operated as a workingmen's residence and was one of the last buildings to be designed by the partnership of Graham & Myers.

28) HING HAY PARK
1975, Sakuma James & Peterson
Maynard Avenue S. & S. King Street

This quarter-block park features an elaborate Chinese pavilion built in Taipei and donated to the community. The park includes a memorial honoring Chinese-Americans who fell in World War II. The dragon mural, by John Woo, illustrates the multicultural nature of the community, with Chinese, Filipinos and Japanese working on the railroads, canneries and farms, and in internment camps. Hing Hay Park is a popular gathering spot and location for community events such as the Chinese New Year celebration and the International District Summer Festival. This early district improvement project was completed with "Forward Thrust" funds.

29) UNION GOSPEL MISSION
(American Hotel)
1925, J.L. McCauley
520 S. King Street

This simple four-story reinforced concrete building was built as the American Hotel and is now operated by the Union Gospel Mission. The building includes 56 rooms, which can provide shelter for up to 90 women and children.

30) HOTEL PUBLIX
1927, J.L. McCauley
504 Fifth Avenue S.

This six-story working-men's hotel features a stuccoed brick façade with central and corner bays marked by flat pilasters and pediments executed in an English Gothic mode. With its location across from Union Station, the Hotel Publix once served many visitors and new arrivals to the International District.

31) UWAJIMAYA VILLAGE
2001, Arai/Jackson Architects
600 Fifth Avenue S.

This two-block retail-residential complex includes 176 market-rate apartments in three buildings, 365 parking spaces, a 60,000 square-foot superstore, food court and 16,000 square feet of retail space. The exterior is clad in stucco with black and orange banding. The roof is covered with blue tiles, a signature of Uwajimaya's retail outlets. Seattle artist Aki Sogabe designed the dragons for the air vent stack and circular stairs connecting the pedestrian plaza to the underground parking. Other artwork includes a moon gate and a fountain sculpted by Gerard Tsutakawa.

Uwajimaya got its start in Tacoma in 1928 when Fujimatsu Moriguchi began selling fishcakes from the back of a truck. He named the business for his home town. After internment, Moriguchi brought his family back to Seattle and established their business in the International District. Uwajimaya is now run by Tomio Moriguchi, son of the founder, who has expanded the business to become the largest Asian-American retailer in the region, with additional stores in Bellevue, Washington and Beaverton, Oregon. The flagship store moved here from its previous location at Sixth Avenue South and South King Street in 2001.

32) OPUS CENTER AT UNION STATION
2000, NBBJ; Landscape Architect: Murase Associates
Between Fifth & Fourth Avenues S. and S. Weller & S.
Dearborn Streets

The three-building Opus Center office park incorporates the nine-story Opus Center West, the four-story Opus Center East and the triangular, eleven-story Opus Center South. The buildings feature extensive glazing and red brick veneer, relating them to the nearby historic buildings. This complex and the neighboring 505 Union Station are built over the bus tunnel lid, the King Street train station tunnels and a parking structure. The site demanded the use of innovative structural systems, including a system engineered by Seattle-based Coughlin Porter Lundeen, which employs a rubber membrane running beneath the Union Station complex that is analogous to a giant rubber band; in a seismic event, the structures will be stabilized by this system from the movement beneath. The Asian-inspired landscaping is by Murase Associates.

33) 505 UNION STATION
2000, NBBJ
505 Fifth Avenue S.

This unconventional eleven-story office building features a curving green glass wall ascending its northern façade, juxtaposed with an angular glass wall on the western façade that leans toward Fourth Avenue South. The dynamic curved and angled curtain walls appear to cascade over or jut out, respectively, from the more solid structure to which they are attached. 505 Union Station was developed as part of the Union Station Complex by Union Station Associated, LLC and is home to the offices of Vulcan Northwest.

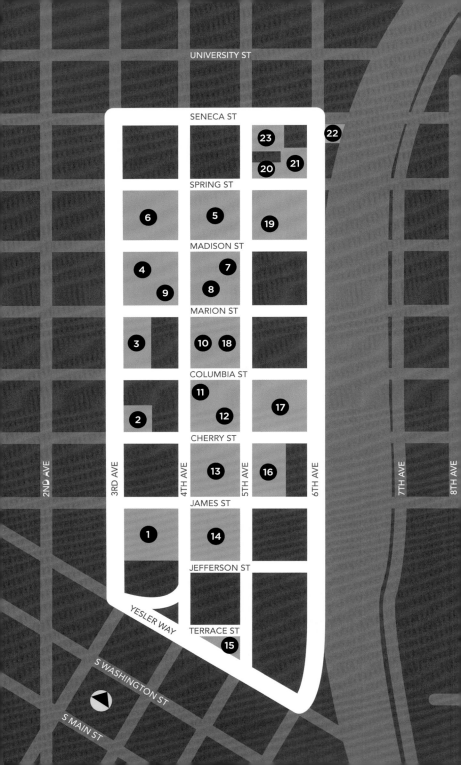

CHAPTER 3

FINANCIAL/CIVIC DISTRICT

Seattle's Financial and Civic District contains City and County government buildings as well as Seattle's tallest skyscraper, Columbia Center. Although the area is characterized by a dense concentration of twentieth and twenty-first century office towers, traces of early twentieth-century Seattle can still be found scattered among them. Efforts to develop a cohesive center of government buildings have had a long legacy in the district and have shaped many of its southern blocks.

The site of the present Financial and Civic District was logged and cleared in Seattle's first years. Its old-growth timbers were processed at Yesler's mill and exported to San Francisco, initiating the city's first industry. Throughout Seattle's first three decades, this area was the residential outskirts of downtown. Churches and gabled clapboard houses surrounded by picket fences with gardens and orchards occupied these blocks. Late-nineteenth century streetcar lines facilitated development of residential areas east to Lake Washington and north to Queen Anne and Green Lake at a time when the city's population grew tenfold from 3,533 in 1880 to 42,800 in 1890.

After Washington became a state in 1889, Seattle produced its first home rule City Charter, which expanded City government and significantly enlarged City Council. Seattle's first City Hall was destroyed in the Great Fire and government administration offices were located in various temporary locations. In 1891, City Hall moved into the former County Courthouse, located on Third Avenue between Yesler Way and Jefferson Street. The City quickly outgrew the building, necessitating a series of ad hoc additions,

Seattle City Hall in "Katzenjammer Castle."

leaving it with an awkward appearance that earned it the nickname, "Katzenjammer Castle."

In 1892, Mayor George Hall suggested purchasing the University of Washington site (see Retail District Tour) for development as a civic center, but the idea failed to find support. Katzenjammer Castle became severely overcrowded and its wood frame construction made it unsafe for keeping public records. A new, "fireproof" City Hall was finally completed in 1909 on the triangular lot between Fifth Avenue, Yesler Way and Terrace Street (now the 400 Yesler Building).

A 1911 proposal by City Engineer Virgil Bogue to construct a civic center in the Denny Regrade (see Belltown tour) was rejected by voters in 1912 in favor of a six-story City-County building (now the King County Courthouse). City Hall moved into the City-County Building in 1916, and the 1909 building became the Public Safety Building, housing the Health Department, City Hospital, Police Department and City Jail. The construction of the Public Safety and City-County buildings established the vicinity of the government center that would develop over the next one hundred years.

Social and educational clubs and associations constructed buildings on the northern blocks between 1904 and the 1930s, including the Rainier Club, the YMCA, YWCA and the Women's University Club. The Arctic Club constructed the terra-cotta-clad Arctic Building in 1916. A handsome Beaux Arts Seattle Central Library, designed by P.J. Weber of Chicago, was built in 1906, establishing its location as the site of two subsequent Seattle Central Libraries.

After World War II, efforts to create a cohesive municipal center were renewed. In 1945, the City Planning Commission hired St. Louis City Planner Harland Bartholomew to create a plan for a proposed public buildings area to be set aside as the location of government offices. Only one building was constructed from the plan, the 1951 Public Safety Building (destroyed) designed by Naramore Bain Brady & Johanson with Young & Richardson

The Public Safety Building became downtown's first international-style building in 1951.

and B. Marcus Priteca. The design of the 12-story building featured an asymmetrical composition, converging masses and functional expression, making it the first international-style building to be constructed downtown. A second Modern building was introduced to the district with the 1959 completion of a new Seattle Central Library building (destroyed) designed by Bindon & Wright and Decker Christenson & Kitchin.

The 1960s and 70s saw continued development of the government center. In 1962, the City to move out of the City-County Building and into a new 12-story Municipal Building (destroyed) designed by Damm Daum & Associates and J.M. MacCammon of Dallas, Texas. The King County Administration Building followed in 1971.

The 1960s and 70s brought a larger scale to the Financial and Civic District with the 1969 completion of the 50-story Seattle First National Bank Building (now Safeco Plaza) and the 41-story Bank of California Building (now 901 5th Avenue Building) in 1974. A high-rise boom in the 1980s brought the 76-story Columbia Center to the district and a rapidly increasing scale that alarmed Seattle residents; this lead to the passage of the "Citizen's Alternative Plan" (CAP) in 1989, which limited building height and density. However, since the technology boom of the 1990s, Seattleites have become more comfortable with their big-city status and have accepted that, given downtown's limited amount of land, there is no place to go but up. Height restrictions were lifted in 2006 from 450 feet to 700 feet in the central business district to encourage taller, thinner buildings.

In 1999, the City adopted the Civic Center Master Plan, which links multiple buildings and open spaces into a municipal campus. Development began in 2000 along the three blocks between Third and Sixth Avenues and Cherry and James Streets. One of the goals of the project, which incorporates open spaces, public art and neighborhood services, was to bridge the gap between Pioneer Square, the International District and the Commercial core.

Providing a model for sustainability was another goal of the plan, which mandated that buildings in the Civic Center achieve a minimum Leadership in Energy and Environmental Design (LEED) rating of Silver. The Seattle Justice Center, completed in 2002, was the first building constructed under the Civic Center Master Plan. City Hall, designed to service the City for 100 years, followed in 2003.

A third Seattle Central Library opened in 2004 after a 1998 vote to spend $196.4 million in public funds and another $80 million in private donations to replace the Central Library and renovate 27 branch libraries. The new Seattle Central Library brings a striking architectural presence to the district and draws visitors from around the world.

Seattle's Financial and Civic District showcases a broad range of architectural styles from the past 100 years, thanks to the handful of low-rise early-twentieth-century gems that have been preserved. The Civic Center and other recent public buildings hint at the potential direction of Seattle's future built environment, as models for environmentally-responsible design. This potential is bolstered by City programs implemented in 2004, which offer green building education, assistance and incentives to encourage sustainable architecture in the private sector.

1) KING COUNTY COURTHOUSE ⑂

1916, Augustus Warren Gould; addition, 1931, Henry Bittman; renovation, 1967, Harmon Pray Detrich and Paul W. Delaney & Associates
516 Third Avenue

The King County Courthouse was origi-nally built as a five-story Beaux Arts City-County building. In 1929, Henry Bittman was hired to design an additional six stories to the building including the three at-tic stories, which served as the county jail and infirmary. The building was modernized in 1967 with new windows, spandrels and interior renovations. The building's interiors have since been partially restored. The main en-trance, which originally faced City Hall Park, was converted to a loading dock with the 1967 renovation. City Hall Park was established in conjunction with the construction of the King County Courthouse (then known as the City-County building), but the historical significance of the 1.3-acre site dates back to Seattle's earliest years. In January 1856, Native Americans, led by Chief Leschi, fought the "Battle of Seattle" here in retaliation for treaties imposed by the territorial government. The Navy gunship *Decatur* fired cannon balls from Elliott Bay and quickly ended the fight. The King County Courthouse is within the boundaries of the Pioneer Square Historic district.

2) ARCTIC BUILDING ⑂ ⑂

1916, Augustus Warren Gould; restoration 1982, Stick-ney & Murphy; restoration, 1997, Wiss Janney Elstner Associates, Inc.; conversion, 2007, Burgess+Weaver Design Group and Madrona Architecture
700 Third Avenue

The Arctic Building was built as the headquar-ters for the Arctic Club, a business and social organization founded by successful gold rush prospectors that was the center of Alaska trade, which had boomed since the Klondike Gold Rush of 1897. The ten-story, terra-cotta-clad, steel and reinforced concrete building features polychrome terra-cotta ornamentation in an arctic theme; including the walrus heads on the third floor exterior and a life-size polar bear over the Third Avenue entrance, no longer in place. Blue and peach matte terra-cotta enliven the upper story spandrels and elaborate Italianate cornice, making the Arctic Building one of the most colorful terra-cotta-clad buildings in Seattle. The Arctic Building's interior features an opulent dining room beneath a huge stained glass dome, for which it takes its name, "the Dome Room." The Arctic Building, which had been owned by the city since 1988, was sold in 2005 to the Arctic Club Hotel LLC for conversion into a 117-room hotel.

3) CENTRAL BUILDING
1910, C.R. ALDRICH
810 Third Avenue

The Central Building was constructed as an attempt to anchor a new central business district at Third and Marion. The business district had begun moving north from its Pioneer Square hub in the early twentieth century. Despite its abundance of high-end office space, the Central Building could not fight the current of office development on northern blocks. The simulated granite on the façade of this Renaissance Revival building is a terra-cotta product called "granitex," which was often used in the early twentieth century to sheath steel-framed structures because it was more economical than real stone.

The Arctic Building's original terra-cotta walrus tusks were removed years ago as a precaution against potential injury to pedestrians in earthquakes. Fiberglas replcement tusks were fabricated in the 1982 restoration. Thirteen of the walrus heads, which had cracked due to expanding grout where the new tusks were attached, were replaced in the 1997 renovation. The replacement heads were hand sculpted by Boston Valley Terra Cotta near Buffalo, NY, one of only two U.S. companies currently producing architectural terra-cotta.

The beloved terra-cotta walruses adorning the Arctic Building give a playful profile to this ornate historic landmark.

4) FOURTH & MADISON
(IDX Tower)
2002, Zimmer Gunsul Frasca Partnership and Kendall/Heaton Associates
925 Fourth Avenue

Expressed as two intersecting masses, Fourth & Madison stands on a seven-story L-shaped base and rises to a height of 39 floors. The tower responds differently to each street that it faces. To the east, it emulates the strong vertical lines of 901 5th Avenue Building. To the north, the building responds to the grid of Safeco Plaza. To the south, a curved glass curtain wall cantilevers out over the YMCA building, allowing for greater floor space and providing a backdrop to the historic building. To the west, along Third Avenue, a four-story atrium features a glass installation on the window by New York glass artist James Carpenter. As with many buildings in the downtown core, Fourth & Madison provides a public pathway through the building to assist pedestrians in traversing the hills of downtown Seattle. The atrium hall on Third Avenue links the lobby to Fourth Avenue.

5) SEATTLE CENTRAL LIBRARY
2004, OMA (Rotterdam) and LMN; Landscape Architect: Petra Blaisse and Jones & Jones
1000 Fourth Avenue

With its asymmetric, cantilevered volumes, the design of the Seattle Central Library is a radical departure from the rectilinear structures that surround it. The diagonal grid system of the library's mesh-like skin is designed to withstand lateral forces caused by wind or earthquakes. The library includes eleven levels supporting five main "platforms" that are designed for primary library functions. Between these platforms are areas designated for various public uses. The public spaces are arranged around the outside walls to capture views of

Elliott Bay and Mt. Rainier. Preservation of the views, use of natural light and other program-specific requirements were cited by the architects as dictating the library's unusual shape. The Central Library was conceived as a multi-media center containing over 400 public computers and the capacity for 1.4 million books and materials. Many innovative systems were implemented into the library, including the "book spiral," which winds through four floors and makes up the nonfiction collection. The book spiral allows the collection to be updated without disrupting the Dewey Decimal system-based order. A state-of-the-art automated book sorting system uses Radio Frequency Identification (RFID) tags on each of the volumes to organize and reshelf the books. The Seattle Central Library was designed to achieve LEED Silver status. The library offers free architectural tours; inquire at the 5th Avenue visitor's desk.

Henry and Sarah Yesler's 40-room Victorian mansion, designed by William Boone (the site of the house is now the southwest corner of the King County Courthouse), briefly served as the home of the **Seattle Public Library**. *Although completed in 1884, the Yeslers moved in 1886, one year prior to Sarah's death. The Yesler mansion narrowly escaped destruction by the Great Fire of 1889. After Henry Yesler's death in 1892, the house was occupied by Henry Yesler's second wife, Minnie, until she moved out in 1899. The house then served as the* *Seattle Public Library but was claimed by fire on New Year's Day, 1901. Andrew Carnegie's nation-wide library campaign provided the funds for a new library on the site of the current Seattle Central Library, which opened in 1906. The classical, Beaux-Arts building was replaced by a modern library in 1959. The new* **Seattle Central Library**, *designed by the firm of renowned Dutch architect, Rem Koolhaas, opened in 2004.*

Yesler Mansion during its brief stint as the Seattle Public Library.

Vertebrae, by Henry Moore, greets visitors to Safeco Plaza.

6) SAFECO PLAZA
(Seattle First National Bank Building)
1969, Naramore Bain Brady & Johanson and Pietro Belluschi (consulting)
1001 Fourth Avenue

At 50 stories, the Seattle First National Bank Building, now known as Safeco Plaza, was the tallest building in the city upon its completion in 1969. Just slightly taller than the Space Needle, the Seattle First National Bank Building was nicknamed "the box the Space Needle came in." The building's curtain walls were designed as vierendiel trusses, which transfer loads to the four huge pylons at its corners and allow for open interiors and better views. The pylons taper as they ascend the building and their load decreases; visually, this structural expression intensifies the verticality of the building. The original art collection of the Seafirst Building was nearly as impressive as the building itself and included the Henry Moore sculpture, "Vertebrae," located in the plaza along Fourth Avenue and Madison. The Seafirst Building won architectural and structural awards and was praised by New York architecture critic Ada Louise Huxtable as "one of the most urbane buildings in the country." The Seafirst Building was Seattle's tallest building for 15 years after its completion. The plaza was altered by NBBJ in 1986 to reduce wind and provide public amenities at the street level.

7) FIFTH & MADISON CONDOMINIUMS
2007, Ruffcorn Mott Hinthorne Stine; Landscape Architect: Phillips Farevaag Smallenberg
909 Fifth Avenue

The development of this 24-story, 129-unit condominium tower involved the renovation of the adjacent 41-story 900 Fourth Avenue building lobby. The project, which was designed to achieve LEED gold certification for the entire block, included the development of the generous public green space surrounding the building. The tower is clad in high-efficiency clear glazing and textured metal panels. A green roof at the terrace level helps filter storm water runoff and serves as private green space for residents. Fifth & Madison was the first large-scale condominium building constructed in Seattle's financial district, bringing residential development to every downtown neighborhood, thereby cultivating a 24-hour downtown. The building was constructed on the former site of drive-through bank tellers for the adjacent Bank of California Building (now 900 Fourth Avenue). Automated and online banking have made the drive-through teller system obsolete, and the site was unused for many years prior to the development of Fifth & Madison.

8) 901 FIFTH AVENUE BUILDING

(Bank of California) 1974, John Graham & Co.; renovation, 2007, Ruffcorn Mott Hinthorne Stine
900 Fourth Avenue

The 41-story Bank of California building recalls the form of Eero Saarinen's CBS Building in New York with its tightly grouped, beige diamond-shaped columns and lack of formal crown or base, emphasizing its vertical-

The YMCA Building's brick exterior, simple detailing and arched windows suggest Romanesque design. Peaked gables and a hipped copper roof reflect the Collegiate Gothic style, resulting in a building that is a refined example of the eclecticism typical of designs by A.H. Albertson and his associates, Joseph W. Wilson and Paul Richardson. Found-

ity by allowing the columns to rise straight from the ground. Every fourth column is structural; the others are hollow and exist only to maintain the vertical aesthetic. The building's lobby was renovated with the development of the adjacent Fifth and Madison condominium tower and plaza. The renovation and development were designed to achieve LEED gold certification for the entire block.

9) YMCA BUILDING 📖
1931, A.H. Albertson; renovation, 2002, Zimmer Gunsul Frasca Partnership
909 Fourth Avenue

A 2002 renovation to the YMCA included restoration of the original exterior and interior features. Upgrades included the addition of a new pool, gymnasium, sport courts, locker rooms, administrative offices as well as new electrical and mechanical systems, elevator additions and upgrades. A fourth-floor atrium was filled in adding an additional 20,000 square feet of space to the facility, effectively bringing the building up-to-date while preserving its original character.

ed in 1876 through an effort led by Seattle banker Dexter Horton, the Seattle YMCA served as a morally and spiritually-oriented alternative to the saloons and brothels that made up the social diversions available to young men in frontier towns. The present building was an addition to the 1907 YMCA building, which was demolished in 1999 for the construction of Fourth & Madison. By the time of this building's construction, the YMCA's mission had broadened to offering educational and physical training through lectures, vocational courses and gymnasium equipment, and had expanded its outreach to boys, as is indicated by the "boy's entrance" to the building.

10) THE RAINIER CLUB ⑪ ⑪
1904, Cutter Malmgren & Wager; addition, 1928-29, Bebb & Gould
810 Fourth Avenue

Spokane architect Kirtland Cutter applied the Jacobean Revival style, with its characteristic stepped peaks, in his design for Seattle's prestigious gentlemen's club, which was said to have been inspired by Aston Hall, a stately seventeenth-century home in Warwickshire, England. In 1928, Bebb and Gould expanded the five-story building 54 feet southward, utilizing the same vocabulary of clinker brick and stepped gables. The original portion of the club house was constructed of brick masonry; the 1929 addition was constructed of reinforced concrete with brick veneer. Founded in 1888, the Rainier club operated out of leased locations until forming an association in 1902 to finance construction of their own building. The Rainier Club served an important role in reconstruction planning after the Great Fire of 1889, providing a meeting place for Seattle's business leaders. The club offered membership exclusively to men until July 1978, when the first woman was admitted. In scale, materials and texture, the Rainier Club and the nearby YMCA Building offer a glimpse into what this part of the city, now dense with skyscrapers, was like in the early twentieth century.

11) COLUMBIA HOUSE
1909, unknown; addition, 1979, Fred Bassetti; renovation, 2000, S.M. Stemper & Associates
403 Columbia Street

This five-story brick and steel office building, today known as Columbia House, was originally built as the three-story Oakland Hotel, likely constructed to accommodate visitors to the 1909 Alaska-Yukon-Pacific Exposition. The building briefly operated as a brothel as well. At the time of the construction of the adjacent Columbia Center, Columbia House was owned by local architect Fred Bassetti. Bassetti refused to sell the building to Columbia Center developer Martin Selig until 1986, after Columbia Center was completed, thus ensuring that the historic building would not fall victim to the wrecking ball. Bassetti added two stories in 1979; however, the 1909 structure was not able to support additional loads so the two-story addition stands on its own foundation and structural system, straddling the older building. Columbia House and the 76-story Columbia Center remained separate until a renovation in 2000 shifted the entrance to the office space in Columbia House to inside the Columbia Center.

12) COLUMBIA CENTER
1985, Chester L. Lindsey Architects
701 Fifth Avenue

The 943-foot **Columbia Center** *was originally planned to be 1,005 feet tall; however, the FAA demanded that it be shortened because of its position within a flight path to SeaTac Airport. One of the September 11th masterminds, Khalid Shaikh Mohammed, claimed that the "tallest buildings in Washington and California" were among the targets of the original plan, but Osama Bin Laden opted for a "smaller-scale" attack. Although Mohammed did not name the Columbia Center explicitly, his statement clearly implied that it was among the original targets.*

At 76 stories, the Columbia Center is the tallest building in the state of Washington and the tallest by number of stories on the West coast. The dark-gray glazed building is made up of three concave towers of varying height joined by a common mechanical and elevator core. Developed for maximum revenue, nine corner offices are available on each floor below the 43rd floor. The granite base marks the lower three floors, which are occupied by internally focused shops and restaurants not visible from the street. At the time of its construction, many Seattleites were concerned by their rapidly changing skyline and felt that the Columbia Center was out of scale with the other buildings of downtown. Concerned citizens created initiative 31, the Citizen's Alternative Plan (CAP), which limited the height of new office buildings to 450 feet. Somewhat ironically, due to the height restriction, the Columbia Center still dominates the Seattle skyline over 20 years after its completion. In April of 2006, the City Council approved a new downtown zoning plan, allowing taller but thinner buildings; the intent being that denser development would enliven downtown and encourage more people to live downtown and walk or take transit to work, shopping and entertainment. Although the vote repealed CAP, it is unlikely that buildings as tall as Columbia Center will be built given the scarcity of full-block lots available. An observation deck on the 73rd floor can be visited for a small fee.

13) SEATTLE CITY HALL
2003, Bassetti Architects and Bohlin Cywinski Jackson; Landscape Architect: Gustafson Partners and Swift & Co.
600 Fourth Avenue

City Hall is part of a multi-block campus known as the Seattle Civic Center. The building houses the Mayor's office, the City Attorney's offices, City Council Chambers and other city departments. City Hall's curvilinear forms and projecting terraces were designed to capture near and distant views. Transparency and addressing Seattle's natural and built environment were central to the design. Quartzite paving was chosen for the outdoor public space to visually unify the complex and for its color, which is similar to the waters of Elliott Bay. All levels of the building are linked through a stairway that runs from exterior to interior, blurring the outdoor-indoor boundary. Designed to achieve LEED silver certification, City Hall has many environmentally-conscious features, including a green roof with storm water collectors (the roof can be viewed from the elevator lobbies on floors 3-7). Green roof systems decrease storm water runoff into the sewer system, insulate the building, and reduce the "urban heat island effect" because the plants absorb the sun's energy through photosynthesis. The east façade confronts the Justice Center and is faced with the same stone, visually connecting the buildings. The buildings are physically connected by the fountain which originates from the Justice Center and runs under the street to City Hall.

14) KING COUNTY ADMINISTRATION BUILDING
1971, Harmon Pray Detrich
500 Fourth Avenue

The King County Administration Building is made up of a single, rectangular mass elevated above an exposed aggregate podium. The building's unusual diamond-shaped exterior pattern was achieved by the use of a steel lattice frame and the entire façade is clad in porcelain enamel panels. The building was originally planned to be 16 stories but only eight were completed. The skybridge running through the administration building is used to transport inmates from the King County Courthouse to the King County Correctional Facility. Though it is indifferent to the street and often referred to as "homely" or "weird," the King County Administration building always piques the curiosity of visitors to the city.

15) 400 YESLER BUILDING
(City Hall/Public Safety Building)
1909, Clayton Wilson; renovation, 1977,
Mayo Associates Architects; restoration, 2001, BOLA
Architecture+Planning
400 Yesler Way

This six-story Beaux Arts building was originally planned to house the Health Department, City Hospital, Police Department and City Jail, but served as City Hall until 1916 when government moved into the new City-County Building (now the King County Courthouse). The reinforced concrete building is trapezoidal in plan with an engaged round tower at its apex. The first two levels feature rusticated sandstone cladding with three stories of light-colored brick veneer above. A projecting metal cornice with brackets and modillions divides the middle three floors from the top floor, which is surmounted by a squat mansard roof. The City left the building in 1951, after which time it was partially converted to a parking garage. The penthouse level was added in 1977 when the building was converted back to office space. The government purchased the building back in 1991 and it continues to house government offices. A 2001 restoration included cleaning and repair of exterior sandstone and brick masonry veneer, repair and reconstruction of the metal cornice and parapet, and seismic repair of exterior elements. The 400 Yesler Building is within the boundaries of the Pioneer Square Historic district.

16) SEATTLE JUSTICE CENTER
2002, NBBJ; Landscape Architect: Gustafson Partners and Swift & Co.
600 Fifth Avenue

The Justice Center is home to the Municipal Courthouse and Police Headquarters. The glass section on the southern end of the block houses the courts and the masonry section of the Northern end houses the police. The fountain that runs from the Justice Center to City Hall serves to connect the buildings as a complex. A large portion of the building's west façade features a "double skin" glazed curtain wall. This double skin of glass not only provides visual interest but serves as a thermal buffer. Louvers within the air space between the glass planes are automatically controlled and can be closed to create an insulating barrier or opened to vent heat away from the building. Like City Hall, the Seattle Justice Center was designed to achieve LEED silver certification.

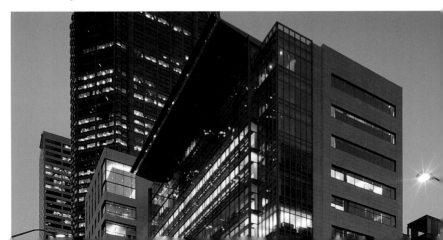

17) SEATTLE MUNICIPAL TOWER
(Gateway Tower, Key Tower),
1990, Bassetti Norton Metler & Rekevics
700 Fifth Avenue

A primary issue for very tall buildings is wind resistance. One way that wind and seismic loads are addressed is through the use of X-bracing, which is evident on the outside of the 62-story Seattle Municipal Tower. The architects chose to express this seismic structure, celebrating the nature of the building's construction and engineering while revealing its strength in this earthquake-prone region. One of the building's most distinctive skyline features is its unusual curved, green glazed rooftop, which houses five floors of office space. Bay windows on the building's façade direct views away from the mass of the Columbia Center across the street. The building, whose name changed from Key Tower to Seattle Municipal Tower on May 17, 2004 when the city purchased it, now houses the City's main offices, which had previously been scattered among various surrounding buildings. An onramp to I-5 northbound express lanes passes directly underneath the building.

18) FIRST UNITED METHODIST CHURCH
(First Methodist Episcopal Church)
1910, James Schack and Daniel Huntington
811 Fifth Avenue

With its massive dome articulating the sanctuary space and rational central plan, this Beaux Arts-style church evokes both Byzantine and Palladian forms. The design was a departure from the Gothic Revival style commonly being applied to church design at the time. The Seattle First Methodist Episcopal congregation was Seattle's first religious congregation. It was founded by pioneers Rev. and

Mrs. David Blaine upon their arrival in November 1853. They established the settlement's first service the following Sunday, November 27, 1853. In 2002, the church announced plans to sell to a local developer who would demolish the building to make way for an office tower. Church leaders described it as an emotional decision that was vital to their survival as a congregation and to the preservation of their mission of outreach to the homeless and victims of domestic violence. They stated that the church was too large and expensive for them to maintain, particularly after it sustained damage in the 2001 Nisqually earthquake. The tide turned in August 2006 when local developers Nitze-Stagen stepped in with an offer that included saving the historic church and building around it.

19) NAKAMURA COURTHOUSE 𐃃
(United States Federal Courthouse)
1940, Louis Simon; renovation, 2008, Weinstein A|U
1010 Fifth Avenue

The Federal Courthouse building is a good example of the stripped-down Federal Classicism of the time, which was defined by central massing, symmetry and vertical strip windows. Its landscaped lawn was the principal open space in downtown Seattle until the 1970's, when the "Forward Thrust," Block Grant and other local, state and federal sources provided funds to build Waterfront Park, Freeway Park, Occidental Park and other public facilities. The open space was the site of many anti-war demonstrations in the 1960s and early 1970s. In 2000, the building was renamed the Nakamura Courthouse in honor of fallen World War II Japanese-American soldier William Nakamura. The United States Federal Courthouse moved to its new 600,000 square-foot building at 700 Stewart Street in 2004 (see Retail District tour). The Nakamura Courthouse now houses the Ninth District Court of Appeals.

20) HOTEL VINTAGE PARK
1923, John Graham Sr.; conversion, 1993, G. "Skip"
Downing Architecture
1100 Fifth Avenue

This 11-story brick and terra-cotta Renaissance revival building was originally built as the Spring Apartment Hotel, which operated as a single-room-occupancy apartment building. Later known as the Kennedy Hotel, the building was converted into a four-star hotel in 1992.

21) WOMEN'S UNIVERSITY CLUB
1922, A.H. Albertson and Édouard Frère Champney
1105 Sixth Avenue

The Women's University Club was formed in 1914 as a social, educational and community-oriented organization for university-educated women, programs that continue to this day. The club held meetings in a temporary building on the current site of the Olympic Hotel before deciding to commission a building of their own. Their Georgian Revival style building features a brick and terra-cotta façade and galvanized iron cornice. Interior features include guestrooms for out-of-town visitors, dining and meeting areas and a theater. Although the Georgian Revival style was not widely used in Seattle, beyond the occasional private residence and apartment building, its presence on many East Coast university campuses and local residential use make it appropriate to the functions of the building.

22) NARAMORE FOUNTAIN
1967, George Tsutakawa
Sixth Avenue & Seneca Street

The design of Naramore Fountain is based on Japanese "obos," which are arrangements of stacked rocks meant as a gesture of thanks to nature. The fountain honors the late Floyd Naramore, a Seattle architect who was a founding partner in the firm Naramore, Bain, Brady & Johanson (now NBBJ).

23) YWCA
1913, Édouard Frère Champney
1118 Fifth Avenue

This eight story, two-toned brick and terra-cotta Renaissance Revival building was begun under Édouard Frère Champney's brief partnership with Augustus Warren Gould but completed by Champney alone. When the YWCA opened in 1913, it offered Turkish baths, a tearoom, pool and a vocational school among other amenities. A roof-top garden and clock tower were part of the original plan but were never executed. The Seattle YWCA was founded in 1894 with the mission of providing single young women with education, healthy social activities and sources of employment. An early nineteen-teens fundraising campaign provided the $400,000 necessary to complete the Seattle YWCA's flagship facility. Part of the capital for the new building was raised through a concession of services provided at the 1909 Alaska-Yukon-Pacific Exposition. Today the YWCA offers programs to help women lead safe and self-sufficient lives as well as programs for children.

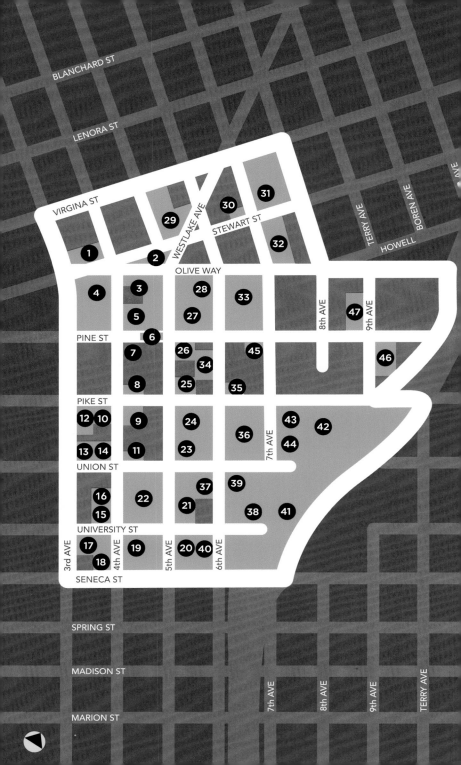

CHAPTER 4

RETAIL DISTRICT

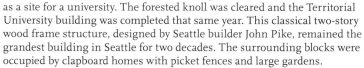

Seattle's retail district is a vibrant urban center with theaters, shops, restaurants, hotels and office towers and, more recently, residential development through adaptive reuse of obsolete office buildings. Much of the area's development took place in the first 30 years of the twentieth century, leaving it with some of Seattle's finest terra-cotta buildings.

In 1861, Charles Terry, Edward Lander and Arthur Denny deeded 10 acres between Third and Fifth avenues and Union and Seneca streets, including a slight rise called Denny's Knoll, to the territorial government as a site for a university. The forested knoll was cleared and the Territorial University building was completed that same year. This classical two-story wood frame structure, designed by Seattle builder John Pike, remained the grandest building in Seattle for two decades. The surrounding blocks were occupied by clapboard homes with picket fences and large gardens.

Seattle's first fashionable retail district began developing along Second Avenue between Madison and Spring streets with the 1893 completion of the Rialto Building (destroyed), which later became home to Frederick and Nelson's first large-scale department store. The retail district continued to spread north along Second Avenue with the completion of the Bon Marché and the Arcade Building in 1900 and 1903, respectively (both destroyed).

While the first retail district was developing, the University (by then the University of Washington) moved to its present site north of Portage Bay in

The Territorial University building, upper left, is surrounded by homes in this 1878 image.

1895. Their hope was to sell the 10-acre tract of their former location to help finance the development of their new campus. Due to the economic depression of the mid 1890s, no buyers surfaced for the land, which was still quite removed from the central business district in Pioneer Square.

By 1900, Gold Rush prosperity was expanding downtown north of Pioneer Square along First and Second avenues. The University Regents began searching for an investor to lease and develop the land. A deal with J. C. Levold fell through after construction began on just one building, a new home for the *Seattle Post Intelligencer* (destroyed). In 1904, Fourth Avenue was regraded, pushing commercial development further north. The University entered into a 50-year lease with Seattle developer James A. Moore that same year. However, Moore was unable to raise the capital to develop the land and the lease was purchased by a group of businessmen in 1907 who organized under the name Metropolitan Building Company (MBC); the land has since been known as the Metropolitan Tract.

The MBC engaged the New York architecture firm of Howells & Stokes to design a master plan for the Metropolitan Tract. The plan called for a "city within a city" having architecturally-unified Beaux Arts brick-and-terra-cotta buildings. The Metropolitan Tract was regraded and the White-Henry-Stuart Block, Cobb Building, Metropolitan Theater, and an Arena were completed by 1916 (all but Cobb are now destroyed). The plan included temporary structures to be rented out until future development could take their place. Social and educational clubs, such as the Women's University Club, occupied many of the temporary buildings. The Women's

The Cobb Building, left, stands across from the White-Henry-Stuart Block in this 1920s view north on Fourth Avenue. Temporary buildings can be seen in the foreground.

University Club later constructed their own building nearby (see Civic/Financial District).

About half of the buildings in the Howells & Stokes plan were completed by the time the United States became involved in World War I. The pre-war construction on the Metropolitan Tract attracted developers to the blocks outside of its boundaries. The 1909 Seaboard Building was among the first major office buildings to be constructed outside of the business and financial hub at Second Avenue and Cherry Street, followed by the Securities and Joshua Green Buildings in 1913 and the Times Square Building in 1915. The Coliseum Theater (now Banana Republic), the region's first major motion picture palace, was completed in 1916.

The 1919 completion of a new Fredrick & Nelson department store (now Nordstrom) at Fifth Avenue and Pine Street initiated a shift of the retail district away from upper Second Avenue to its present location (although some retailers such as J.C. Penney remained on Second Avenue into the 1960s).

The years following World War I saw renewed development on the Metropolitan Tract with the construction of the Stimson Building (1925, destroyed), Skinner Building and the Olympic Hotel, which was built around the Metropolitan Theater on the former site of the Territorial University Building. Buildings outside of the Tract began to take on a grander scale and departed from Beaux Arts style to embrace modernistic design. These Art Deco works include the 27-story Northern Life Tower (now Seattle Tower) and the 15-story 1411 Fourth Avenue Building.

In 1929, the Bon Marché (now Macy's) helped solidify the northward movement of the retail district with a new department store at Fourth and Pine near Frederick & Nelson. But as with all areas of downtown, construction in the retail district and Metropolitan Tract ceased during the Great Depression and did not resume until after World War II, with the notable exception of Woolworth's (now Ross), the five-and-dime store that opened at Third Avenue and Pike Street in 1940.

The prosperous post-war economy allowed the retail district to continue to thrive, leading to the vertical expansion of its major department stores. In 1953, four stories were added to the Frederick & Nelson building; and in 1956, three stories were added to the Bon Marché.

In 1954, the University of Washington leased the Metropolitan Tract to University Properties Company (now UNICO). UNICO hired Naramore Bain Brady & Johanson (now NBBJ) to create a new "master plan 2009" for development through the end of their lease (which has since been extended). Modern office buildings like the Washington Building (now Puget Sound Plaza) and the Logan Building replaced older buildings in and around the Metropolitan Tract in the late 1950s and early 1960s.

Although the UNICO developments fostered a thriving business center in the Metropolitan Tract, the increasing popularity of suburban living and the supremacy of the automobile initiated a decline in the retail district that would challenge the area for the next 30 years. In the early 1960s, construction of Interstate 5 created a canyon that divided downtown from First Hill to the east and destroyed many inner-city homes and apartment buildings. Paul Thiry proposed a plan to cover the downtown stretch of the freeway with a lid, but funding for the plans was not approved. Interstate 5 facilitated more suburban development, including the suburban shopping centers that drew customers away from downtown.

Controversy over the declining area of Westlake and Fourth avenues was also stirring in the early 1960s. Proposals to close off cross streets to create a pedestrian park on the site along Westlake Avenue between Olive and Pine streets were challenged by retailers who feared that less vehicle access would drive even more customers away. This debate went unresolved until 1988.

The 1970s saw significant changes in the Metropolitan Tract and surrounding blocks. The Stimson Building was replaced by the Financial Center in 1972. The proposed demolition of the White-Henry-Stuart Block for the construction of Rainier Square, which included a 28-story office tower and full-block retail plaza, sparked a major controversy and effort to save the historic buildings. Although the University Regents confirmed their right to destroy the older buildings, they agreed that the Cobb Building (the last remaining from the original Howells & Stokes plan), the Skinner Building and the Olympic Hotel could be listed in the National Register of Historic Places, although this does not protect them from demolition. Rainier Square was the last completely new construction in the Metropolitan Tract.

Freeway Park created a partial lid over Interstate 5 and provided a pedestrian connection to First Hill in 1976. The five-acre park, which was paid for with State, private and public "Forward Thrust" funds, cost more to build than it would have cost to lid the entire downtown section of the freeway 15 years earlier.

The bridging of the freeway was expanded after 1988 with the development of the Washington State Convention and Trade Center. The 1980s brought a wave of high-rise construction to Seattle, including the 36-story One Union Square Building, the 44-story US Bank Centre and the 56-story Two Union Square Building in the retail district. The Westlake controversy was also settled at the time with the construction of the Metro Transit Tunnel, Westlake Center and Westlake Park in 1988.

Pine Street was closed to vehicle traffic through Westlake Park in 1990, but was reopened by Seattle voters in 1995, ensuring Nordstrom's relocation of their flagship store to the Fredrick & Nelson Building, empty since 1992. A three-block redevelopment of new or renovated retail stores, including Pacific Place, followed. Many considered the vote to re-open Pine Street to traffic as essential to the revitalization of the retail district, although it is still considered controversial by some. Other major retail developments included the renovation of the Coliseum Theater for a Banana Republic store and new outlets for the Gap, Niketown Seattle and Old Navy, all of which offered more incentives for people to shop downtown.

Recent renovations and adaptive reuse projects have brought a residential element to the retail district. The former Eagles Temple, adjacent to the convention center, was renovated as ACT Theater. The project included rehabilitation of the residential portion of the building into affordable housing. The Cobb and Seaboard buildings have also been adapted for housing, which, along with the high concentration of hotels, restaurants and theaters, assures active streets long after 5 p.m.

The revitalization of Seattle's retail district has been a success story. People continue to shop downtown with its wide variety of stores and the unique experience that cannot be found at a suburban mall. Many have made it a holiday tradition to board the Monorail at Seattle Center to embark upon their gift shopping in the cool open air among decorated store windows with a warm latte in hand. With the recent surge of downtown residential development and the South Lake Union Streetcar line, which connects the South Lake Union neighborhood to Westlake & Fifth Avenue, Seattle's retail district is likely to continue to grow and thrive.

1) SECURITIES BUILDING
1913, John Graham Sr.; addition, 1915,
Frank Allen (engineer)
1904 Third Avenue

With its legible steel-frame grid, clearly articulated base, shaft, crown and restrained classical ornamentation, the Securities Building is typical of the office towers popularized by the Chicago School at the turn of the century. Green terra-cotta cartouches bearing the letter "S" provide an eye-catching diversion from the predominately white façade. The Securities Building represents an early shift in office construction northeast of the financial hub, inspired by successful pre-World War I development on the Metropolitan Tract.

2) TIMES SQUARE BUILDING 𝕿 𝕿
1915, Bebb & Gould; renovation, 1983,
Bumgardner Architects
414 Olive Way

The terra-cotta used on the **Times Square Building** *was manufactured by the Renton-Denny Clay and Coal Company, where Charles Bebb had worked engineering terra-cotta architectural projects for five years before establishing his first architectural practice in 1899.*

By 1915, *The Seattle Times* had grown to be the region's largest circulation daily and had outgrown its original headquarters at Second Avenue and Union Street. The newly-formed partnership of Bebb & Gould was selected to design the new headquarters. This six-story terra-cotta-clad building stands on a triangular parcel and rises from a polished granite base. An arched window arcade continues up three stories of the shaft to maximize natural light. An elaborate light-blue corbelled cornice caps the building. The fine Italian Renaissance detailing and precise horizontal banding on this building reflect Gould's École des Beaux Arts training. A terra-cotta relief on the Olive Street façade represents the newspaper production process. The building was nicknamed "Times Square" for its resemblance to the Flatiron Building in New York and because originally the east side opened onto a large plaza that functioned like New York's Times Square, where people gathered to get the latest news and baseball scores. The Times Square Building housed *The Seattle Times* until 1931, when the newspaper moved into a larger facility at Fairview and John streets.

3) MAYFLOWER PARK HOTEL
(Bergonian)
1927, Stuart Wheatley
401 Olive Way

This 12-story, 171-room hotel building is clad in red brick and features restrained Renaissance Revival terra-cotta ornamentation at its base, string courses and parapet. Originally opened as the Bergonian, the Mayflower Park Hotel is among Seattle's oldest continually-operating hotels. The lobby features a five-tiered crystal chandelier, which was originally located in the Grand Ballroom of the Olympic Hotel (see # 19).

4) MACY'S ⑪
(Bon Marché), 1929, John Graham Sr.; addition,
1956 John Graham & Co.
1601 Third Avenue

This full-block, sandstone building was the second location of the Bon Marché department store, founded in Seattle in 1890. Natural imagery was incorporated into the decorative details, including native ground cover above the first floor windows and a frieze depicting sea life on the copper canopy that wraps the building. Originally built to four stories, three more floors were added in 1956 by John Graham & Co., then being run by John Graham, Jr. The addition resulted in the loss of the band of Art Deco ornamentation that ran along the upper cornice as well as the original corner windows. The addition is clearly visible as the new stone is not an exact match with the original. This combination of stylized natural motifs neatly contained within geometric forms and sleek lines was typical in Art Deco design. Though altered, the main sales floor retains some if its Art Deco features, particularly its wave-like coffered ceiling, decorated column capitals and mahogany-paneled elevator bay.

5) WESTLAKE CENTER
1988, RTKL (Baltimore)
1601 Fifth Avenue

Westlake Center is the result of decades of debate over how to develop the site along Westlake Avenue between Olive and Pike Streets. Several plans had been proposed since 1960, including a luxury hotel, a new location for the Seattle Art Museum (which was then at its original location on Capitol Hill), as well as an attempt to preserve the site as an open, public green space. The four-story Westlake Center mall was modeled after the urban shopping center trend of glassed-in "festival marketplaces," which were intended to create a connection to exterior surroundings. A twenty-one-story office tower rises from the retail base, which sits atop parking spaces and access to the underground Metro Transit Tunnel. An unusual agreement between the developer and the city allows for the building's common spaces to be used before and after retail hours to allow pedestrian passage through the building to the Metro Transit Tunnel and monorail. Westlake Center was developed by the Rouse Co. of Baltimore, Maryland (with Koehler McFadyen & Co of Bellevue, WA), who developed similar shopping centers throughout the country.

6) SEATTLE MONORAIL 🚝
1962, Alweg Co. (Cologne, Germany)

The Seattle monorail line was built for the 1962 Century 21 World's Fair (see Seattle Center tour) as a vision of the future of urban transportation. The Seattle Center Monorail was the nation's first full-scale urban commercial monorail system. The Seattle trains are direct descendants of the first test train developed by the Alweg Company. The original southern terminus of the monorail was removed from its original location on Pine Street (at what is now Westlake Park) and a new station was built into the Westlake Center development in 1988.

7) WESTLAKE PARK
1988, Hanna/Olin (Philadelphia)
Fourth Avenue & Pine Street

Westlake Park was created in conjunction with the development of Westlake Center and the construction of the Metro Transit Tunnel. The angle of the park responds to the former alignment of Westlake and Fourth Avenues. The design of the granite pavers that dominate Westlake Park was inspired by a Salish Indian basket weave pattern. The red granite sculpture on the south end of the park, "Seven Hills" by Robert Maki, alludes to the seven hills between Elliott Bay and Lake Washington on which the city was built. The water wall serves as a screen from the street, blocking the views and sound of passing traffic. The park features a grid pattern of Japanese Zelkova trees. The park's combination of elements alluding to Native American art, Japan, water and topography reflect Seattle's natural environment, native culture and Pacific Rim location. Seattle's Westlake Park is the primary open space in the retail district and the favored location for street musicians, protests, and public rallies.

8) THE SEABOARD BUILDING 🏛 🏛
(Northern Bank and Trust Building)
1909, William Doty Van Siclen; renovation,
2001, NBBJ
1500 Fourth Avenue

Built as the Northern Bank and Trust Company, the Seaboard Building was one of the first major office buildings to mark the expansion of Seattle's commercial and banking district northeast of its then-hub on lower Second Avenue. The trapezoidal shape of this ten-story building was dictated by the angles created by the former convergence of Fourth and Westlake Avenues. The base of this Beaux-Arts building has been altered, however the string course and cornice retain the building's original lively terra-cotta ornamentation, which includes garlands, lions and shields among other decorative flourishes. The Seaboard building was renovated in 2001 as a mixed-use development, housing retail on the ground floor, commercial office space on the next five floors and luxury condominiums on the upper floors and a new penthouse.

9) FOURTH & PIKE BUILDING 🏛
(Ligget Building)
1927, Lawton & Moldenhour
1424 Fourth Avenue

This ten-story terra-cotta-clad concrete and steel-framed office building is nearly identical in design to the Melbourne Tower at Third Avenue and Pike Street (see West Edge tour), although its stylistic treatment differs greatly from the French Renaissance-styled Melbourne Tower. The Fourth and Pike Building's Gothic-inspired terra-cotta ornamentation includes arches with multifoil tracery at the parapet, terminating in finials at the peaked corners. The multifoil arches are repeated over the lobby entrance on Fourth Avenue. Quatre-foils in the spandrels carry the theme up the shaft of the building.

10) THE JOSHUA GREEN BUILDING
1913, John Graham Sr.
1425 Fourth Avenue

This ten-story, terra-cotta-clad, steel-frame building is typical of early twentieth century commercial architecture. Baroque ornamentation is contained within the spandrels, which are recessed behind vertical piers with decorative pilasters. The structural grid remains legible and dominant. The building originally featured an Italianate cornice, which was removed after the 1949 earthquake. It is named for prominent Seattle businessman Joshua Green, who was a sternwheeler captain, a leader in the Puget Sound shipping and ferries industries as well as a successful banker.

11) MEN'S WEARHOUSE
(Great Northern Building)
1929, R.C. Reamer
1404 Fourth Avenue

This four-story Indiana limestone-clad building originally housed the ticket office of the Great Northern Railroad. Its ground floor display windows were modeled after the green and tan train car interiors of the Orient Express. A motif suggesting Native American feather headdresses is carried along the top frieze. The building's imagery combines classical and modernistic motifs, exemplifying this architect's skill in handling many diverse architectural vocabularies. A rather charming and unusual feature is the window mullions in the shape of Art Deco skyscrapers, perhaps meant to suggest the exciting destinations that could be reached by rail. The box-like simplicity of the building, its incised and neatly contained ornamentation and lack of overhanging cornice, signal a move away from the classically-inspired office building and anticipates modernism.

12) ROSS
(Woolworth's)
1940, Harold B. Hamhill (New York)
301 Pike Street

The Seattle Woolworth's building was based on a standard company design that was repeated throughout the country. At the time it was built, Seattle's was the largest Woolworth's on the West Coast. The warm beige and salmon terra-cotta cladding, Art Deco design and floral petal corner tower give the building a distinctive presence. The Woolworth's building was one of the last terra-cotta-clad buildings to be built in downtown Seattle as post-war architecture was moving toward Modernism with its emphasis on glass, steel, and concrete.

13) JOSEPH VANCE BUILDING
1929, Victor Voorhees; renovation, 2006, Zimmer Gunsul Frasca Architects
1402 Third Avenue

The 14-story, terra-cotta-clad Joseph Vance building was originally planned as a hotel but opened instead as an office building. The Art Deco style building's vertical piers terminate in ornamental fern fronds and a decorative band of light blue and pink terra-cotta enlivens the façade in the spandrels below the upper-story windows. A checker motif occurs at the parapet. The building is named for Seattle lumber magnate and real estate developer Joseph Vance.

14) 1411 FOURTH AVENUE BUILDING 𝍌 𝍌
1929, R.C. Reamer
1411 Fourth Avenue

At 15 stories, 1411 Fourth Avenue was the tallest edifice in the city to be built entirely with stone facing (native gray sandstone). The boxlike form is defined by recessed spandrels, unadorned vertical piers, gently setback parapet pillars, with Art Deco and Celtic ornamentation at both the base and crown. At the time it was built, 1411 Fourth Avenue was the location for railroad and steamship company sales offices. These tenants, along with the offices of many major insurance companies and brokerage houses, made the corner of Fourth Avenue and Union Street the city's transportation headquarters and a financial hub.

15) COBB BUILDING 𝍌
1910, Howells & Stokes (New York) and A.H. Albertson; renovation, 2006, GGLO
1301 Fourth Avenue

The Cobb Building is the last surviving element of the original development plan for the "Metropolitan Tract," a multi-block development at the heart of downtown. The building is named for Charles H. Cobb, one of the original investors in the development. The building is thought to be the first on the West Coast designed as a medical office building, intended exclusively for physicians and dentists, as the plaque of Hippocrates at the main entrance attests. The exterior materials and details of the eleven-story steel and reinforced concrete Beaux-Arts building reflect the initially intended pattern for all Metropolitan Tract buildings. The most notable feature is the terra-cotta Native American heads

adorning the frieze; these were considered "symbolic of the characteristics of the American Indian, and indicative of the strength and vigor of the West." The Cobb Building was converted into apartments in 2006. In order to seismically upgrade the structure, the Cobb Building was tied to a new tower on the inside corner of the L-shaped building. Like many older office buildings, its small floor plates lack the space required by contemporary offices, but can be converted to apartments, providing new residential space to add to the liveliness of Seattle's downtown core.

16) PUGET SOUND PLAZA
(Washington Building)
1960, Naramore Bain Brady & Johanson; renovation, 1969 & 1986, NBBJ
1325 Fourth Avenue

The Washington Building is an early example of Corporate Modern architecture in downtown Seattle. Unlike the many airy glass and steel towers suspended over open plazas emerging at the time, the Washington Building tower is a solid and elegant marble slab juxtaposed with an equally solid two-story horizontal base that extends up to the street wall. For the construction of the building, pre-cast concrete beams were used up to the fourth floor then steel thereafter to complete the 22-story building. This construction resulted in 223,000 square feet of column-free rentable space. The Washington Building was among the first completely enclosed air-conditioned buildings in the Northwest.

17) SEATTLE TOWER ᴛ ᴛ
(Northern Life Tower)
1929, Albertson Wilson & Richardson
1218 Third Avenue

With its muscular vertical piers and tapering setbacks, the Northern Life Tower is considered Seattle's quintessential Art Deco skyscraper. Now known as the Seattle Tower, this 27-story edifice was originally built as the headquarters for the Northern Life Insurance Company. The client wanted a building that would be a symbol of reliability and permanence and the architects responded with a building that was intended to suggest the mountains that surround Seattle. The multicolored brick becomes gradually lighter as it reaches the top of the building and the piers are finished with light terra-cotta resembling snow-capped rocky peaks. Stylized metal rods resembling evergreen trees crown the building. The lobby was conceived as a tunnel-like space carved out of rock. The elegant materials of the richly decorated interior space include incised bronze panels, marble and a gilt ceiling. Exterior lighting, which had been removed decades ago, has recently been restored to the building.

18) FINANCIAL CENTER
1972, Naramore Bain Brady & Johanson
1201 Fourth Avenue

The twenty-eight-story Financial Center is an example of the brutalist architecture that emerged in the late 1960s and 1970s. Architects working within the brutalist movement were exploring the expressive possibilities of concrete. Over 34,000 cubic yards of concrete went into the structure, which is supported on each side by two columns straddling a glass and steel lobby. The Financial Center stands above the Great Northern train tunnel, constructed in 1905. To stabilize the foundation of the building and the Fourth Avenue slope, massive caissons were sunk below. The caissons, in depth and volume, were the largest in the world at the time. The building is located on the former site of the Stimson Building (Albertson Wilson & Richardson, 1925).

19) THE OLYMPIC HOTEL 🏛
1924, George B. Post & Sons (New York) and Bebb & Gould; Fifth Avenue wing addition, 1929 and penthouse addition, 1930, R.C. Reamer; renovation, 1984, NBBJ
411 University Street

The Olympic Hotel, the grande dame of Seattle hotels, stands as the result of the efforts of a group of local businessmen who banded together in 1922 to develop an elegant community hotel. The hotel was completed in 1924 at a cost of $5 million and was named for business leader C.D. Stimson's favorite yacht, *Olympic*. Based on Italian Renaissance Palazzo design, the hotel is clad in brick and terra-cotta to simulate the characteristic rusticated stone base. Roman arched windows define the public rooms, complemented by classical molding and balustrades. The Olympic immediately became "the" hotel for Seattle society and an east wing was added in 1929. In 1982, NBBJ was commissioned to reduce the number of rooms in order to increase room size, to restore the principal public rooms and develop the main entry courtyard on University Street in a $55 million refurbishment for the Four Seasons chain. The Olympic Hotel is now managed by the Fairmont Hotels & Resorts, based in Toronto, Canada.

The Metropolitan Theater once stood at the location of the **Olympic Hotel** *auto court and the main entrance to the hotel was on Seneca Street. The U-shaped hotel (East wing added in 1929) was built around the 1911 theater. The Metropolitan Theater was torn down in 1956 to make way for an automobile entrance.*

The Metropolitan Theater during its 1956 demolition.

20) IBM 5TH AVENUE PLAZA
1964, Minoru Yamasaki (Detroit) and Naramore Bain Brady & Johanson
1200 Fifth Avenue

Structurally, this building was a precursor to Yamasaki's World Trade Center towers in New York City. Rather than the traditional steel column and beam skeleton, perimeter loads are carried by tightly spaced, small-scale steel pipes covered in precast concrete sleeves. Yamasaki was a controversial architect in the 1960s and 1970s because of his decorative rather than purely functional approach to Modernism. The arched arcade at the bottom of this building is an example of this tendency; however, the steel arches do carry some perimeter loads, as the small columns bear on diaphragms above the arches. The absence of corner columns announces that the arches do not carry loads in the traditional sense and call attention to the structural innovation of the building. A portion of the half-block site was reserved for the adjacent sunken plaza in order to preserve light to the street and provide open public space among the high-rise buildings. The plaza features a black bronze fountain by Seattle artists James Fitzgerald.

21) SKINNER BUILDING/5TH AVENUE THEATER 門
1926, R.C. Reamer and J.L. Skoog (interior design consultant); renovation, 1979, Richard McCann
1326 Fifth Avenue

The eight-story Skinner
Building was executed
in a restrained version of
the Italian Renaissance
Revival mode popular in
the 1920's. The building
is faced with sandstone
and features a false
loggia and a red tile roof. The 5th Avenue Theater
is located at the south end of the building. Its magnificent interior is said to have been modeled after
various locations in Peking's Forbidden City and
offers an excellent rendition of traditional Chinese
timber architecture. The choice of this theme reflects
Seattle's prominence as a gateway to the Pacific Rim
nations of Asia.

22) RAINIER SQUARE
(Rainier Bank Tower)
1978, Minoru Yamasaki (Detroit) and Naramore Bain Brady & Johanson
1301 Fifth Avenue

Rainier Tower was one of
the last significant works
by University of Wash-
ington-trained architect
Minoru Yamasaki, best
known for designing
the World Trade Center
Towers in New York City.
Yamasaki's work often
reflected his interest in
structural innovation
and Rainier Tower is no
exception. The building
appears to balance precar-
iously on its slender base,
but it is stabilized by a
massive below-grade con-
crete base that is heavier
than the steel-frame structure above. Close inspection
reveals that the concrete pedestal is covered with tiny,
white, octagonal mosaic tiles. A pedestrian corridor
under Rainier Square runs below Fifth and Sixth Avenues to the One and Two Union Square Buildings.

23) LOGAN BUILDING
1958, Mandeville & Berge
500 Union Street

The ten-story Logan Building exemplifies the stripped-down International Style Modernism popular in the post-war years. The building is similar in appearance to the Norton Building (see West Edge tour) with its minimal façade articulated by the window mullions and gray spandrel panels. A series of construction photos is on display in the second floor breezeway to the adjoining US Bank Centre Building.

24) US BANK CENTRE
1989, Callison Architecture
1420 Fifth Avenue

The US Bank Centre reflects the postmodern approach common in the 1980's. The 44-story building is embellished with such eclectic historical references as a French Mansard roof topped with finials in the shape of Egyptian obelisks at each of its four corners. The reflective glazing creates an interesting play with the changing daylight. Accordion-like window protrusions at the center of the building's façade heighten this effect and provide 180-degree views, compensating for the lack of unobstructed corner office windows. The City Centre shops at the base of the US Bank Centre are a successful integration of a retail shopping center into an office tower. The environmental design package that ties art, signage and colors together within the public spaces of the building was developed by Paula Rees of Seattle-based Maestri Design.

25) BANANA REPUBLIC ᵀ ᵀ
(Coliseum Theater)
1916, B. Marcus Priteca; renovation, 1995, NBBJ
500 Pike Street

The Coliseum Theater was one of Seattle's earliest theaters developed exclusively for film, and has been credited with being among the first major motion picture palaces in the United States. Its Renaissance Revival terra-cotta façade originally featured an opulent, cupola-capped half dome at the corner, which was replaced in the 1950s with a more conventional neon marquee. The Coliseum became unprofitable as a movie theater by the mid-1980s and saving it from demolition required adaptive reuse. The building was renovated for use as a Banana Republic retail outlet in 1995. The renovation involved restoration of the façade and replacement of the neon marquee with the present canopy and inverted bay window above. Most of the theater's original interior detail remains above the neutral retail interior.

26) GAP
(O'Shea Building)
1914, Louis Mendel; renovation, 2001,
Callison Architecture
1524 Fifth Avenue

This four-story retail and office building features a white terra-cotta-clad base and Italianate cornice. Delicate, tan brick piers facilitate large window openings. A motif of white terra-cotta rectangles on the spandrels accentuates the extensive glazing. The O'Shea Building was the location of Seattle-based retailer Jay Jacob's flagship store from 1965 until they went out of business in 2000. The building was remodeled for use as a Gap retail outlet in 2001 and features a two-story corner atrium at the main entrance.

27) NORDSTROM 🍴
(Frederick & Nelson Building)
1918, John Graham Sr.; addition, 1953, John Graham
& Co. and Skidmore Owings & Merrill; remodel, 1998,
Callison Architecture
500 Pine Street

This terra-cotta Renaissance Revival building was originally five stories and topped with an elaborate copper cornice. The top four stories were added in 1953. The addition was compatible in design but features simplified detail and resulted in the loss of the original cornice. The line of terra-cotta medallions beneath the original windows was not replicated on the additional stories. After Frederick & Nelson closed its doors in 1992, the building sat empty for several years, evidencing a decline in Seattle's retail core and prompting the closure of other stores. Nordstrom agreed to remodel the building as their new flagship store after voters approved the reopening of Pine Street to vehicle traffic in 1995. This move by Nordstrom was critical to the revitalization of the retail core that has occurred since the mid-1990s. The 1998 remodeling included all new interiors, the addition of an interior atrium, cleaning and restoration of the exterior terra-cotta detail and a new street-level façade.

Prolific commercial architect John Graham, Sr. designed this building for the Frederick & Nelson department store when the Seattle-based retailer moved from its previous location on Second Avenue between Madison and Spring Streets. Although considered a risky move in 1918, other retailers soon followed, effectively shifting the retail core to its present location.

28) MEDICAL & DENTAL BUILDING 🍴
1925, John A. Creutzer and A.H. Albertson
(consulting); addition, 1950, William H. Fey
505 Olive Way

This 18-story, terra-cotta-clad, reinforced concrete-framed high-rise features Gothic-style ornamentation. Continuous projecting ribbed piers ascend the height of the shaft and terminate at a blind story with coupled ogee arches framing sky blue terra-cotta. The building steps back to a tower at the top three floors and continues the motif of blue terra-cotta and coupled ogee arches. Originally an L-shaped building standing on a two-story podium with a beveled edge conforming to the site, an L-shaped east wing was added in 1950, resulting in the present u-shaped structure. The 1950 addition utilized ceramic veneer terra-cotta cladding in the same color as that of the original building; however, the addition is flat and unadorned, reflecting the modern trend of its era. The two-story base of the entire building was altered with the 1950 addition.

29) WESTIN SEATTLE
(Washington Plaza Hotel)
1969 & 1982, John Graham & Co.
1900 Fifth Avenue

*The first **Westin Hotel** tower stands on the former site of the magnificent Orpheum Theater, designed by B. Marcus Priteca. The Orpheum, which boasted outstanding acoustics, was one of several theaters that were constructed around the bustling new retail district in the 1920s. The second tower replaced the Benjamin Franklin Hotel.*

Opened as the Washington Plaza Hotel, the 891-room Westin Seattle includes two cylindrical towers with a combined total of 87 floors. The north tower was added in 1982. The building's unusual structural system utilizes three concentric rings per floor, tied together by six-inch concrete slabs rather than radial beams; these slabs form the floors. The steel was fabricated into three-story-high column trees to expedite construction. Because of its distinctive shape, the Westin Hotel is nicknamed "the curling irons" and "the corn cob towers."

Orpheum Theater was replaced by the first Westin Hotel tower in 19

30) HOTEL MAX SEATTLE
(Vance Hotel)
1927, Victor Voorhees; interior renovation, 2005,
Corso/Staicoff
620 Stewart Street

Hotel Max, formerly the Vance Hotel, exemplifies the restrained Renaissance Revival mode popular in the 1920s. The 10-story building is clad in light-colored brick with low-relief terra-cotta ornamentation. A terra-cotta stringcourse divides the top two floors and cornice from the unadorned shaft. The east-of-center hotel entrance is marked by light cream-colored terra-cotta ornamentation, including fluted pilasters, swags, and fern fronds topped by a fourth-story cartouche bearing the letter "V". The building was designed for lumber and real estate magnate Joseph Vance by Victor Voorhees, who designed several buildings for the Vance Company. Voorhees was also responsible for the 10-story Lloyd Building on the southeast corner of Sixth Avenue and Stewart Street.

31) UNITED STATES FEDERAL COURTHOUSE
2004, NBBJ
750 Stewart Street

The 23-story United States Federal Courthouse building is made up of three primary components: courtroom tower, judicial chambers and office bar. The transparent courtroom tower is flanked by the more solid judicial chambers and office bar, resulting in a symbolic yet functional expression. Birch trees and reflecting pools in the full-acre public plaza along Seventh Avenue provide transition from the street into the Courthouse. Planning began for this building several years prior to the September 11 terrorist attack, but as with all Federal government buildings, security concerns and standards are addressed throughout. The building is supported and reinforced through a redundant structural system, engineered by Seattle-based Skilling Ward Magnusson Barkshire. The 15 by 60-foot lobby reflecting pool separates secure and non-secure areas. The pool permits a clear view of the entire lobby while controlling access through the security check point, yet fosters a serene environment. The United Stated Federal Courthouse building meets the challenge of achieving a high level of security while remaining welcoming and refined.

32) 1700 7TH AVENUE BUILDING
2001, Callison Architecture
1700 Seventh Avenue

This 24-story, steel-frame building features 22 floors of office space over a two-story retail space and lobby. The building is made of medium and high-rise portions. The high-rise portion on the north end of the site achieves a strong sense of verticality with its setbacks and uninterrupted piers. The main corner entrance of the southern, low-rise portion of the building is marked by an engaged round tower, which terminates at a roof terrace. 1700 Seventh Avenue was the first building in Seattle to feature structural design for a 2500-year seismic event.

33) PACIFIC PLACE
1998, NBBJ
600 Pine Street

Constructed as a single building, the exterior of Pacific Place is made up of several false façades that differentiate the storefronts of its many retail outlets. Although the façades were carried out in a variety of styles—some with cornices and classical details, others with a modern appearance—continuous stringcourse, or in some cases incised, lines unify the building. The interior of Pacific Place focuses on a sky-lit, half-circle atrium. A skybridge connects Pacific Place to the adjacent Nordstrom building. The city paid for the parking garage below Pacific Place to help support the revitalization of Seattle's retail district.

34) DECATUR BUILDING
1922, Henry Bittman and Harold Adams
1511 Sixth Avenue

The four-story, terra-cotta-clad Decatur Building features Beaux Arts classical ornamentation including pilasters running the height of the top three stories to an entablature and cornice featuring rosettes, a dentil band and a parapet crowned with acanthus crests. A motif of flowers and acanthus leaves is contained within the spandrels. Eight continuous retail bays at the street level are framed by subtle arches. The Decatur Building was built for Louisa Denny Frye, daughter of city founder Arthur Denny. The developer of the adjacent building at Sixth Avenue and Pike Street purchased the rights to the developable space above the Decatur Building, resulting in a part of the new building looming above the southern end of the Decatur Building.

35) NIKETOWN SEATTLE
1996, BOORA Architects (Portland, OR)
1500 Sixth Avenue

Part retail outlet and part sports memorabilia museum, Niketown Seattle represents a highly specialized type of retail design. The flat concrete exterior gives way to a fully glazed street-level storefront. The corner entrance is marked by a double-height glass pavilion. The design aims to create a theatrical experience for shoppers moving through the interior spaces, which feature chain-link mesh and steel pipe, reminiscent of playgrounds and sport courts. Niketown Seattle was only the sixth to open in the world and contributed to the revitalization of the retail district. BOORA Architects of Portland, Oregon have designed several Niketowns.

36) SHERATON HOTEL & TOWERS
1982, John Graham & Co.; addition, 2007,
Callison Architecture
1400 Sixth Avenue

A 31-story triangular tower rising from a three-story horizontal base makes up the strong geometrical composition of the Sheraton Hotel & Towers. The controversial building was criticized upon completion for its fortress-like façades along Pike Street and Seventh Avenue. A second, 25-story tower was added in 2007, making the Sheraton Hotel & Towers Seattle's largest capacity hotel with 1,253 rooms. The additional capacity makes this hotel an important anchor to the Washington State Convention and Trade Center, as the only hotel capable of providing lodging to conventions of more than 1000 people.

37) WASHINGTON ATHLETIC CLUB
1930, Sherwood Ford
1325 Sixth Avenue

This 23-story Art Deco building houses the Washington Athletic Club and the 112-room Inn at the WAC. At the time of its completion, the WAC towered over its neighbors. Open-winged eagles spanning the upper corners contribute to the building's confident presence. The recessed spandrels, setbacks and emphasized verticals, typical of Art Deco skyscrapers, underscore its loftiness.

*At the **Washington Athletic Club** in 1955, Seattle City Councilman Al Rochester—who had frequented the 1909 Alaska-Yukon-Pacific Exhibition as a boy—discussed his idea for a second World's Fair in Seattle over lunch with two members of the Chamber of Commerce and an editor for the Seattle Times. It was this informal meeting that led to the Century 21 exposition of 1962.*

38) ONE UNION SQUARE
1981, TRA Architects
600 University Street

The rectangular shape of this 36-story, aluminum-clad building is trimmed at the corners, creating a subtle deviation from the common boxlike modern office tower. Another uncommon feature is the touches of yellow that appear at the top of the building. The One Union Square building reflects the trend of modern skyscrapers constructed after the energy crisis of 1973, with the reflective glazing limited in relation to the width of the spandrels. The glass curtain walls of modern skyscrapers built in the 1950s and 1960s were anything but energy efficient, but were built at a time when energy was seemingly abundant and inexpensive. Today, advances in HVAC systems and energy-efficient glazing have allowed for a return to extensively glazed façades and buildings with a less weighty appearance. One Union Square and Two Union Square were developed as "sister structures" eight years apart.

39) TWO UNION SQUARE

1989, NBBJ; Landscape Architect: Thomas Berger & Associates
601 Union Street

The 56-story Two Union Square is a modern skyscraper designed to make abstract allusions to the Puget Sound region. The curving form of the tower suggests sails and airplane wings, while the white, angled penthouse configuration references sailboat sails and the mountains surrounding the city. More overt regional inspiration can be found in the retail courtyard. The naturalistic landscape design includes a two-story rock waterfall reminiscent of a mountain stream. The retail courtyard provides an open, landscaped public space away from traffic, reflecting urban design trends that emerged in the 1980s to improve the street-level environment and make urban centers more livable. Two pedestals at the entrance to the courtyard bear plaques in the shape of the footprints of the One and Two Union Square buildings.

40) PLYMOUTH CONGREGATIONAL CHURCH
1967, Naramore Bain Brady & Johanson.
1217 Sixth Avenue

Plymouth Congregational Church is a rare example of a modern church building in a downtown commercial core. The building replaced the congregation's original 1912 neoclassical building. With the construction of the freeway and the development of the adjacent IBM Tower, the congregation chose to construct a new building that would be architecturally integrated with the surrounding area. The asymmetrical arrangement of rounded and square volumes reflects the building's interior spaces and functions. The dominant exterior decoration is achieved through blocks, which are inlaid with shapes inserted into the sanctuary walls. The shapes on the blocks are commonly seen as doves, although some maintain that they are purely abstract forms. Three memorial windows, a stained-glass medallion that graced the sanctuary ceiling, and the cross that topped the belfry of the old church were incorporated into this building. The columns from the old church now stand at Plymouth Pillars Park, which adjoins Boren Avenue between Pike and Pine Streets.

41) FREEWAY PARK
1976, Landscape Architect: Lawrence Halprin & Associates (San Francisco) and Sakuma James & Peterson; renovation, 1982, Danadjieva & Associates.

This 4.5-acre park is an example of brutalist modern landscape architecture and features cast-in-place concrete paving, cast-in-place board form retaining walls and fountain and a variety of ornamental trees and shrubs. Most of the large evergreen trees are Deodar cedars. The complex forms of the cascading fountain and retaining walls suggest the jagged rock formations of the surrounding mountains, while their cubist geometry echoes the city skyline to the west. The fountain is an example of the interactive, "playable" fountains developed by Halprin in the 1970s. This freeway-spanning park was the first of its kind in the country and has inspired similar projects in other US cities. The park opened July 4, 1976, as part of the U.S. Bicentennial celebration.

State and Federal plans to build the Interstate Highway adjacent to downtown Seattle sparked a major controversy in the early 1960s. Residents worried the highway would create an ugly canyon that would destroy the fabric of the city and sever downtown from Capitol Hill. Many citizens were in favor of covering the downtown section of the highway with a lid, but funding to carry out the idea did not materialize. In 1976, Federal, State and "Forward Thrust" funds were combined with private funding to construct at least part of the lid that was proposed 15 years earlier, resulting in **Freeway Park.**

42) WASHINGTON STATE CONVENTION AND TRADE CENTER
1988, TRA Architects; addition, 2001, LMN
Seventh Avenue & Pike Street

The Washington State Convention and Trade Center straddles I-5 between Pike and University streets, expanding on the lidding of the freeway that began with Freeway Park. The 371,000 square-foot facility is an unusual example of a building designed specifically to fit with an adjacent public open space. The Convention Center was planned several years after Freeway Park was in place. The complex cubist forms of the park's retaining walls and fountains were carried over to the design of the Convention Center. Towering green glass walls blur the distinction between indoor and outdoor spaces, making the building seem to flow organically out of the park. The Convention Center features a large collection of art, inside and out, which is well worth a tour. A massive addition was completed in 2001, which more than doubled the convention center's size to nearly one million square feet.

A massive addition to the Convention Center was completed in 2001.

43) ONE CONVENTION PLACE
2001, Callison Architecture; Pike Street Canopy,
2001, LMN
701 Pike Street

One Convention Place was constructed as part of the massive Convention Center expansion plan. The 16-story office tower, designed as two intersecting glass and steel masses, is built atop the Convention Center's new entrance, placing the first office floor 120 feet above the street.

The expansion (which includes but is not limited to this building) doubled the Convention Center's size and included the controversial truck and pedestrian bridges, as well as the 10-story glass canopy that stretches over Pike Street between Seventh and Eight avenues. The City Council approved the hotly-debated features but shortly after their completion, approved a ban on skybridges that would impair views in designated downtown view corridors.

44) ACT THEATER
(Eagles Temple Building)
1924, Henry Bittman and Harold Adams; renovation,
1998, Callison Architecture and GGLO (LL) (NR)
700 Union Street

This Renaissance Revival-style building was designed to house the Fraternal Order of Eagles, Seattle Aerie No.1, as is indicated by the eagles at the front and back entrance to the building. The terra-cotta ornamentation was likely designed by Harold Adams, whose deft hand with classical motifs graces many of Seattle's finest terra-cotta buildings. The building's original interior facilities included hotel rooms surrounding a grand ballroom, meeting rooms, restaurants, cocktail lounges, performance spaces, billiard rooms and a boxing ring. The Eagles sold the building in the early 1980s but development plans were not carried out and the building sat vacant and neglected for years. The Eagles Temple Building was renovated in 1998 to provide two new performance spaces for ACT Theater and low-income housing within the complex. The renovation also involved restoration of the exterior terra-cotta ornamentation.

45) ROOSEVELT HOTEL
1929, John Graham, Sr.
1531 Seventh Avenue

The 20-story Roosevelt Hotel features a terra-cotta-clad base giving way to a brick shaft, which steps back to a brick and terra-cotta penthouse. There was originally dark bronze Art Deco ornamentation on the recessed spandrels below the windows of the 151 guest rooms. The ornamentation at the tops of the setbacks and penthouse is typical of Graham's work of this period.

46) PARAMOUNT THEATER 〼 〼
1928, Rapp & Rapp (Chicago) and B. Marcus Priteca;
renovation, 1995, NBBJ
911 Pine Street

Opened as the Seattle Theater, the Paramount Theater was developed by Paramount Pictures, which began constructing movie palaces throughout the country in the mid-1920s. The building was designed by Rapp and Rapp–who designed many of Paramount's Theaters–with local famed theater designer B. Marcus Priteca, who was responsible for design of the residential studios to provide housing for performing artists. The building's façade is quite restrained; however, this simplicity belies the lavishly decorated spaces within. The French Renaissance interior is said to have been inspired by Versailles, the opulent palace of Louis XIV. The 1994 restoration expanded the stage and staging facilities and included the installation of a state-of-the-art flooring system that can change from raised to flat seating.

47) CAMLIN HOTEL 〼 〼
1926, Carl J. Linden; Conversion, 2005,
Callison Architecture
1619 Ninth Avenue

This 11-story Tudor Revival building features a brick façade with terra-cotta ornamentation. In 1949, the top floor was converted from a penthouse into a restaurant named "The Cloud Room" for its lofty views of the city. The Cloud Room was the only restaurant to offer 360-degree views of the city until the opening of the Space Needle in 1962. The years since have seen taller and taller buildings rise around the Camlin, and the eventual loss of its sweeping views. The Cloud Room closed in 2003 when the Camlin Hotel was purchased for conversion to a private vacation resort.

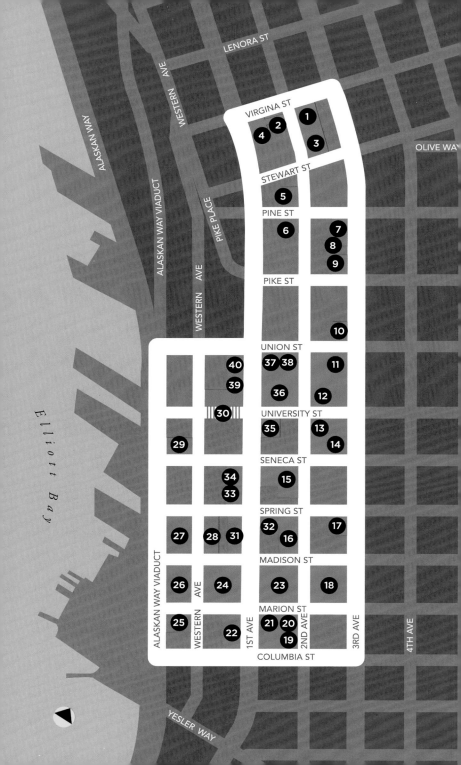

CHAPTER 5

WEST EDGE

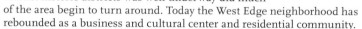

The name "West Edge" was not derived from a historical pattern of development, but was given to the blocks from Third Avenue to the Waterfront between Pioneer Square and Belltown by the Downtown Seattle Association in 2001 in an effort to strengthen the neighborhood's identity. However, the neighborhood now known as West Edge encloses an area that experienced rapid growth sparked by the Klondike Gold Rush and a steady decline after the 1930s. Not until preservation of the Pioneer Square and Pike Place Market historic districts was well underway did much of the area begin to turn around. Today the West Edge neighborhood has rebounded as a business and cultural center and residential community.

Among the earliest of Seattle's many regrades took place in 1876, on First Avenue (then Front Street), which was the only overland route between downtown and Belltown. Streetcar and cable car lines introduced along First and Second avenues between 1884 and 1889 were a welcome alternative to navigating Seattle's muddy streets on foot or horseback between Pioneer Square and the largely residential areas to the north. Improved transportation sparked the early development of an "uptown" retail district along Second Avenue north of Yesler Way. The Rialto, designed by Skillings & Corner (1893, destroyed), was a two-story retail building that stretched 240 feet along the west side of Second Avenue between Madison and Spring streets, and boasted over 40 stores under one roof.

The central business district remained firmly in Pioneer Square; however, with the construction boom after the Great Fire, First and Second avenues experienced some significant development outside of the historic core, most notably with the 1891 completion of the quarter-block Burke Building (destroyed), designed by Elmer Fisher, which stood on the northwest corner of Second and Marion (now the site of the Jackson Federal Building). The Seattle Athletic Club Building and Dobson

The Burke Building, designed by Elmer Fisher for Judge Thomas Burke, 1891.

and Denton Hotel buildings (1892-93, destroyed), all designed by John Parkinson, created a continuous street-wall along the west side of Front Street (now First Avenue) from Seneca to University. But the Panic of 1893 halted construction and further expansion of the central business district.

When Klondike Gold Rush prosperity hit Seattle in 1897, the rapid expansion of the central business district began. Because the city was still hemmed in by First Hill, Denny's Knoll, Denny Hill and tideflats to the south, much of the growth spread northward along First Avenue where several businesses catering to Gold Rush prospectors and transient laborers were established.

By the turn of the century the beach along Elliott Bay was filled, creating more land for development. Warehouses were then constructed along West Street (now Western Avenue) by railroads, produce brokers and merchants for the transfer of goods by rail and by sea. Second Avenue was regraded in 1902, followed by Third Avenue in 1907, facilitating growth north of Pioneer Square and east of First Avenue. The central business district began shifting to Second Avenue between Cherry and Marion streets at this time, with the construction of "modern" office buildings such as the 1904 14-story Alaska Building (see Pioneer Square tour).

With the first phase of the Denny Hill Regrade (see Belltown tour), a new fashionable retail and theater district began to coalesce along upper Second Avenue near Virginia and Stewart streets. Upper Second Avenue would remain the theater and retail hub into the 1920s when the area was challenged by development on the Metropolitan Tract and surrounding blocks (see Retail District tour).

The 23-story Exchange Building on Second Avenue and Marion Street, completed in 1929, was the last skyscraper to be constructed in downtown Seattle prior to the Great Depression. The 1933 Federal Office Building was one of the very few significant buildings constructed downtown during the following years. Thereafter, First Avenue declined and by the 1940s had become lined with run-down hotels and bars, adult entertainment businesses and pawn shops. The warehouses along Western Avenue were also falling into disrepair as shipping activity was increasingly concentrated south of the Central Waterfront. The 1953 completion of the Alaskan Way Viaduct did nothing to improve the quality of First and Western avenues, and several of the historic warehouses in its shadow were demolished in the 1960s to make room for parking lots.

Second and Third avenues fared better in the post-war years, although major construction was slow to return. In 1950 the Federal Reserve Bank was completed on Second Avenue and in 1959 the 19-story Norton Building, at Second Avenue and Columbia Street, became the first skyscraper to be constructed in downtown Seattle since the adjacent Exchange Building, completed 30 years earlier.

In 1974, the 37-story Henry M. Jackson Federal Office Building replaced the Burke Building and introduced an increasing scale to the area. The high-rise boom of the 1980s brought the 48-story First Interstate Bank (now Wells Fargo Center) in 1983 and the 55-story Washington Mutual Tower, Seattle's second-tallest skyscraper, in 1988.

The preservation movement of the 1960s and 70s that saved Pioneer Square and Pike Place Market began to effect positive change along Western and First avenues in the late 1970s. Cornerstone Development Co.'s Waterfront Place project included the renovation of several his-

toric buildings, such as the Grand Pacific Hotel and the Agen Warehouse, as well as construction of new mixed-use buildings like the Watermark Tower, increasing the retail and residential presence in the area. A "furniture row" developed along Western Avenue, with home décor and furniture stores occupying several historic warehouse buildings.

The 1991 opening of the Seattle Art Museum's new building on First Avenue and University Street was a major boost to the rebounding neighborhood. The completion of Benaroya Hall in 1998 further established the University Street corridor as a cultural hub. The completion of the first phase of Harbor Steps in 1994, a project that had been in the works for two decades, created a direct pedestrian link to the waterfront lined with shops and restaurants. Its large apartment buildings added a major residential element to the area. The proximity of these projects to Pike Place Market, the Seattle Art Museum, Benaroya Hall and downtown employers has been a draw for people who want to avoid commuting and live in an active urban center.

More recently, the construction of the 42-story WaMu Center has brought a larger scale as well as a major downtown employer to Second Avenue and Union Street. The decision by the Four Seasons chain to locate their Seattle hotel and condominium development at First Avenue and Union Street is a testament to the positive long-term impact that the preservation of Seattle's historic districts has had on the revitalization of the area.

The West Edge neighborhood is facing major transformations in the coming years with the replacement of the Alaskan Way Viaduct and development on the Central Waterfront. Though these are likely to have a positive effect on the quality of life of those who live and work in the area, careful planning will be needed to ensure sensitivity to the scale of historic structures and pedestrian environment as well as affordable housing options.

1) MOORE THEATRE & HOTEL 🎭 🎭
1907, Edwin Houghton
1932 Second Avenue

The eleven-story Moore Theatre and Hotel is constructed of reinforced concrete and faced with white glazed brick. Subtle touches of Renaissance and Byzantine detail executed in tan terra-cotta enliven the simple façade. These motifs were carried forth with exuberance into the lavishly detailed lobby and auditorium spaces. The building gained national recognition for its innovative construction, which allowed for a column-free auditorium with excellent sight lines. This and other innovations such as exiting ramps in the theatre as well as sports equipment for the hotel, including a basement swimming pool, put the facility ahead of its time. The Moore is the oldest theater in Seattle still operating for its original purpose, hosting a variety of performance genres and community events.

2) TERMINAL SALES ANNEX
(Puget Sound News Building)
1915, Bebb & Gould
1931 Second Avenue

This four-story, terra-cotta-clad building was executed in a simplified English Gothic style. The cornice features a stepped parapet with terra-cotta tiles fading from blue to peach. The tiles are recessed behind a tightly-spaced arcade of trefoil arches above a trefoil-arched corbel table framing blue terra-cotta tiles. The spandrels of the central bay are ornamented with a pattern of recessed blue terra-cotta and shields. A large arched window spans the central bay at the street level. Built for the *Puget Sound News*, the niches framing the arched window once housed terra-cotta figures in the form of newsboys.

3) THE JOSEPHINUM 🏛 🏛
(New Washington Hotel)
1908, Eames & Young (St. Louis), renovation, 1991,
Stickney & Murphy
1902 Second Avenue

This fourteen-story Renaissance Revival hotel was financed by Seattle developer James A. Moore, who developed the adjacent Moore Theater and Hotel. Now known as the Josephinum, the New Washington Hotel replaced Moore's Washington Hotel (1890-1906) that was demolished with the regrading of Denny Hill. Most of the embellishment occurs at the ground level where an arched window arcade featuring terra-cotta ornamentation is punctuated by smaller, pedimented openings. The building was purchased by the Catholic Archdiocese in the 1970s to provide low-income housing for people in transition and renovated in 1991.

Photo montage of the Denny Hill regrade showing the old and New Washington hotels.

4) TERMINAL SALES BUILDING 🏛
1923, Henry Bittman and Harold Adams
1932 First Avenue

Henry Bittman's background as an engineer is evident in this eleven-story warehouse building with its legible structural grid, expansive industrial sash windows and large open interior spaces despite the building's height. At the time it was built, the Terminal Sales building was the tallest flat-slab structure west of the Mississippi. Flat-slab construction utilizes a reinforced concrete slab at each floor that is designed to span, without any beams or girders, to supporting columns. The building's original use, as a sales and display warehouse for manufacturers and wholesalers, was well served by the maximized daylight and open interior spaces. Cream-colored terracotta pilasters with neo-Gothic ornamentation define the base and crown of the building while uninterrupted brick-faced piers ascend the shaft. Terra-cotta spandrels are present throughout the façade and, in contrast with the brick piers, emphasize the building's structural grid while balancing its verticality. The Terminal Sales Building was among the first constructed under the zoning ordinance adopted in 1923, which encouraged setbacks to preserve light at the street level.

5) BROADACRES BUILDING
(Standard Furniture Co.)
1907, Augustus Warren Gould, renovation, 1961, Arnold G. Gangnes
1601 Second Avenue

This nine-story reinforced concrete-framed high rise was modernized in 1961, resulting in the loss of most of its terra-cotta ornamentation; however, cartouches bearing the letter "S" still dot the spandrels below the upper story. Such alterations were not uncommon in Seattle at the time, as the city was preparing for the futuristic-themed Century 21 exposition of 1962 and had not yet come into the era of preservation that would soon follow.

6) DOYLE BUILDING 🎋 🎋
(J.S. Graham Store)
1919, Doyle & Merriam (Portland, OR); restoration, 1973, Ibsen Nelson & Associates
1527 Second Avenue

Located near the heart of Seattle's historic retail district, the Doyle Building was originally built as the J.S. Graham women's apparel store. This four-story, reinforced concrete frame building is now named for its designer A.E. Doyle, Portland, Oregon's leading architect of the early twentieth century. The cream-colored terra-cotta-clad building reflects Doyle's skill with Italian Renaissance design. The three stories above the ground-floor retail bays are unified by continuous piers rising to form an arcade of paired arched window bays divided by spiral mullions. The building is topped with an elaborately ornamented entablature and projecting cornice. The Doyle building is among the finest Renaissance Revival buildings in Seattle.

7) OLYMPIC TOWER 🎋 🎋
(United Shopping Tower)
1931, Henry Bittman and Harold Adams
217 Pine Street

This twelve-story, reinforced concrete building is clad in terra-cotta and composed of a two-story retail and office base supporting a setback, ten-story tower. The polygonal crown creates large terraces and a loggia around the Penthouse offices. Art Deco ornamentation in a stylized floral motif adorns the base and crown. With its strong verticality, set-back tower and Chicago-style windows, the Olympic Tower displays the prevailing architectural trends of its time. Despite the building's original name, it has been occupied mainly by offices above the first floor.

8) FISCHER STUDIO BUILDING
(Fischer Music Building)
1912, Bebb & Mendel; 1915, Bebb & Gould
1519 Third Avenue

The eight-story, terra-cotta-clad Fischer Studio Building was the first design to come from the partnership of Bebb & Gould. The project was initiated during Bebb's partnership with Louis Mendel. Construction began under Mendel's design and had been built to the third floor when Gould redrew the plans adding a music hall on the seventh and eight floors. These floors feature Venetian Gothic-inspired terra-cotta ornamentation. Blind windows are treated with a diamond motif and are divided by fluted pilasters. Fleur-de-lis and finials in the shape of grotesque masks adorn the cornice. Black cast iron urns flank the bays at the second story. The street-level façade has been altered.

9) MELBOURNE TOWER
(Republic Building)
1928, Lawton & Moldenhour
1511 Third Avenue

This eleven-story office tower is nearly identical in form to Lawton & Moldenhour's design for the Fourth & Pike Building (see Retail District tour); however, the Melbourne Tower's terra-cotta-clad façade was executed in a French Renaissance mode rather than the Gothic styling of the Fourth & Pike Building. The most dramatic ornamentation occurs at the attic story, with finials in the shape of shields dotting the peaked corner parapets. False quatrefoil windows below the peaks frame blue terra-cotta tiles. Coronets rising from the dentil band are set above windows corresponding to ornamental balconies with wrought-iron balustrades.

10) MANN BUILDING 🏛
(Embassy Theater)
1926, Henry Bittman; renovation, 1998, NBBJ and Ron Wright & Associates
1401 Third Avenue

This two-story, terra-cotta clad-building, executed in the English Gothic style, was built as the Embassy Theater and housed retail and office space on the above-ground levels with the theater space below. The Embassy Theater served as a venue for vaudeville productions and was one of many that made up a vibrant theater district on upper Second Avenue. After years of neglect, the Mann Building was renovated for use as restaurant space and a musical performance venue. The renovation included cleaning and restoration of the terra-cotta exterior ornamentation, seismic reinforcing and replacement of the original interiors.

11) BENAROYA HALL
1998, LMN
200 University Street

The various functions of this symphony hall can be read on the exterior, from the dominant façade element of the curving glass wall enclosing the lobby to the angled roof over the main auditorium, which mimics the slope of the seating within. The building is set back from the south and west edge of its site, creating open space and preserving views along the University Street

Benaroya Hall is the Seattle Symphony's first real home since its inaugural 1903 performance in Christensen Hall, which was located at the current site of the Seattle Art Museum. The symphony performed at the Moore Theater starting in 1906 and moved to various locations over the next fifty years. Since the opening of the Century 21 Exhibition in 1962, the Opera House (see Seattle Center tour) had been the symphony's primary venue.

corridor. Renowned acoustician Cyril Harris worked with the architects to create an auditorium space conceived as a "box within a box," which buffers noise and vibration from the Third Avenue transit tunnel, the Great Northern Railroad tunnel and surface traffic. Benaroya Hall boasts a collection of art commissioned specifically for the building, including chandeliers by Northwest glass artist Dale Chihuly and a mural titled "Echo" by Robert Rauchenberg. The building is named for a major benefactor.

12) GARDEN OF REMEMBRANCE
1998, LMN; Landscape Architect: Murase Associates

The black granite engraving wall, which runs along the east side of this garden, lists the names of fallen servicemen and servicewomen, which were transferred from the previous war memorial site at the now demolished Public Safety Building. 3,000 names that had been left off the original list were added. The landscape design features granite benches and fountain, Katsura and Japanese maple trees, rhododendrons, azaleas and other northwest-native plants. The Garden of Remembrance exists because of the effort led by Priscilla "Patsy" Bullitt Collins (1920-2003). A prominent Seattle citizen and philanthropist, Bullitt Collins headed the effort to raise $3.5 million to build this half-acre memorial to Washington's War dead. Out of respect for the fallen, Bullitt Collins demanded assurance from the city that no commercialism, politicizing or alcohol use would be allowed at the site.

1201 Third Avenue (the old Washington Mutual Tower) reflected in the skin of the new Wa Mu Center.

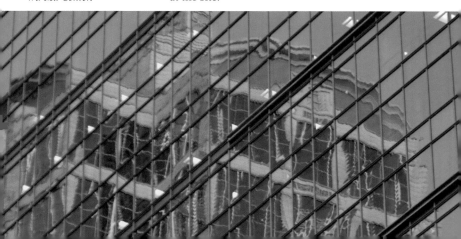

13) BROOKLYN BUILDING
ca. 1890, unknown
1222 Second Avenue

This four-story brick building is a fine example of Richardsonian-Romanesque architecture, which was popular among Seattle architects during reconstruction after the Great Fire of 1889. Distinguishing stylistic features include its massive masonry construction, heavy rounded arches and lack of ornamentation. The Brooklyn Building was constructed for street-level commercial business with apartments above, suggesting the residential character of Second Avenue before it became a thriving commercial district. Only the façades fronting Second Avenue and University Street are original. Once the location of a party wall, the south-facing side was incorporated into the Washington Mutual Tower.

14) 1201 THIRD AVENUE BUILDING
(Washington Mutual Tower)
1988, Kohn Pedersen Fox (New York) and McKinley Architects
1201 Third Avenue

This 55-story postmodern skyscraper, Seattle's second tallest, was formerly the world headquarters of the Washington Mutual Bank, which has moved into its new building on Second Avenue and Union Street, although some of their offices remain here. The 1201 Third Avenue building is a highly stylized and rigidly symmetrical composition with a tower rising from a granite base which accommodates the change in grade along University and Seneca Streets. Its first 45 stories are conceived as a glass cylinder encased in a granite box. The tower steps back at the peak to its distinctive pyramidal top. The Washington Mutual Tower was originally planned to stand at the exact center of the site but the desire to save the Brooklyn Building and preserve views to and from the historic Seattle Tower required shifting it slightly south.

15) SECOND & SENECA BUILDING
1992, Zimmer Gunsul Frasca Partnership
1191 Second Avenue

The tiered form of this 22-story office building was a response to varying height limits within the block as well as an effort to relate to the differing scale of its neighbors. The green dome that caps the cylindrical portion of the building is illuminated after dark, providing a distinctive spot on the skyline that has earned this building the nickname, "the Ban Roll-on Building."

16) FEDERAL RESERVE BANK OF SAN FRANCISCO
1950, Naramore Bain Brady & Johanson
1015 Second Avenue

This simple, six-story building was built for the twelfth Federal Reserve District, which includes nine western states with branches in Los Angeles, Salt Lake City, San Francisco and Seattle. The Federal Reserve Bank acts as the nation's central bank; it holds cash reserves and moves currency in and out of circulation. The building's limestone veneer façade and granite base give the building a solid, weighty feeling somewhat analogous to a bank vault. The Federal Reserve Bank moved to a new facility twelve miles south in Renton in 2007.

17) EXPEDITORS INTERNATIONAL HEADQUARTERS
(City Light Building)
1931, Earl W. Morrison; addition, 1953, Jones & Bindon Architects; renovation and addition, 1999, Weinstein A|U
1015 Third Avenue

This 13-story, half-block building was originally constructed for Seattle City light. The existing nine-story building was renovated for Expeditors International in 1999. Floor plates were increased and four stories added to expand the square footage of the building from 140,000 to 225,000 square feet. Problems with alignment of the cladding and a deteriorating skin were resolved by stripping the building to its structural frame and re-cladding with granite panels and installing a new storefront system at the base. The tower portion was given a new curtain wall, resulting in the building's contemporary appearance. The renovation also included interior reconfiguration and mechanical and electrical upgrades.

18) WELLS FARGO CENTER
(First Interstate Building)

1983, McKinley Architects
999 Third Avenue
The form of this 48-story office tower is an elongated hexagon rising from a terraced, three-story plaza. Its flush exterior surface is clad in alternating continuous bands of tinted glass and spring rose granite panels. The unconventional shape of the tower allows for six corner office spaces on each floor, a desirable feature in the fiercely competitive office rental market of the 1980s. The base of the tower reflects

the urban design ordinances of the time, which were concerned with how tall buildings meet the street and what public amenities they provide. The terraced outdoor spaces include areas for sitting, gathering, view points as well as food and retail services. The escalators at the base of the public space offer a "hill climb assist".

19) NORTON BUILDING
1959, Skidmore Owings & Merrill (San Francisco office) and Bindon & Wright; Plaza renovation, 1987, Loschky Marquardt Nesholm; Landscape Architect: Thomas L. Berger & Associates
801 Second Avenue

When the 19-story Norton Building opened, it was the first skyscraper to be built in downtown Seattle since the adjacent Exchange Building (1929), and was downtown Seattle's introduction to the glass curtain wall. The rectangular glass block of the building straddles a glass lobby and rises from a granite base. The Norton Building was innovative and widely published. It was the first building in the United States over six stories to utilize prestressed concrete beams, permitting open floor spans of 70 feet and eliminating the need for interior structural columns. Its curtain wall, composed of alternating bands of clear and gray spandrel glass, was assembled from preglazed window units. Uninterrupted anodized aluminum mullions run the full height of the building and terminate the curtain wall at the corners. The lead design architect for the Norton Building was Myron Goldsmith of Skidmore Owings & Merrill, a student of Mies van der Rohe. The Second Avenue plaza and entrance were renovated in 1987 with the addition of granite pavers, a metal trellis, landscaping and a new lobby on the north end of the building.

20) KEY BANK 〒
(Bank of California)
1924, John Graham Sr.; restoration, 1982,
The Callison Partnership
815 Second Avenue

The Bank of California Building is a fine example of the Greco-Roman style popular for bank design at the time as well as a testament to John Graham Sr.'s skill with classical motifs. Its Roman temple façade and four ionic fluted columns are clad in "granitex", a terra-cotta product that simulates the look and texture of granite. The sky-lit interior features a polychrome coffered plaster ceiling; the skylight, which had been blacked out since the 1940's, was brought back with the 1982 restoration.

21) EXCHANGE BUILDING 〒
1929, John Graham Sr.; renovation, 2002, Mithun
821 Second Avenue

This 23-story Art Deco building is clad in a warm-toned, cast concrete product called "Romanite" that simulates sandstone. The Exchange Building was the second tallest reinforced concrete structure in the nation when it was completed. Built to house the Northwest Commodities and Stock Exchange, many of the ornamental reliefs were designed to represent Washington State's agricultural products. Comparison with the neighboring Bank of California building of 1924 reveals this architect's skill with various styles and building scales. The renovation of the building involved technology upgrades, restoration of the elevator lobbies, public areas and mill work as well as cleaning and re-anchoring of the exterior cast-stone panels.

The Colman Building prior to the 1906 addition.

22) COLMAN BUILDING 𝍀 𝍀
1890, Stephen Meany; remodel and addition, 1906, August Tidemand; remodel, 1929, Arthur Loveless; restoration, 1982, Hewitt Daly Isley
811 First Avenue

The six-story Colman Building, built on the site of the original Colman block that burned in the Great Fire of 1889, was begun in 1890 as a Classical Revival structure with an arcade of round arched windows flanking the protruding central bay. Only two stories were completed, however. The building was remodeled and four stories were added in 1906. With its large window openings and lack of classical ornamentation, the 1906 remodel and addition reflect the influence of commercial architecture being built in Chicago and eastern cities at the turn of the century. Only the cast iron columns between the storefront bays were retained from the 1890 façade. A 1929 remodel for Peoples Bank & Trust Company incorporated Art Deco elements at the south corner of the building. A large-scale reproduction of the bronze bank doors (removed) can be seen on the main level at Macy's. The Colman Building, built for Seattle business leader James Colman, played an active role in Seattle's Klondike Gold Rush prosperity. Klondike clothing outfitter Rochester Clothing Co., Seattle Hardware Co., and grocer Louch, Augustine & Co. occupied the building at the time.

23) HENRY M. JACKSON FEDERAL OFFICE BUILDING
1974, Fred Bassetti & Co. and John Graham & Co.;

Landscape Architect: Richard Haag Associates
915 Second Avenue
The designers of this 37-story concrete office building aimed to create a high rise with sensitivity to human scale and environment at the street level. The façade piers turn inward at the ground level, provid-

ing human-scaled entries into the lobby. The H.M.
Jackson Federal Office Building was among the
first buildings in downtown Seattle to enhance the
street-level appearance on all four sides of the site.
Entry-level plazas were provided at both First and
Second avenues and are connected by stairs and landings enhanced with native vegetation, which provide
public open space along the sloping site. Stone and
terra-cotta from the Burke Building, which formerly
occupied the site, were incorporated into the outdoor
spaces, including the Burke's arched Romanesque entry facing the Second Avenue. Alterations made to the
First and Second avenue entrances to heighten security after the September 11, 2001 terrorist attack have
compromised the integrity of the original design.

24) OLD FEDERAL OFFICE BUILDING 🏛
(Federal Office Building), 1933, James A. Wetmore
(Washington, D.C.)
909 First Avenue

This nine-story Art Deco
building is a departure
from the Neoclassical
style that was typi-
cally applied to federal
buildings at the time;
however, the Old Fed-
eral Office building does
incorporate the classi-
cal elements of base,
column and entablature,
but here they have been
reinterpreted into an Art
Deco composition with
its characteristic stepped massing and vertical emphasis. Cream-colored terra-cotta capping the piers
of the red brick façade heightens the cascading effect
of the building's form and suggests the irregular
rock formations of the surrounding mountains. The
spandrel panels on the Old Federal Office building
are thought to be the first extensive use of aluminum
as a construction material on the West Coast.

Decorative urns adorn the Old Fed-
eral Office Building.

25) COMMUTER BUILDING
1906, unknown
815 Western Avenue

Originally known as the Castens Building after its owner, Thomas Castens, this four-story brick store-and-loft building operated as a cold storage warehouse for wholesale dairy products. The building was later converted for office and retail use. The name of the Commuter Building, as it has been known since the 1930s, comes from the pedestrian bridge connecting to the ferry terminal at the north side of the building.

26) MARITIME BUILDING
1910, unknown
911 Western Avenue

This five-story reinforced concrete building is a fine example of early warehouse architecture. Its extensive wood sash windows allow for ample light to its open interior spaces. The Maritime building played an important role in the Western Avenue wholesale district, housing offices and showrooms for manufacturers and distributors of goods as diverse as John Deere plows and office supplies. The building now houses home décor and furniture retailers on its ground floor, part of the "furniture row" that has developed along Western Avenue. The floors above are office space.

27) WATERFRONT PLACE
1984, Bumgardner Architects
1011 Western Avenue

This thirteen-story building houses retail on the ground floor, three levels of parking, and six floors of office space topped with twenty penthouse condominium units. Waterfront Place was built as part of the Waterfront Place project by Cornerstone Development Co., which involved the renovation of old buildings as well as the construction of new buildings in the formerly run-down area bordered by Madison and Seneca streets and First and Western avenues.

28) NATIONAL BUILDING ⊓
1904, Kingsley & Anderson; renovation, 1983,
Hewitt Daly Isley
1008 Western Avenue

The National Building is the oldest survivor of a group of six-story brick commercial buildings built by the Northern Pacific Railroad to accommodate Seattle's growing produce trade. The site, near the railroad tracks and piers, was crucial to the efficient transportation of goods to retailers by rail or by sea. This building was the center of activity for the National Grocery Company, one of the West Coast's largest grocery wholesalers. Most of the warehouses constructed by Northern Pacific were demolished in the 1960s for parking lots. The National Building was renovated for use as retail and office space as part of the Cornerstone Development Co.'s Waterfront Place project.

29) WESTERN BUILDING Ⅷ
(Agen Warehouse)
1910. John Graham Sr.; addition, 1911, John Graham
Sr.; renovation, 1987, Hewitt Daly Isley
1201 Western Avenue

Originally built as a four-story building, two stories were added in 1911 to accommodate John Agen's growing dairy industry. Brick piers rising from the base to the fourth floor of the bearing-wall structure are treated as pilasters, terminating in capitals of herringbone-laid brick forming vertical swags. Concrete-framed decorative brick and tile adorn the spandrels of the original four stories, with galvanized metal panels on the spandrels of the 1911 addition. Shields flanking the cast concrete arched Western Avenue entrance bear the letter "A" for its original owner. Agen, known as the father of the dairy industry in the Pacific Northwest, shipped goods produced and stored in this plant from his own pier (now Pier 56) to locations in the United States and abroad. The Western Building was converted for use as office space as part of the Waterfront Place project by Cornerstone Development Co. The building shell and interior were completely renovated and a penthouse office space and roof-top deck were added.

30) HARBOR STEPS
1994-2000, Arthur Erickson Architectural Corp.
(Vancouver, B.C.), Callison Architecture and
Hewitt Isley Architects
1221-1301 First Avenue

Harbor Steps complex was twenty years in the making. Approval of the master-use permit went through in 1990, nearly two decades after the 2.3 acre site was acquired. Harbor Properties, Inc., developed the project, which was carried out in phases over six years and incorporates apartments, retail space, hotel and parking facilities flanking the public open space created by Harbor Steps Park. The block of University Street between First and Western avenues was closed off

*The site of the **Harbor Steps** development was the shoreline of Elliott Bay until around 1900 when the beach was filled in to create more land for development. The early twentieth century buildings that occupied the site had become neglected as this area had fallen into decline and gained the reputation as being a seedy part of town. Preservation of the Pioneer Square and Pike Place Market districts in the 1970s inspired the development of residential, retail and office spaces along First Avenue. These developments and the presence of the Seattle Art Museum and Benaroya Hall have transformed this area into a cultural center and urban residential neighborhood.*

to construct the grand stairway, providing direct pedestrian access to the waterfront from downtown. The outdoor spaces include pre-cast concrete paving, cast-in-place concrete retaining walls, and cascading fountains lined with green slate tiles. Flowering cherry, flowering pear and Italian cypress trees soften the appearance of the curving concrete steps and a series of plazas, landings and ledges were included along the steep 60-foot grade. A plaza where the steps intersect with Post Alley connects the park to the Pike Place Market. Retail and building entrances step down with the plazas, and public elevators make them accessible. The design of the glass and concrete towers, ranging in height from 16 to 26 stories, features exposed concrete framing with extensive glazing and balconies to capture views of Elliott Bay and the Olympic Mountains from the apartment and hotel units and an uncommon use of color on a modern building. The southwest tower was completed in 1994, followed by the southeast tower in 1997 and the northeast and northwest towers in 2000.

31) ALEXIS HOTEL/ARLINGTON BUILDINGS 𐊕 𐊕
(Globe Building, Beebe Building, Hotel Cecil)
1901, Max Umbrecht; renovation, 1983, Bumgardner Architects
1007-1023 First Avenue

These three buildings form the last intact, continuous block of circa 1900 buildings on First Avenue between the Pioneer Square and Pike Place Market Historic Districts. They form an individualized yet harmonious street frontage and display their architect's skill with Renaissance-derived, eclectic detail. All three buildings are faced in tan pressed brick. These buildings were constructed in a period of rapid growth northward along First Avenue and responded to the demand for transient worker housing created by the Klondike Gold Rush. Being close to the historic commercial district, these buildings, particularly the Globe Building (now Alexis Hotel), catered to businessmen as well. The buildings were renovated and their façades restored as part of the Waterfront Place project by Cornerstone Development Co. The Globe Building was renovated for reuse as a hotel after having been used as a parking garage since the 1940s. The Beebe Building and Hotel Cecil (now Arlington Buildings) were renovated into apartments and condominiums.

32) HOLYOKE BUILDING 🎵 🎵
1890, Bird & Dornbach
1022 First Avenue

This five-story brick masonry building is a good example of Victorian commercial architecture with its characteristic tall, narrow windows and closely spaced piers emphasizing its verticality. Cast iron and rusticated stone define the base of the building, while continuous pilasters terminating in carved stone capitals unify the top four floors. Excavation for the Holyoke Building began just prior to the Great Fire of 1889. The deep hole served as a fire stop preventing the spread of the fire further north. Subsequently, the Holyoke Building was one of the first office buildings to be completed after the fire and represents an early northward expansion of the commercial district, which would take off after the Klondike Gold Rush of 1897. The Holyoke Building housed Seattle's first conservatory for the arts in the 1920s. The building is named for Richard Holyoke, a successful Seattle lumberman turned real estate investor.

33) WATERMARK TOWER
1984, Bumgardner Architects
1109 First Avenue

This 20-story retail and condominium tower incorporates the terra-cotta façade of the 1915 Coleman Building designed by Bebb & Gould at the southern portion of the building. With its sculpted rooflines, setbacks, vertical articulation and geometric ornamentation, the Watermark Tower recalls the form and detailing of the Art Deco period. The Watermark Tower was constructed as part of the Waterfront Place project by Cornerstone Development Co.

34) GRAND PACIFIC CONDOMINIUMS 🏛
(Grand Pacific Hotel)
ca. 1898, unknown; renovation, 1983, Bumgardner Architects
1115-1117 First Avenue

Originally known as the First Avenue Hotel, the Grand Pacific Hotel was one of the last buildings in Seattle to be built in the Richardsonian Romanesque style, which had fallen out of fashion by the time of the building's completion. Rusticated limestone blocks and voussoirs make up the heavy entrance arch and recessed spandrels dividing the two-story arcade. The eight, round cut-stone arcade arches spring from compact stone capitals; these features are typical of Richardsonian Romanesque architecture. The Grand Pacific Hotel, along with other First Avenue hotels, filled a growing need for retail space and transient worker housing during the Klondike Gold Rush years. The Seattle Woolen Mill, which outfitted miners with blankets and clothing, operated out of the street-level commercial space of the Grand Pacific Hotel. The Grand Pacific Hotel's exterior was restored and the building was joined internally with its Renaissance Revival neighbor to the north, the Colonial Hotel, in a renovation to condominiums as part of the Waterfront Place project by Cornerstone Development Co.

35) YALETOWN SOFA
(Diller Hotel)

1890, Hetherington Clements & Co.
1224 First Avenue
This four-story brick masonry building is one of the oldest buildings in downtown Seattle, constructed immediately after the Great Fire of 1889. Although most post-fire buildings were

The Diller Hotel was named for its owner, Leonard Diller. Diller's first Seattle hotel, the Hotel Brunswick, in the Pioneer Square area, was destroyed in the 1889 fire. He immediately built this hotel several blocks north on the site of his family home.

inspired by the Richardsonian Romanesque style, the Diller Hotel was executed in the Victorian mode more common to pre-fire buildings. The three bays of its primary façade feature tall, narrow windows and are divided by brick piers treated as pilasters, which terminate in brick capitals at each story. Its corner entry arch is made of lightly rusticated limestone. The three-story corner bay is another Victorian flourish and a very unusual feature in post-fire Seattle. Large storefront windows divided by cast-iron columns that originally faced First Avenue in each of the street-level bays have been filled in; and, like many historic buildings in Seattle, its cornice was removed after the 1949 earthquake. The Diller Hotel was an early local work of Louis Mendel, who was then employed with Hetherington Clements & Co., and would later become a prominent Seattle architect.

36) SEATTLE ART MUSEUM
1991, Venturi Rauch & Scott-Brown (Philadelphia) and Olson Sundberg Architects; renovation, 2001, Allied Works Architecture (Portland, OR) and LMN 100 University Street

The postmodern Seattle Art Museum building exemplifies Venturi's concept of the "decorated shed," in which the building's functions are contained within a utilitarian shell adorned with decoration and symbolism. The limestone exterior is incised with fluting and monumental lettering announcing the building's function. The limestone mass of the building is countered at the street level with a base of granite, sandstone and bluestone. Polychrome terra-cotta frames the arched entry ways, which draw on Venetian Gothic, Persian and other sources. The application of terra-cotta alludes to Seattle's rich history of use of the material on early twentieth century buildings. Zoning required the architects to keep a view corridor along University Street. Their response was the broad staircase that parallels the interior stair. The stairs create a processional experience and blur the indoor-outdoor distinction. The 48-foot sculpture at the corner of First Avenue and University Street is "Hammering Man" by Jonathan Borofsky.

37) SEATTLE ART MUSEUM EXPANSION
2007, Allied Works Architecture (Portland, OR), NBBJ and LMN
1300 First Avenue

Four interlocking L-shaped walls make up the form of the sixteen-story Seattle Art Museum expansion, which on the exterior appear as a series of layered planes. The clefts created by these intersections on the northern façade feature full-length windows providing water and city views. Tightly grouped steel dividers run uninterrupted the full height of the building, accentuating its verticality against the adjoining 42-story WaMu Center. A four-story sunscreen of "brise-soleil" panels along First Avenue shifts to accommodate changes in daylight or to be tailored to exhibits. A rooftop garden creates an open space at the seventeenth floor of the adjacent WaMu Center. The main entrance to the museum was relocated from the old museum building to the corner of First and Union. The SAM expansion was designed to be occupied by the museum in phases over the next twenty years. When it fully occupies the 12 floors designated for its use, the museum will have tripled its space to 450,000 square feet. The Seattle Art Museum, the SAM expansion and WaMu Center make up a full-block complex with distinct exteriors.

38) WAMU CENTER
2006, NBBJ
1301 Second Avenue

At 589 feet, the 42-story WaMu Center building is the tallest office block constructed in Seattle since the Seattle Municipal Tower in 1990 (see Civic/Financial District tour). The form of the building incorporates three narrow rectangles, which are offset to capture views. The base-levels of the WaMu Center are clad in glazed terra-cotta, establishing a connection with Seattle's architectural past and maximizing light at the street level during Seattle's grey and rainy months. The glazed rectangular forms on the east and west façades of the building sandwich the denser center core, giving the building a transparent yet solid appearance. Floor-to-ceiling glass curtain walls are treated with individualized grid patterns at the various elevations, relating to the surrounding and adjoining structures. WaMu Center was built to house the headquarters of Washington Mutual Bank.

39) LUSTY LADY
(Seven Seas Hotel)
1900, unknown
1315 First Avenue

This three-story masonry building is another of the few circa 1900 survivors outside of the Pioneer Square and Pike Place Market Historic Districts. The building was constructed as a seamen's hotel and bar called the Seven Seas Hotel. The ground floor space, except for the columns, has been altered. The Lusty Lady adult entertainment center has occupied the ground-floor space since the early 1980s and has amused passersby with puns on its marquee such as, "Obi wanna disrobie?" and "Our birds have no dressing." The Lusty Lady is a lone survivor of the adult entertainment district that once thrived on First Avenue. The owners of the building sold the rights to the air space above to the developers of the adjacent Four Seasons Seattle. The arrangement ensures that views to the south of the hotel and condominium building will not be blocked by future development on this site.

40) FOUR SEASONS SEATTLE
2008, NBBJ
First Avenue & Union Street

Having just 146 guestrooms and 36 residential units, the 21-story Four Seasons Seattle is the smallest hotel-condominium development in the Four Seasons chain. The building is U-shaped to maximize water views. It steps down at the northern end in response to the scale of the neighboring Pike Place Market. Four Seasons Seattle was kept below its height allowance to preserve views from the WaMu Center rooftop garden. The street level houses lobby and retail space, with ten floors of hotel guestrooms above. A protruding bay along First Avenue contains a glass elevator, allowing views to the street and adding an element of motion to the façade. The hotel portion of the building is clad in metal with punched windows; the ten-story condominium level is encased in a glass curtain wall with clear, translucent and opaque finishes. The building's west façade centers on a terrace courtyard and swimming pool. The adjacent Union Street Plaza was part of the Four Seasons development. This public plaza provides a stair connecting upper and lower Union Street.

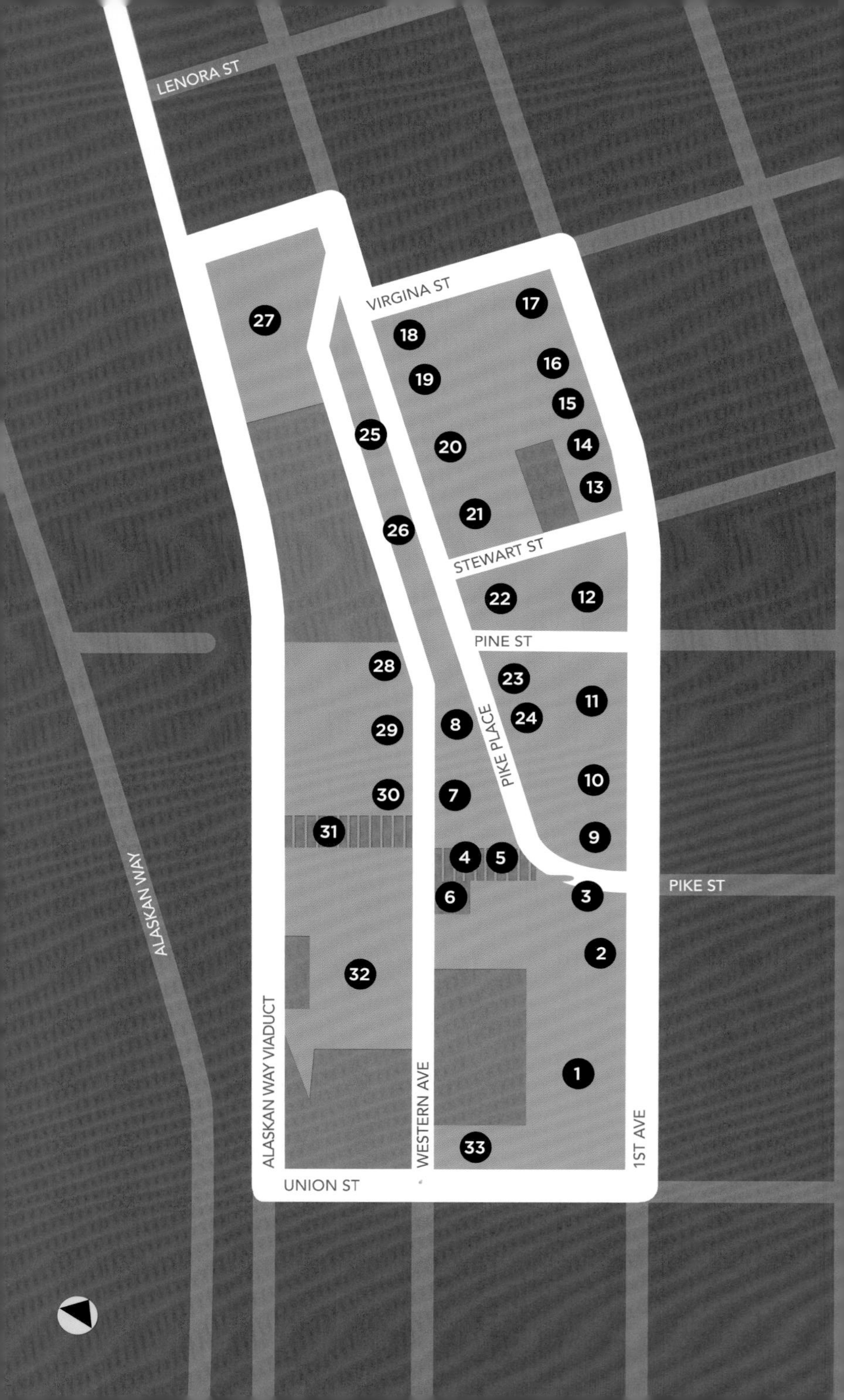

LENORA ST

VIRGINA ST

(27)

(17)

(18)

(16)

(19)

(15)

(25)

(14)

(20)

(13)

(21)

(26)

STEWART ST

(22)

(12)

PINE ST

(28)

(23)

(29)

(8)

(24)

(11)

PIKE PLACE

(30)

(7)

(10)

(31)

(9)

(4) (5)

(6)

(3)

PIKE ST

(2)

ALASKAN WAY

(32)

ALASKAN WAY VIADUCT

(1)

WESTERN AVE

1ST AVE

(33)

UNION ST

CHAPTER 6
PIKE PLACE MARKET

A walk through Seattle's Pike Place Market is a rich multi-sensory experience. The sounds of thousands of voices swirling beneath the shouting fishmongers and street musicians; the scent of fresh bread, exotic spices and fresh-cut flowers; and the sight of colorful produce in tightly packed crates conspire to create the timeless atmosphere of a bazaar in the midst of a modern city. This special place that is loved by Seattle-ites and tourists by the millions was born of necessity at a time when America's working class was being squeezed by unfair labor and business practices.

Farmers from the Rainier Valley, river valleys to the north and south, the Puget Sound islands, and the Cascades foothills, had for years been making trips into Seattle to sell their produce to the commission men who worked out of warehouse buildings along Western Avenue. The price they fetched for their produce was determined by these middlemen, who were increasingly accused of flagrantly cheating the farmers, then turning around and charging consumers exorbitant prices. Many felt that they were sending the best produce out of Seattle, leaving local consumers to pay top dollar for low-quality food.

By 1907 the consumers and the farmers found a sympathetic ear in newly-elected City Councilman Thomas P. Revelle. It was the era of Theodore Roosevelt's trust-busting campaigns, and Revelle was politically like-minded. He believed that a public market allowing farmers to sell directly to consumers would increase both profits and savings, and force the commission men to "clean up their act." Revelle discovered a dormant City Council ordinance adopted in 1896 that allowed for the establishment of a public market "somewhere" in Seattle. He proposed the newly-planked Western Avenue and Pike Place as a logical choice, providing easy access to farmers arriving either by mosquito fleet or traveling to Western Avenue in their wagons. This location also had a generous amount of undeveloped land north of the Leland Hotel that could potentially be used to expand the market in the future. The location was several blocks away from what was then the heart of downtown, keeping the odors of produce and fish at a comfortable distance.

City Council approved the location and a few weeks later, on August 17, 1907, the Pike Place Public Market opened for the first time. Fewer than a dozen farmers parked their wagons along the curb in front of the Leland Hotel on that rainy morning. They were quickly overwhelmed by the thousands of people, mostly women, who showed up to shop. The farmers sold everything they had in what was described as a "clamorous fiasco."

The *Seattle Times*, which had run editorials in support of the public market, blamed intimidation by the corrupt commission men for the poor

This image of vendors on Pike Place illustrates the market's chaotic first days.

farmer turn-out. But the throngs of people willing to crowd the rainy streets for affordable produce sent a clear message that there was demand. The following Saturday, 70 farmers' wagons bypassed the commission men and headed up Western Avenue toward the public market. They too sold all of their produce that day and the Pike Place Market was born.

Demand for sheltered market space quickly surfaced, but city council lacked the funds to construct it. Relief from the drizzle and downpours would come from an entrepreneur named Frank Goodwin.

Goodwin had moved to Seattle from Washington, D.C. in 1897, to profit from Gold Rush trade. He and two of his brothers instead decided to go directly for the gold and headed to Dawson City. He returned to Seattle the following year with a $50,000 fortune, and with his brothers established a thriving real estate business. Among their holdings were the Leland Hotel and the undeveloped land along the bluff west of Pike Place, which they purchased in September 1907. Frank Goodwin saw opportunity in the market and devised a plan for an arcade with 76 stalls that could be rented to farmers monthly. His brother John, an engineer, helped him come up with the design. They had the arcade built and opened by November 30, 1907.

The city funded an adjoining arcade that extended north to Virginia Street in 1910. The stalls in this publicly-owned portion of the market were rented to farmers by the day. Stalls were assigned in a daily lottery held by the "Market Master," a custom that continues today.

Councilman Revelle's hopes that the market would bring fair prices to farmers and consumers were realized almost immediately. A 1909 *Seattle Times* article about the market proclaimed it "a blessing to Seattle people." It went on to read, "So keen did the market make competition that the human food stores of the city were forced to meet the market prices or lose

A view of Pike Place Market taken in the first weeks of operation, prior to the construction of Goodwin's arcade.

business. The result is that a generally lower price for foodstuffs prevails all over the city." (*The Seattle Times*, 2/14/09).

In 1910 Goodwin and his partners established the Public Market and Department Store Co. to manage and develop Goodwin Real Estate's holdings in the market area. By 1914 they had built the vertical labyrinth known as "Down Under" descending the hillside to Western Avenue. Like all of their market structures, utility and economy guided the design. In 1916, they converted the former Bartell Building (built in 1900) into the Economy Market. The Corner Market was constructed in 1912. In 1913, a new ordinance designated a portion of Post Alley for public market use. By 1917, the Pike Place Market had taken a form similar to that we see today.

Pike Place Market continued to thrive but by 1920 increasing congestion of trucks and automobiles prompted a proposal to move the Public Market to a larger, more accessible space on Westlake Avenue. The vendors formed the Associated Farmers of Pike Place Market to fight the relocation and were successful. The first attempt at closing the Public Market at Pike Place was thwarted.

The Market was an important source of affordable food and a social gathering spot throughout the Great Depression. Those who could not afford to spend a quarter for a bag of groceries, waited for closing time when vegetables, cheese and meat scraps sold for pennies. Sailors and longshoremen appreciated the affordable lodging at the many workingmen's hotels in the area. Artist Mark Tobey became captivated by the Market in the late

1930s and devoted years to sketching and painting its vibrant and ever-changing tableau.

Joe Desimone, an Italian immigrant farmer who had been selling at the market for years and had become Vice President of the Public Market and Department Store Co. in 1927, took control of Goodwin Real Estate's holdings in the Market in 1941. Desimone drafted a will prohibiting his heirs from selling his market properties, Pike Place Public Market, Inc.; his son took over after his death in 1946. The end of the Goodwin era coincided with an event that would impact both the market scene and the entire United States.

The December 7, 1941, attack on Pearl Harbor brought America into the war and cast suspicion on thousands of innocent Japanese-Americans. Within a few months of the attack, the Japanese-American farmers, who made up over 60 percent of Market merchants, were forced to relocate first to Puyallup and then to the internment camp at Minidoka, Idaho. Their sudden absence meant market shoppers were greeted by hundreds of empty stalls. Due to the dearth of vendors, the Municipal Market Building was used for rummage sales, antique shops and other purposes. By the time the Japanese-American farmers were able to return (and many did not), new challenges faced Pike Place Market.

The years following the war were marked by increasing suburbanization. Downtown streetcar service, which for decades had shuttled people down First Avenue directly to the market, had ceased in 1941. Affordable home refrigeration and the establishment of supermarkets weakened demand for the fresh foods sold at the Market. Many began to view Pike Place Market as an obsolete relic of a bygone age.

In 1950 an urban renewal plan was proposed to raze the Market and

Victor Steinbrueck leading a 1971 "Save the Market" demonstration.

replace it with parking garages. The 1953 construction of the Alaskan Way Viaduct created a barrier to the once vital relationship between the Market and the waterfront. A plan proposed in 1963 called for doubling the width of the Viaduct and replacing the Market with parking structures and office buildings.

Fortunately, there were those who recognized the unique character and sense of place that Pike Place Market brought to Seattle and they organized to fight the urban renewal plans. Allied Arts (an urban design activist group), architect and preservation activist Victor Steinbrueck and attorney Robert Ashley formed "Friends of the Market" in 1964, "dedicated to saving and renewing the historical Pike Place Market and district through a program of community planning." They began an aggressive campaign to raise public awareness about the danger of losing the Market. In 1968 Victor Steinbrueck published his *Market Sketchbook*, which captured the character of the market and raised public interest.

In 1970, Steinbrueck proposed a 17-acre Pike Place Market Historic District; but only a 1.7-acre district was approved, which would have allowed urban renewal plans to proceed. The Friends of The Market fought back again, proposing a 7-acre historic district, which was approved by voters in November 1971. A local historic district was formally established later that year, and the district was listed on the National Register of Historic Places in 1973. (The local district was expanded westward in 1984 and 1991.) The Pike Place Market was saved, but the question of what to do with it presented another major hurdle.

The Pike Place Market Public Development Authority (PDA) was established in 1973 to purchase and manage buildings in the Market and develop property in the surrounding area. George Rolfe was named the first director of the PDA. The enormous task of rehabilitating and upgrading the public market buildings fell to George Bartholick, who was named supervising architect in 1974. He, along with several other local architects, rehabilitated or replaced buildings in the district over the following several years.

Preserving the buildings in their original form, as much as possible, was a guiding principle of the rehabilitations projects. The Market Arcade was almost entirely reconstructed in its original form. Other buildings, such as the Corner Market building, were preserved and structurally reinforced. The buildings that could not be rehabilitated were replaced by new construction that adhered to design guidelines requiring the use of scale and materials compatible with the historic buildings.

Creating a viable pedestrian retail environment was another major component to revitalizing the Market. Prior to 1974, Pike Place ran one-way south, funneling traffic onto Pike Street and First Avenue. This had become a common route into downtown for people living in West Queen Anne, Magnolia and Ballard. The commuters took Fifteenth Avenue West to Western Avenue, using Pike Place as a "cut through" into downtown and causing major congestion in the Market. Traffic was reversed one-way north eliminating the cut-through and dramatically alleviating congestion. Pike Place was paved with brick, slowing traffic and making a walk through the space more appealing. Parking areas, later garages, were created along Western. The addition of the Hillclimb Corridor in 1976 created a link to the waterfront and the newly developed Seattle Aquarium and Waterfront Park. Market Park, now named Victor Steinbrueck Park, was built atop one of the parking garages in 1982 providing access to views to Elliott Bay, Puget Sound and the Olympic Mountains. Recent construction, such as the Heritage House senior housing facility, has included additional links from parking to the Market Arcade.

The Market Foundation, a non-profit organization, was established in 1982 to support services for the market community, including a senior center, food bank, childcare and a preschool.

Infill projects, such as the Pike and Virginia Building, were developed with sensitivity to the character of the Market. Condominiums and market-rate apartments began developing in the immediate surrounding areas in the 1980s, creating a diverse residential population that, along with millions of tourists, supports Market merchants and businesses. The Pike Place Market Heritage Center was added in 1999, offering a place for visitors to see the history of Pike Place Market.

The revitalization of the Market has also helped transform First Avenue from a strip of marginal buildings and businesses into an attractive urban neighborhood and cultural center. The Market was an important factor in the selection of the site on First Avenue and Union Street for the Four Seasons Seattle development (see West Edge tour). The preservation of the Market has helped effect positive change all along the Pike-Pine corridor, including the revitalization of the Retail District (see Retail District tour).

It is difficult to imagine Seattle without Pike Place Market. Its familiar neon clock and sign have become as recognizable a symbol of the city as the Space Needle (see Seattle Center tour). Many who visit the Market today are unaware of how very close we came to losing it in those pivotal years in the 1960s and 70s. It is a local gem, a major tourist attraction, a supportive community for low-income and elderly residents, and the oldest continually-operating farmer's market in the United States.

The buildings listed in this section are all within a city historic district, the Pike Place Market Historic District. Some of them are also local landmarks or are listed in the National Register, as noted in the text.

1) 98 UNION/SOUTH ARCADE
1985, Olson/Walker
98 Union Street

This mixed-use complex includes 81 condominium units and over 40,000 square feet of retail space. The 13-story residential tower features steel-framed balconies, peach cladding and a set-back penthouse level creating large corner terraces and a form suggesting Art Deco design. 98 Union was an early large-scale residential development in the Market vicinity. The first level of the complex connects to the Pike Place Market South Arcade and the Economy Market.

2) ECONOMY MARKET ATRIUM
(Bartell Building)
1900, unknown; remodel, 1916; John Goodwin (engineer) and Andrew Willatsen; rehabilitation, 1978, George Bartholick

The Economy Market Atrium was constructed as the Bartell Building in 1900. The original Market developer, Frank Goodwin, acquired the building in 1916. Andrew Willatsen, who began overseeing Market improvements in 1915, designed the conversion to provide space for more vendor stalls and permanent businesses. The 1978 rehabilitation created a covered gathering space within the atrium and provided an entrance into the building from the adjacent 98 Union South Arcade development.

3) INFORMATION BOOTH AT FIRST AVENUE AND PIKE STREET

The information booth is located at the site of the original Market that opened on a rainy August morning in 1907. One can inquire here about guided Pike Place Market tours. The ramp below leads to Lower Post Alley, where the Market Theater and Alibi Room are located; the "wall of gum" was created over the years by people waiting in line for shows.

4) PUBLIC MARKET CENTER CLOCK AND SIGN
ca. 1930

The Market clock and neon sign, one of Seattle's oldest neon signs, has served as a landmark and rendezvous point since it was erected. During the Depression years, this was a popular location for political dissidents to preach to the bustling crowds.

5) "RACHEL"
1986, Georgia Gerber

Rachel is a life-size, 550-pound bronze piggy bank. Money deposited in Rachel helps support the Market Foundation's human services programs. Rachel accumulates between $6,000 and $9,000 worth of change every year. Some of the change even comes in Dinars, Rials, Euros, Yen, Won, Pesos and Shillings. Rachel receives a constant flow of visitors eager to pose with her for snapshots. Just beyond Rachel is *Pike Place Fish*, famous for its boisterous, fish-throwing crew.

6) LASALLE HOTEL
(Outlook Hotel)
1908, unknown; rehabilitation, 1977, George Bartholick
87 Pike Street

The Outlook Hotel offered low-cost housing to workers and seamen and ran as a legitimate hotel until 1942, when its Japanese-American operators were interned. The lease was then taken over by Nellie Curtis, who had been running a bordello at the Camp Hotel on First Avenue and Virginia since 1933, the first such establishment to be tolerated north of Yesler Way. Nellie changed the name to the LaSalle Hotel and catered to her patrons here for nearly a decade. The 1977 rehabilitation joined the hotel internally with the Cliff House (c. 1901) , creating a nine-story complex with low-income housing on the upper levels, shops and the Market PDA office on the lower level.

7) LELAND HOTEL/BAKERY COMPLEX
1900, unknown; renovation, 1907, John Goodwin (engineer); rehabilitation, 1977, George Bartholick

The three-story Leland Hotel was purchased by original Market developer Frank Goodwin in 1907 and its ground floor was integrated into the construction of the Main Market Arcade (Fairley Building). The building houses apartments on the top two floors and open Market space below.

8) MAIN ARCADE AND DOWN-UNDER SHOPS
(Fairley Building)
1907, John Goodwin (engineer); addition, 1914, John Goodwin; improvements to addition, 1915, Andrew Willatsen; rehabilitation, 1977, George Bartholick

Original Market developer Frank Goodwin purchased the land north of the Leland Hotel (as well as the hotel) in September of 1907. Frank's brother John Goodwin designed the 76-stall structure, which is primarily utilitarian with ornament limited to the column capitals. The structure opened on November 30, 1907, and was immediately inadequate as 120 vendors arrived to fill the stalls. In 1914, three lower levels were built down the hillside and linked in a labyrinth fashion by a system of ramps. These came to be known as the Down-Under shops. Architect Andrew Willatsen was brought in to supervise improvements to the addition the following year. The Main Arcade was rehabilitated in 1977 by George Bartholick, who was named Pike Place Market's first supervising architect in 1974.

9) CORNER MARKET
1912, Harlan Thomas & Clyde Grainger; rehabilitation, 1975, Karlis Rekevics
Northwest corner of First Avenue & Pike Street

The three-story, concrete-frame Corner Market building was constructed to meet the growth of the Market in its early years and provided open stalls for vendors and space for larger businesses. Concrete with brick inlay create architectural interest on this utilitarian building. Arched windows are framed in concrete and form a continuous arcade along the third story. Bands of concrete divide the bays and frame the windows from the ground up. Brickwork in the spandrels provides a motif of diamonds flanking rectangular bands. The parapet rises to a peak at the center of the First Avenue and Pike Street façades, framing a clock on the central bay. The second floor opens out onto First Avenue and originally provided open-front shops (later converted to closed-front) for larger businesses. The Pike Street and Pike Place sides have always had smaller, open-front businesses.

The Three Girls Bakery is the first known business to operate out of the **Corner Market**. *Shoppers gathered around the bakery windows to marvel at Seattle's first automatic doughnut maker. The bakery is still in business today in the adjacent* **Sanitary Public Market** *building.*

10) SANITARY PUBLIC MARKET
1910, Daniel Huntington; reconstruction, 1942, McClelland & Jones; rehabilitation and addition, 1981, Bassetti Norton Metler
1515-1521 Pike Place

This building reputedly takes its name for being the first in the market where horses were not permitted. The original 1910 four-story building was severely damaged by fire on December 15, 1941, resulting in the loss of the top two stories. The Sanitary Public Market was quickly reconstructed as a two-story building with rooftop parking and reopened in October of 1942. The 1981 rehabilitation eliminated the parking and added two residential levels above ground-level vendor stalls.

The Sanitary Public Market *fire raised suspicions and fueled resentment toward the market's many Japanese-American vendors, as it occurred one week after the attack on Pearl Harbor. Many suspected that it was sabotage intended to disrupt the food supply to Seattle. The fire took place within a paranoid climate, and reinforced the kind of thinking that would escalate to the internment of thousands of innocent West Coast Japanese-Americans.*

6 PIKE PLACE MARKET

153

11) POST ALLEY MARKET /FIRST & PINE BUILDING
1983, Bassetti Norton Metler
1529-1529 First Avenue

The five-story First &
Pine Building includes
ground-level shops with
housing and offices
above. This relatively
new building maintains
a sense of the utilitarian simplicity of the historic
Market buildings. Originally constructed as a privately-owned retail and low-income apartment
building, the First & Pine Building was purchased by
the Pike Place Market PDA in 2005.

12) INN AT THE MARKET
1985, Ibsen Nelson & Associates
1609 First Avenue

This six-story hotel building features red brick
veneer cladding and a
concrete base incised
with horizontal banding,
suggesting the style of
the nearby historic buildings while remaining
contemporary in its lack
of ornamentation. Bay
windows maximize views
of downtown, the Market
and Elliott Bay from the
guestrooms. The Inn at the Market is built around a
central courtyard and steps down in height as it de-
scends Stewart Street toward Pike Place, relating it in
scale to the historic Market buildings.

13) FAIRMOUNT HOTEL
**1914, W.E. Dwyer; rehabilitation, 1977, Ralph
Anderson & Partners**
1907 First Avenue

When the six-story Fair-
mount Hotel opened in
1914, it boasted fireproof
construction, command-
ing marine views and
modern rooms equipped
with bath and phone.
The Enumclaw Creamery originally operated out of
the ground-level space. The Fairmount Hotel was
rehabilitated for office space in 1977.

14) ALASKA TRADE BUILDING ҭ
1909, J.O. Taft; rehabilitation, 1977, Ralph Anderson
& Partners
1915-1917 First Avenue

The four-story Alaska Trade Building was one of the first steel and concrete-frame buildings to be built in the Market area. It was home to press operation of the nation's first labor-owned daily newspaper, *The Seattle Union Record,* from 1921 until the end of its run in 1928. The *Record* was instrumental in inciting the nation's first general labor strike on February 6, 1919, two days after having published Anna Louis Strong's appeal to Seattle workers to launch the strike. People stocked up on food and supplies in anticipation of a several-week strike. Streetcars stopped running and shops closed as 65,000 sympathizers joined 35,000 shipyard workers striking for a post-war salary increase. But the strike officially lasted only until February 11, 1919. The Alaska Trade Building was renovated in 1977 for retail and office space.

15) BUTTERWORTH BUILDING ҭ
1903, John Graham, Sr.; rehabilitation, 1977, Ralph Anderson & Partners
1921 First Avenue

This three-story brick and stone building is a fine example of the materials and craftsmanship of the early twentieth century. The rusticated stone base features a wide arched portico flanked by two narrow arched openings. Red brick piers terminate in scroll brackets supporting a projecting cornice and parapet featuring an arched balustrade. The Butterworth Building was John Graham, Sr.'s first commercial

Edgar Butterworth's undertaking business was the first to offer a horse-drawn lacquered hearse and formal funeral services to the citizens of Seattle. Butterworth's business boomed and he became highly respected in his field. He is generally credited with coining the terms "mortuary" and "mortician." Perhaps not surprisingly, the **Butterworth Building** *has earned the reputation of being one of Seattle's most haunted places.*

building commission in Seattle as well as Seattle's first modern mortuary. The building is named for undertaker Edgar R. Butterworth and functioned for its original purpose until 1923 when the business moved to Capitol Hill. The building was rehabilitated in 1977 for retail and office space.

16) SMITH BLOCK BUILDING
1906, unknown; rehabilitation, 1977, Ralph Anderson & Partners
1923 First Avenue

This 1906 building was jointly restored with the adjacent Butterworth and Alaska Trade buildings. Records of its original use are unclear; from 1920 on, the building served as the offices and lodge hall of the Marine Engineers Benevolent Association. Today the Smith Block Building houses ground-level commercial space and a bed and breakfast on the upper floors.

17) LIVINGSTON-BAKER APARTMENTS
(Hotel Livingston)
1901, unknown; rehabilitation, 1977, Harader & Mebust
1925-1937 First Avenue

The three-story Hotel Livingston features bay windows on both of its upper stories and a round corner turret, providing views of the street and Elliott Bay. The ground floor has always served as a bar, and has been the Virginia Inn since 1908 (originally named the Virginia Bar). During prohibition it remained open as a card room. The Livingston Hotel and the adjacent Baker Apartment building now provide 96 low-income housing units.

18) PIKE AND VIRGINIA BUILDING
1978, Olson/Walker
87 Virginia Street

The seven-story Pike and Virginia building was the first entirely new building completed in the Market district. It is one of very few buildings within the historic district with an overtly modern appearance, but in its scale and industrial materials the Pike and Virginia building fuses nicely with its historic surroundings. The building houses 14 condominium units above ground-level retail space.

19) CHAMPION BUILDING
1928, unknown; rehabilitation, 1977,
Champion/Turner Partnership
1924-1928 Pike Place

The Champion Building was constructed for the Dollar Cab Company and originally served as a parking garage. The building later served as a meat packing business. The Champion Building was renovated in 1977 creating ground-level retail space with office space above.

20) SOAMES-DUNN BUILDING
1918, unknown; rehabilitation, 1976, Arne Bystrom
1912-1922 Pike Place

Dunn's Seeds operated out of this building, selling seeds to farmers and home gardeners. Dunn's also provided storage space for farmers vending their produce at the Market. Soames Paper Company operated out of the adjacent building, selling paper bags to Market farmers. The two buildings were joined in the 1976 rehabilitation, creating retail space. Among the current tenants is the Original Starbuck's Coffee shop, opened here in 1971.

21) STEWART HOUSE
(Stewart House Hotel)
1902-1911, unknown; rehabilitation and addition,
1982, Ibsen Nelson & Associates
84-86 Stewart Street

The Stewart House Hotel was built as a working-man's hotel and offered affordable, short-term housing to the many seamen, longshoremen and dock workers in the area. The hotel operated until 1977 when it was closed for fire code violations. Originally built as a two-story wood-frame building, a one-story brick retail space was added in 1911. The 1982 rehabilitation involved extensive foundation repair, reconstruction of the main façades, rehabilitation of the original wooden structure and a four-story addition faced in red brick veneer. The building contains retail space on the ground floor and low-income housing above.

22) SEATTLE GARDEN CENTER
1908, W.C. Geary; rehabilitation and addition, 1980,
Arne Bystrom
1600 Pike Place

The Seattle Garden Center was built for the Gem Egg Market; it became the Seattle Garden Center in 1946. Built as a simple, two-story utilitarian structure, Art Deco flourishes such as fluted columns and zig-zag coping were added in the 1930s. Architect Arne Bystrom and two merchants purchased the building and saved it from demolition in the late 1970's. Bystrom added a third-story office level while rehabilitating the original building. Its pink and green paint provide a vibrant backdrop to the bustling Market activity and highlight the building's Art Deco touches.

23) SILVER OAKUM BUILDING
1910, unknown; rehabilitation, 1977, Fred
Bassetti & Co.
1530-1534 Pike Place

This three-story brick masonry building was constructed for the Market Hotel, which operated from 1910 to 1972. The hotel was frequented by seamen and owned by Ben Silver. It is believed that the building takes its name from the original owner and oakum, a fiber used by seamen for caulking seams in wooden ships. The building was joined internally with the Triangle Market and renovated into one-bedroom apartments above retail space in 1977.

24) TRIANGLE MARKET
1908, Thompson & Thompson; rehabilitation, 1977,
Fred Bassetti & Co.
1530-1534 Pike Place

The shape of the two-story Triangle Market building was dictated by the irregular lot created by the intersection of upper Post Alley and Pike Place. The building was constructed to house the South Park Poultry Company. Chickens once hung from the ceiling for inspection by shoppers and egg crates were stacked on the floor. The building was joined internally to the adjacent Silver Oakum Building in the 1977 renovation and now houses ground-level Market shops with a restaurant above.

25) NORTH ARCADE
1911 &1922, John Goodwin (engineer); rehabilitation,
1977, George Bartholick

The market was extended 1,200 feet north of the Main Market (Fairley Building) in 1911. Further extension in 1922 accommodated the overflow of farmers and moved their carts off of Pike Place into covered stalls, providing parking space for Seattle's growing number of motor vehicles. The new arcade created an additional 160 stalls. Today the North Arcade is used by farmers as well as flower and craft vendors.

26) DESIMONE BRIDGE ENCLOSURE
1985, James Cutler Architects

Desimone Bridge spans Western Avenue and was originally constructed across Western Avenue in 1925 to connect the market with the Municipal Market Building (1924, destroyed). The bridge was enclosed in 1985 as an extension of the North Arcade and replicates its utilitarian design. The enclosure is primarily used by craft vendors. The bridge is named for Giuseppe "Joe" Desimone, a farmer and Market vendor who took over management of the Market in 1941 after having been Vice President of Public Market and Department Store Co. since 1927.

27) VICTOR STEINBRUECK PARK
(Market Park)
1982, Victor Steinbrueck; Landscape Architect: Richard Haag
Western Avenue & Virginia Street

This 0.8-acre park is built over three levels of Market parking. The park offers picnic tables, benches and expanses of grass for taking in views of Elliott Bay and the Olympic Mountains. The two totem poles were designed by Quinault tribe member Marvin Oliver and carved with the help of James Bender (1984). Originally developed as Market Park, it was renamed to honor its architect and leading Pike Place Market preservation activist Victor Steinbrueck after his death in 1985.

Hillclimb Corridor & Lower Market Buildings
To access the Lower Market sites, head south of Victor
Steinbrueck Park down Western Avenue.

28) PIKE PLACE MARKET HERITAGE CENTER
1999, Scot Carr and Thomas Schaer
1531 Western Avenue

Located above the
Market's food bank, this
950-square foot, steel-
frame structure was
designed to mimic the
Main Arcade's industrial
materials and multiple
entrances. Coiling doors open the building to the
public. Its irregular form fits the available site
and responds to the spatial order of the Market. The
Pike Place Market Heritage Center was designed
and constructed by Scot Carr and Thomas Schaer as
their University of Washington Master of Architecture thesis.

29) HERITAGE HOUSE AT THE MARKET
1990, Bumgardner Architects
1533 Western Avenue

This assisted living
facility includes 62 apartments on three floors
with ground floor com-
mon spaces. Its simple
form and materials
relate to the surround-
ing buildings along
Western Avenue. The de-
velopment included the
footbridge that connects
the parking garage below
to the Market Arcade.
Managed by the Sisters
of Providence, this facility addresses an important
aspect of the mission of the Market Foundation,
providing social services to the elderly in addition to
managing a food bank and low-income housing. The
parking garage below was designed by Seattle-based
engineers Skilling Ward Magnusson Barkshire and
constructed in 1989.

30) MADORE BUILDING
1916; Architect: unknown; rehabilitation, 1979,
Bumgardner Partnership
1505 Western Avenue

This three-story re-
inforced concrete
building served various
warehouse and light
manufacturing uses over
the years. In its 1979
conversion to office and
retail use, a storefront and extensive glazing replaced
the blank Western Avenue façade. The building was
jointly rehabilitated with the adjacent Fix Building,
forming the Fix-Madore complex.

31) HILLCLIMB CORRIDOR
1976, Calvin & Gorasht

Hillclimb Corridor was
built to replace the 1912
wooden overpass that
once connected the Mar-
ket to the piers and was
used by Market farmers
and customers arriving
by boat. The Hillclimb Corridor was completed as
part of the "Pc2" Pike Place Market rehabilitation and
is one of the earliest projects to re-establish downtown's link to the waterfront.

32) HILLCLIMB COURT
1982, Olson/Walker
1425 Western Avenue

This five-story devel-
opment integrates
condominium and office
space situated around a
landscaped courtyard.
The modern, modular
design of Hillclimb
Court distinguishes it from the surrounding buildings but its use of industrial materials and stepped
volumes compliments its neighbors and the adjacent
Hillclimb corridor. The completion of Hillclimb
Court brought some of the first new residential development to the Market area.

33) 84 UNION

(U.S. Immigration Building)
1915, Bebb & Gould; renovation, 1987, Hobbs Architecture Group
84 Union Street

This four-story wood-frame red brick masonry building features cream-colored terra-cotta ornamentation. The cornice is decorated with terra-cotta cartouches and diamond-shaped panels. A herringbone brick pattern marks the corners. 84 Union was constructed for the regional headquarters of the federal Immigration service and was a portal of entry for thousands of people. The building was used to house aliens who arrived without documentation or in poor health as well as serving as the location of the bureau offices until the Immigration service moved to a new building on Airport Way South in 1931. From the 1930s until 1946, this building was the location of the headquarters of the Cannery Workers and Farm Laborers Union. It was used as a hiring hall and social center for ILWU members until 1986. 84 Union housed a 125-bed youth hostel from 1987 until 2007; the building's owners, Harbor Properties, plan to convert the upper floors into apartments.

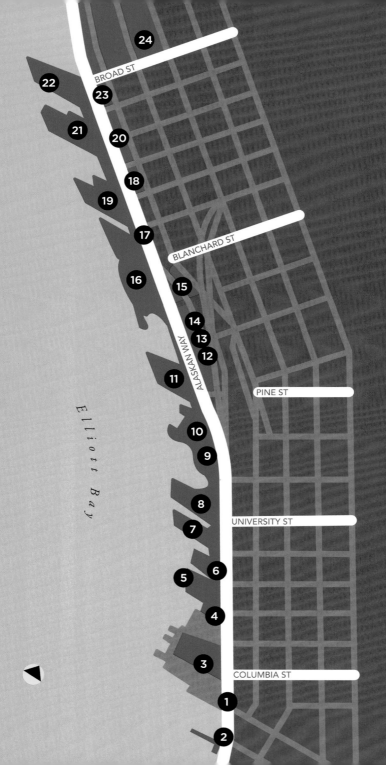

CHAPTER 7
WATERFRONT

Seattle's waterfront has shaped the city as much as Seattle's growth has shaped the waterfront's form. Like most major port cities, Seattle's shoreline is a made one, its physical features altered to accommodate the needs of expanding industry and population. The waterfront, as Seattle's gateway to the outside world, fostered the city's emergence as the "Queen City" of the Pacific Northwest. The network of railroad tracks, wharves and warehouses constructed along the shoreline was essential to the city's economic development.

When Arthur Denny, Carson Boren and William Bell set foot on the east side of Elliott Bay in 1852, they encountered a small area of flat land where Pioneer Square is located today. The natural shoreline ran approximately along what is now First Avenue South. A grassy marsh between today's Yesler Way and South King Street was separated from Elliott Bay by a narrow peninsula of about eight acres, which at high tide became an island known as "Denny Island." To the south, tideflats stretched from the base of Beacon Hill to the Duwamish River delta. Forested hillsides extended east and north of this vast wetland, and the shoreline took a turn in a northwest direction approximately along what is now First Avenue. The topography was less than ideal for building a city. But the deep protected waters and vast old-growth timber outweighed the area's physical challenges in the minds of the ambitious settlers.

As soon as Yesler's Wharf, Seattle's first wharf, was completed in 1853, exportation of lumber to California began. Regular steamboat service to Olympia also began in 1853; regular service between Seattle and other Puget Sound towns began in 1858 with the arrival of the sidewheel steamer, *Eliza Anderson*. The earliest filling of the marsh and tideflats also began at this time, as debris from Yesler's mill and cargo ship ballast were dumped around the wharf, mostly for the purpose of stabilizing the rickety structure. The plank-on-piling wharf was extended in an ad hoc manner over the next several years.

By 1877, Yesler had extended his wharf 900 feet from shore, giving it the capacity to accommodate up to six ships at one time. The wharf was occupied by several warehouses, coal bunkers, a grist mill, steamboat offices and a saloon, among other facilities. Yesler's Wharf was the center of passenger travel and cargo shipping, but it was not the only one in town. Smaller, subsequent wharves began to line the waterfront in a non-uniform, saw-tooth fashion. The Pike Street coal bunker was constructed in 1871 to accommodate the burgeoning coal exportation industry.

The construction of Seattle's first railroad, the Seattle & Walla Walla, in 1875, was an attempt to mitigate the blow to the city's growth when

Tacoma was selected as the terminus of Northern Pacific Railroad's transcontinental line. The intrastate line never made it anywhere near Walla Walla, however, but was instead diverted south to the coal mines in Renton. A 120-foot-wide railroad right-of-way was established from King Street north along the waterfront, and a curving trestle was constructed over the tideflats south of downtown. The generous right-of-way facilitated the construction of subsequent rail lines, which extended north to Smith Cove (now Pier 91) by 1885. In 1887, the Northern Pacific line across the Cascades was complete, and after 1889 allowed Seattle's port to compete equally with other West Coast cities.

Colman Dock was constructed at the foot of Madison Street in 1882 to accommodate the bustling flotilla known as the "mosquito fleet," the privately-owned steamers that transported cargo, mail and passengers to the towns that dotted the inland waters of Puget Sound and the San Juan Islands. Piers and trestles connected by planks nailed to pilings began filling the Central Waterfront. The spaces between the wharves and shoreline became landfills of ship ballast and debris. So much rock ballast was dumped at the foot of King Street that an island formed, aptly named "Ballast Island."

The Great Fire of 1889 claimed the early wharves between Union and King streets, which were immediately rebuilt in the same haphazard manner, jutting in various directions from the shoreline. A small fire station equipped with the fireboat *Snoqualmie* and a hose wagon was constructed at the foot of Madison Street in 1891.

In 1893, the Great Northern Railroad brought Seattle its second transcontinental link, which assured its ascendancy over other Pacific Northwest port cities.

Seattle's waterfront was the location of two pivotal events that would define the course of the city's future. On August 31, 1896, the *Miike Maru* from Japan was greeted with much fanfare at Schwabacher's Wharf (at the location that is now Waterfront Park), beginning trade between Seattle and Japan and establishing Seattle as a gateway to the Far East. Although the arrival of the Japanese ship brought Seattle international importance, the arrival of another ship one year later would spark an era of unprecedented population growth and economic prosperity that would firmly establish Seattle as the commercial center of the Pacific Northwest.

On July 17, 1897, the SS *Portland* arrived at Schwabacher's Wharf with the famed "ton of gold" from the Klondike in her hold. People from Europe and across the United States abandoned their lives and boarded ships and trains destined for Seattle, which was successfully marketed as the point-of-departure for the gold fields of Alaska.

By spring 1898, local merchants raked in $25 million by selling the year's-worth of supplies that each prospector was required to have before entering Canadian territory. The Moran Brothers, whose ship-building business was prospering on government contracts in the 1890s, turned their attention to the Gold Rush trade and made a fortune refitting old boats and constructing a Yukon River fleet of 14 steamers and four freight barges.

In the midst of this flurry of waterfront activity, the shoreline was being aggressively transformed. Reclaiming of the tideflats had begun in 1895 with landfill and regrading projects. Within ten years, the tide flats were filled, adding 300 acres south of downtown; and Harbor Island, at the mouth of the Duwamish River, then the world's largest man-made island, was complete by 1905.

By 1900, the wharves needed to be rebuilt again following an 1897 replat of the tidelands between Washington and Mercer streets. The city mandated a parallel pattern of piers extending east-west at a 45-degree angle from shore, resulting in the present, uniform pattern. The piers were assigned numbers north of Yesler Way and letters south of Yesler Way, rather than being named for the companies that constructed them. The new piers, some of which survive today, typically had a single large shed surrounded by an apron of open space for cargo handling. Rail lines often came onto the pier to expedite the transfer of goods, which longshoremen moved in individual crates on handcarts.

By this time, Railroad Avenue (now Alaskan Way) was

Prospectors depart for the gold fields of Alaska in this 1901 image.

Steamers being constructed at the Moran Brothers shipyard, 1898.

a chaotic and congested plank-on-trestle roadway with only three safe pedestrian overpasses at Bell, Pike and Marion streets. Cargo and passenger trains often had to wait for hours before departing the crowded waterfront. To alleviate this problem, the Great Northern and Union Pacific Railroads split the cost of building a tunnel beneath the city from Washington Street at the south, emerging near Virginia Street at the north; the tunnel was completed in 1905. Passengers could bypass the Railroad Avenue congestion through the tunnel with the completion of the beautiful new King Street Station (see Pioneer Square tour) in 1906.

Railroad Avenue, however, was still as busy as ever; and many of the pilings on which it was built were badly deteriorating because of teredos, a

Railroad Avenue when it was still a congested, plank-on-piling roadway.

wood-boring mollusk resembling a worm. Between 1911 and 1917, the city constructed a concrete seawall from Washington to Madison streets in order to provide some protection, and a sidewalk was built to provide safer access to the piers. This project established the present shoreline between South Washington and Madison streets. Railroad Avenue was gradually backfilled with earth from the Jackson Street regrade, creating more space for development.

In 1911, due to increasing resentment of shipping and railroad monopolies on the waterfront, the voters of King County established the Port of Seattle, with the power to own, build and operate harbor improvements and levy property taxes in the public interest. The new agency acquired the less developed land north of Pike Street and in 1914 constructed the Bell Street Wharf (now Pier 66), and to the north, a warehouse and port office building.

During World War I, maritime trade and steam ship traffic continued along the Central Waterfront, and the ship-building industry boomed to the south, near the Duwamish River. After the war, maritime activity declined; this trend continued through the Great Depression.

The Depression years did see major physical development of the Central Waterfront, however. In 1933, the City Engineering Department developed an innovative seawall design that involved the assembly of several components, including steel sheet piling, wooden piling, a relieving platform and three types of pre-cast concrete panels. A pre-cast concrete railing was mounted on top of the wall. Construction from Madison Street north to Broad Street was complete by 1936, and Railroad Avenue was at last a paved roadway on fill, and renamed Alaskan Way. The completion of the seawall project established the shoreline as it is today.

Seawall under construction showing braces behind the wall, 1934.

By the 1920s, passenger ferries were losing patronage until ferries that carried vehicles were introduced, although passenger-only ferries operated into the 1930s. Passenger-only ferries were discontinued by the beginning of World War II.

Most of the significant war-related activity, such as ship building and embarkation of troops, occurred north and south of the Central Waterfront. The pier identification system was changed by the Federal Government in 1944 because the previous system resulted in duplicate numbers when new piers were added, causing confusion. The current numbering system was established with numerical gaps where future piers might be constructed. Cargo handling on the Central Waterfront had been advanced by this time with the use of slings and gasoline-powered carts; after the war, pallets and fork-lifts sped up shipping.

By the late 1950s, shippers began consolidating cargo in larger shipping containers, which could be transferred directly from ships to trucks and trains via large gantry cranes. The containerization system was adopted in Seattle in 1960. Containerized shipping requires fewer workers, but much more land. Shipping activity was moved from the Central Waterfront to consolidated piers south of downtown. By the 1950s, air travel largely eliminated the need for coastal and ocean-going steamers. The old piers and transit sheds became obsolete and the Central Waterfront was thrust into an era of uncertainty and decline. The piers were primarily occupied by maritime industry businesses, such as the Fisheries Supply Co., the Fishing Vessel Owners Association, and warehouses for canneries. Washington State took control of the ferry system in 1951, consolidating auto-ferry activity to its present location at Pier 52.

Another major change to the Central Waterfront came with the 1953 opening of the Alaskan Way Viaduct. The double-decker Viaduct was constructed above the once-congested railroad tracks, which were infrequently used after World War II. Trucks and automobiles were replacing freight and passenger rail travel. The Viaduct facilitated auto and truck movement by providing a bypass around downtown congestion. It also whisked people past waterfront businesses, creating more uncertainty about the future of the waterfront.

Recreation and tourism became the primary use for the Central Waterfront in the 1960s, and the piers were gradually converted for retail and restaurant uses. Ivar Haglund's restaurant, which he had established on Pier 54 in 1938, was a harbinger of tourist-related waterfront businesses. Ferry service to Canada and Elliott Bay boat tours also launched from the central piers, as they do today.

The Shoreline Management Act of 1971, passed by the Washington State Legislature, called for planned, coordinated development to protect and preserve the shorelines of Washington State. The legislation focused on appropriate uses of both privately and publicly-owned shoreline to protect its ecology and provide better public access to publicly-owned areas, and to protect the shoreline for water-related uses. Along Seattle's waterfront, the Act was reflected in civic improvements in the 1970s, including the construction of Waterfront Park and the Seattle Aquarium.

Vintage waterfront streetcar service was added in 1982, running between Pier 70 and Pioneer Square. The service was later named the "George Benson Waterfront Streetcar" for the former City of Seattle and Metro Council member who worked to implement the line. The streetcar line was extended into the International District in 1990. The streetcars were temporarily replaced by buses in 2005 for the construction of the Olympic Sculpture Park, and the resumption of service has not been determined.

The 1990s brought major changes to the north end of the Central Waterfront with the demolition or redevelopment of piers 64-66 and 69 by the Port of Seattle. Their new headquarters and the Pier 66 complex were completed, and Port-owned land across Alaskan Way was developed in partnership with private developers. The completion of the Waterfront Landing condominiums in 1997 brought the first residential element to the Central Waterfront and stirred controversy about public versus private use of waterfront land.

Seattle's Central Waterfront, although firmly established as a tourist and recreational district, is once again in a state of uncertainty, with many factors potentially affecting its future. The Alaskan Way Viaduct and Seawall Replacement Project will have the most obvious physical impact. Options are also being considered for the replacement or redevelopment of Waterfront Park, the Seattle Aquarium and Piers 62-63.

Many decisions will be made by voters and the elected officials of the City of Seattle and Washington State. Now, as throughout Seattle's history, the waterfront will be shaped by the people and industries that thrive here, just as the waterfront shaped Seattle into the great city that it is today.

1) ALASKAN WAY VIADUCT
1953, Ralph W. Finke (City of Seattle), Ray M. Murray, George Stevens (Washington State Department of Highways)
First Avenue & Battery Street to South Dearborn Street

Looming 60 feet above former Railroad Avenue, the double-decker Alaskan Way Viaduct is a monument to the supremacy of the automobile in post-World War II America. The downtown bypass, which connects the suburbs to the north with the industrial district to the south, was planned in 1948. City Engineer R.W. Finke warned, "It won't be pretty" when he submitted his plans to City Council and clearly, he was right. The "motorist's dream," spanning 2.2 miles, required over 58,000 cubic feet of concrete, 7,460 tons of reinforcing steel, 472 tons of structural steel, and over 170,000 linear feet of piling. The viaduct opened in 1953, and the following year connected Aurora Avenue, which formerly terminated at Denny Way, to Highway 99 with the completion of the Battery Street tunnel. The viaduct was effective in its original conception as strictly a bypass; however, demand for ramps in and out of downtown quickly surfaced. An off-ramp was added at Seneca Street in 1961 and an on-ramp was added at Columbia Street in 1966.

2) WASHINGTON STREET PUBLIC BOAT LANDING 🕎
1920, Daniel Huntington
Washington Street & Alaskan Way

This boat landing, featuring a galvanized iron roof supported by 16 steel columns, established a new waterfront landmark upon its completion in 1920. The structure served a number of purposes over the years, including a landing for ferries, the U.S. Navy's official shore-leave landing and departure point, and as the headquarters of the Seattle Harbor Patrol. Boats tied up to a small finger pier at the water level, which was removed after suffering storm damage. Today, the Washington Street Public Boat Landing is the

The 2001 Nisqually quake damaged the viaduct, which has since shifted more than four inches. Experts estimated that had the 6.8-magnitude quake lasted just 15 seconds longer, the viaduct would have collapsed. The structure is built on fill dirt from regrade projects, which is held in place by a deteriorating concrete seawall completed in 1936. A strong earthquake threatens liquefaction—when solid fill-land turns to mud— and failure of the structure. Construction of a replacement for the **Alaskan Way Viaduct** *is likely to begin in 2010.*

A plaque at the **Washington Street Public Boat Landing** *memorializes the wreckage of the sidewheel steamer* Idaho, *which served as a hospital for the destitute on this site from 1900-1909.*

7 WATERFRONT

last remnant of the once vital link between Pioneer Square and the waterfront. The structure was designed by Daniel Huntington during his employment as city architect (1912-1921).

3) PIERS 50-53
(Colman Dock/WA State Ferries)
1966, Jones Lovegren Helms & Jones; Passenger deck remodel, 2004, LMN
801 Alaskan Way

Colman Dock's famous clock tower was found floating in the harbor the day after the 1912 accident. Its face and works are now on display on the upper passenger deck.

Colman Dock has a long history as the hub of Puget Sound ferry transportation. In 1882, Scottish Engineer James Colman built a dock to accommodate "mosquito fleet" steamship traffic, which was the primary mode of transporting goods, mail and people throughout the region. The dock was destroyed in the Great Fire of 1889 and quickly rebuilt. In 1908, the Colman Dock clock tower and waiting room were added. The dock was again destroyed in 1912, when struck by the S.S. *Alameda*. It was immediately rebuilt with an even grander clock tower and domed waiting room. Colman Dock was later acquired by the Puget Sound Navigational Co., which had consolidated control of the privately owned ferries in the 1920s. Under the name of the Black Ball Line, the company modernized the dock in 1936 in an Art Deco style to complement its signature ferry, *Kalakala*. In 1951, Washington State took over the ferry system and later built the present modern terminal. The terminal was expanded north into the space where the Grand Trunk Pacific Pier once stood to create more auto waiting areas. A 2004 passenger deck remodel involved demolition of the former office spaces to provide more food services and dining areas as well as new ticket booths and restrooms. Planning is now underway for expansion of the ferry dock.

The SS Idaho *serving as the Wayside Mission Hospital.*

4) FIRE STATION NO. 5
1963, Durham Anderson & Freed
925 Alaskan Way

The site of Fire Station No. 5 has been the moorage for Seattle's fireboats since 1891, when the first fireboat *Snoqualmie* was built in the wake of the Great Fire of 1889. The present modern station was built in 1963. The building features an exposed aggregate exterior with an exposed concrete frame, overhanging flat roof and a four-story hose tower. It is the third station to occupy the site since 1891. The station houses eight firefighters, one engine and two fireboats.

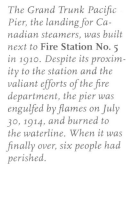

The Grand Trunk Pacific Pier, the landing for Canadian steamers, was built next to **Fire Station No. 5** *in 1910. Despite its proximity to the station and the valiant efforts of the fire department, the pier was engulfed by flames on July 30, 1914, and burned to the waterline. When it was finally over, six people had perished.*

Historic Wooden Piers (Piers 54-59)

Piers 54, 55 and 56 were built by the Northern Pacific Railroad in 1900 to accommodate cargo in transit during the heyday of Seattle's maritime commerce. Piers 57 and 59 were constructed by local merchants for the transfer and storage of goods. The wooden transit sheds were built on finger piers over timber pilings soaked in creosote to discourage damage by teredos, a wood-boring, worm-like mollusk that can make very quick work of untreated timbers. The sheds, which served as open warehouse spaces, feature various timber truss systems to transfer vertical loads to the side walls, eliminating the need for interior columns. Roof monitors atop the sheds create clerestory windows to bring natural light and ventilation into the large spaces. Cargo was transferred manually between the ships, sheds and the many trains that once crowded Railroad Avenue (now Alaskan Way). The finger piers became obsolete for shipping after World War II and shipping activity moved south of the Central Waterfront. Piers 54-59 recall the Central Waterfront's rich history and vital role in the commercial development of Seattle.

5) PIER 54
1900, built by the Northern Pacific Railroad; rehabilitation, 1985, Bumgardner Architects
1001 Alaskan Way

Pier 54 was originally known as Galbraith Dock, named for James Galbraith who rented the pier from the Northern Pacific Railroad for his Galbraith-Bacon hay, feed and building supply business. It soon after became the port-of-call for the Kitsap Transportation Company's "mosquito fleet," which was owned by Galbraith's son, Walter. In 1966, Pier 54 was purchased by Seattle folk singer and restaurateur Ivar Haglund, who had opened a small aquarium and fish-and-chip counter here in 1938. The aquarium was removed in 1946 to make room for his "Ivar's Acres of Clams" restaurant. A sculpture by Richard Beyer on Pier 54 immortalizes Haglund feeding the seagulls, a practice that he encouraged. Ivar's now shares Pier 54 with "Ye Olde Curiosity Shop," a novelty and souvenir store that first opened on the Colman Dock in 1899.

6) PIER 55
1900, built by the Northern Pacific Railroad; rehabilitation, 1985, Anderson Koch & Duarte
1101 Alaskan Way

Pier 55 was originally known as the Arlington Dock, named for the Arlington Dock Company, which served as ticketing agent for steamships serving West Coast cities from South America, Alaska and Europe. On September 14, 1901, less than one year after it was built, Pier 55 collapsed, taking 2000 tons of cargo down with it. Fortunately, no one was injured. Lack of adequate lateral support was to blame for the failure. Northern Pacific quickly rebuilt the present pier. Pier 54 was occupied by the Fisheries Supply Company from 1938 until the early 1980s. The pier was rehabilitated in 1985 and now houses restaurants and shops.

Seattle's Ivar feeds the gulls.

7) PIER 56
1900, built by Northern Pacific; rehabilitation, 2000,
Daly & Associates and Mithun
1201 Alaskan Way

 Pier 56 first housed
Frank Waterhouse & Co.,
which provided steam-
ship service to Alaska,
Hawaii, Russia and the
Mediterranean. The pier
was briefly the location of
an aquarium in the 1960s and later an import store.
Rehabilitation in 2000 involved the development of
an innovative system to pipe in power lines through
the seawall in order to provide enough energy to the
office space being created in the pier shed as well as
retrofitting the structure.

*A view of Pier 56 from the
water.*

8) BAY PAVILION (PIER 57)
1902, built by John P. Agen; rehabilitation, 1974, Bumgardner Partnership
1301 Alaskan Way

 Pier 57 was built by John
P. Agen, a major food
wholesaler, primarily for
shipping eggs and dairy
products to Alaska. The
dock was taken over by
the Chicago, Milwaukee
and St. Paul Railroad in 1909 and later served coastal
steamers. Pier 57 was redeveloped in 1974 as part of
Waterfront Park and is now known as the Bay Pavilion, housing an amusement arcade and a restaurant.

9) WATERFRONT PARK (PIER 58)
1974, Bumgardner Partnership
1401 Alaskan Way

 Waterfront Park was
built on the former site
of Schwabacher's Wharf,
where the August 31,
1896, landing of the
Miike Maru established
trade between Seattle
and Japan. One year later, on July 17, 1897, the SS
Portland arrived holding two tons of gold, sparking
the Klondike Gold Rush and an unprecedented boom
for Seattle. The area between Pier 57 and Pier 59
comprises a 4.8-acre public park. Curving railings

and a creosoted wooden deck surface dotted with benches and public art provide views from the West Seattle Bridge to the south and the Olympic Mountains to the north. The 1968 "Forward Thrust" bond issue provided the funds to construct Waterfront Park and the neighboring Seattle Aquarium, which was completed two years later. Waterfront Park and the Aquarium were the first effort to create civic spaces on the Central Waterfront. Waterfront Park will eventually be reconfigured with the expansion of the Aquarium.

10) SEATTLE AQUARIUM (PIER 59) 🏛
1896, built by Ainsworth & Dunn; rehabilitation, 1976, Bumgardner Partnership; Aquarium, 1976, Fred Bassetti & Co.; expansion, 2007, Miller/Hull Partnership and Mithun
1483 Alaskan Way

Pier 59 is the oldest extant pier on Seattle's waterfront, built for the Ainsworth & Dunn fish packing business, which also built Pier 70 at the north end of the waterfront. In 1903, the original one-story transit shed was replaced with the present two-story shed. The pier was occupied by the Pacific Marine Supply Company and a variety of businesses serving the maritime industry from around 1916 until the 1960s. The pier shed was renovated as part of the Waterfront Park and Seattle Aquarium development project in 1976 to house aquarium support facilities. The 1976 Aquarium design juxtaposes a steep, angular wooden roof with a spiraling concrete mass (which houses a salmon ladder) resulting in a dynamic waterfront structure that compliments the angles and curves of the adjoining Waterfront Park. The expansion of the Seattle Aquarium increased the facility by 30 percent, adding 18,000 square feet in the Pier 59 shed. The project required replacement of 760 rotting creosote-soaked pilings with 270 steel and concrete piles under Pier 59 and stabilization of the shed with new concrete aprons. The historic Pier 59 façade was removed and rebuilt in 2006 to allow for remodeling of the interior and creation of a new entrance as part of the Aquarium expansion project.

11) PIERS 62 & 63
North of the Seattle Aquarium

The former Gaffney and Virginia Street pier sheds were purchased by the city and demolished in 1989. The sheds had become dilapidated and Pier 62 was subsequently damaged by fire. The city cleared the space for public use. The pier aprons served as the site of the popular "Summer Nights at the Pier" concert series until 2004, when it became clear that rotting pilings had rendered the aprons structurally unsafe. At the time of this writing, several options are being considered for the possible replacement of the pilings and piers and redevelopment of the Waterfront Park complex.

12) WATERFRONT LANDING
1997, GGLO
1950 Alaskan Way

The Waterfront Landing Condominiums are the only residential development on Seattle's Central Waterfront. The three U-shaped, five-story wood-frame buildings were built in three phases and consist of 235 units. A single, continuous masonry unit (cmu) wall runs behind the complex to buffer sound from freight trains that emerge from the tunnel at Virginia Street twice an hour. The tunnel can be seen from the public parking lot behind Waterfront Landing.

13) LENORA STREET FOOTBRIDGE
1996, Hewitt Isley

The Lenora Street Footbridge incorporates the remains of the Lenora Street vehicle ramp, which was constructed in the 1930s as a freight route to the former Lenora Street Pier. The bridge connection and pier were demolished in the 1980s and the ramp that remained was called "the bridge to nowhere." The Port of Seattle had

The Great Northern and Union Pacific Railroad tunnel was built in 1905 to permit passenger trains to bypass the freight trains clogging Railroad Avenue (today's Alaskan Way). Trains enter the tunnel at Washington Street from King Street Station and travel under downtown, exiting at Virginia Street. Upon its completion, the tunnel became known as the "world's longest tunnel," since it runs all the way from Washington to Virginia. The tunnel is now used by the Burlington Northern-Santa Fe Railway and Amtrak.

the footbridge and elevator built onto the concrete ramp as part of their Central Waterfront Development Plan. The bridge and glass elevator offer views from West Seattle to the Olympics and an accessible connection between the waterfront, Pike Place Market and Belltown.

14) SEATTLE WATERFRONT MARRIOTT
2003, FMSM Design Group (Albuquerque, NM); Jensen/Fey Architecture
2100 Alaskan Way

The eight-story, 358-room Seattle Waterfront Marriott is one of only two hotels on Seattle's Central Waterfront. The reinforced concrete frame building is E-shaped, with all guestrooms facing toward Elliott Bay, providing views and buffering sound from the railroad tracks behind. A 250-foot concrete shear wall was cast along the rail corridor to provide an additional acoustic barrier. The development of this hotel sparked controversy over concerns about disrupting views from Victor Steinbrueck Park (see Pike Place Market tour) and about the nature of the development of the Central Waterfront. As a result, its height was limited to eight stories.

15) WORLD TRADE CENTER WEST & EAST
1998 & 1999, Zimmer Gunsul Frasca Partnership
2200 Alaskan Way

World Trade Center (WTC) West and East were the first two completed phases of the WTC complex; WTC North was the final phase. The glazed office complex presents simple forms and repetitive bays similar to the warehouses that once lined the Central Waterfront. WTC West, developed by the Port of Seattle and Wright Runstad & Co., is reserved primarily for international agencies. The four-story building is divided from WTC East by the railroad tracks. WTC East rises to six stories from behind, elevated on a five-story concrete parking garage. WTC East, developed by Wright Runstad & Co. alone, is currently occupied by Microsoft and was their first office location west of Lake Washington.

16) BELL STREET PIER (PIER 66)
1996, Hewitt Isley

Pier 66, known as the Bell Street Pier, was central to the Port of Seattle's Waterfront Development Plan. Built on 1,600 concrete and steel pilings, the pier consists of the Bell Harbor International Conference Center, the Odyssey Maritime Discovery Center, a trio of Anthony's restaurants, a small grocery and deli, and the Bell Harbor Marina (a short-stay public marina with 33 slips). The pier also operates a cruise ship terminal with 1,900 linear feet of moorage. The complex was designed to give the various components a distinct yet harmonious presence through the use of broken massing, blocks of color and various materials. The colors are said to have been inspired by shipping containers. A staircase at the ground-level plaza connects to the conference center, footbridge and public roof plaza, which offers views of the city, sound and mountains from elevated benches.

17) BELL STREET FOOTBRIDGE
1996, Hewitt Isley

This two-level footbridge was constructed as part of the Port of Seattle's Central Waterfront Development Plan to connect the Art Institute of Seattle and its parking garage on the east end to the Bell Street Pier on the west. The bridge is the most visible part of the Bell Street project from Alaskan Way and makes a bold statement with its exaggerated structure featuring oversized bolts, plates and connections.

A cruise ship docks at Bell Street Pier.

7 WATERFRONT

18) SKYWAY LUGGAGE BUILDING
(Booth Fisheries/US Radiator Corporation)
1910 & 1911, unknown
2501 Elliot Avenue/10 Wall Street

The Skyway Luggage Building is the last remaining intact industrial complex of many that once stood on the Central Waterfront. The brick masonry building was constructed in 1910, shortly after the Belltown fire destroyed much of the area. The building was purchased by the Kotkins family, Skyway Luggage owners, in 1943. Skyway expanded into the Booth Fisheries building to the north, built in 1911, in the 1960s and remained there into the 1990s. The Booth Fisheries building is the last fish processing building in the area.

19) THE EDGEWATER (PIER 67)
1963, John Graham & Co.; remodel, 1969, James Barrington (Arcadia, CA); remodel, 1990, The Callison Partnership
2411 Alaskan Way

Built on the site of the former Galbraith-Bacon Dock and the Booth Fisheries Pier, this four-story, 234-room hotel is Seattle's only over-water hotel, built before shoreline regulations prohibited such developments. Plans for the building were drawn up in January 1962, in hopes of having it ready for the World's Fair of the same year, but the hotel was not completed until 1963. Originally designed in a distinctly 1960s modern style, the exterior was significantly remodeled in 1969 and again in 1990 and now features a rustic Northwest motif. The hotel famously hosted the Beatles in 1964 but has also housed the Rolling Stones, Frank Zappa and Bill Clinton. The Edgewater originally advertised on the building's north elevation that guests could fish from their room and even offered fishing poles for their use.

20) SEATTLE INTERNATIONAL TRADE CENTER / REAL NETWORKS
(American Can Company)
1917, O. B. Pries (engineer); renovation, 1977, Ralph Anderson & Partners; renovation 1999, Zimmer Gunsul Frasca Partnership
2601 Elliot Avenue/2600 Alaskan Way

This five-story building originally housed the American Can Company, which supplied the local canning industry. It was linked by skybridge to Pier 69, the former site of their warehouse. The structure is a reinforced concrete frame with bays separated by brick infill. The building was renovated in 1977 for the Seattle International Trade Center and again in 1999, when extensive upgrades were made to the building to accommodate the needs of the Real Networks software company.

21) PORT OF SEATTLE HEADQUARTERS (PIER 69)
1931, built by the American Can Company; renovation, 1993, Hewitt Isley
2711 Alaskan Way

The Pier 69 renovation was the first project completed in the Port of Seattle's Central Waterfront Development Plan. The pier itself, built in 1931, was originally home to the American Can Company, and at the time of its construction, was the only cast-in-place concrete pier on the waterfront. The three-story concrete warehouse was vacated by the Can Company in the 1970s and sat largely empty while a series of development projects were proposed but not completed. The Port of Seattle purchased the pier in 1989 and began converting the old warehouse in 1991. The three-story, 180,000 square-foot building's alternating bands of green glazing and white cladding intermittently punctuated with small punch-card rectangular windows, have a distinctly nautical character and suggest the look of the many cruise ships that dock nearby. The pier is also the terminus for the high-speed Victoria Clipper catamarans.

22) PIER 70
1902, built by Ainsworth & Dunn; renovation, 1972, Barnett Schorr & Co.; renovation, 2000, Fuller-Sears
2801 Alaskan Way

Pier 70 was constructed in 1902 by Ainsworth & Dunn to transfer and store products for their fish packing company. Fish packing on the Elliott Bay waterfront had largely ended by the 1970s and in 1972, the Pier 70 shed was the first of the piers to be renovated for use as a shopping mall with stores and restaurants. The 2000 renovation of the pier involved replacement of all windows, the addition of metal cladding and expansion of the structure. The pier is now occupied by a law firm in the upper stories and restaurants below.

23) OLD SPAGHETTI FACTORY
(Ainsworth & Dunn warehouse)
1902, Saunders & Lawton; renovation, 1970, Sally Dussin (OSF co-founder and interiors supervisor).
2801 Elliot Avenue

This two-story brick masonry warehouse was built by Ainsworth & Dunn, a major fish trading and packing company, across Railroad Avenue (now Alaskan Way) from their pier for additional storage. The original exterior is largely intact and retains its arched windows and original arched freight doors along Alaskan Way. Three arched basement windows on the Broad Street elevation have been filled in, possibly during the first Denny Regrade. The building's post-and-beam structure remains exposed on the interior, although partitions were added when the Old Spaghetti Factory opened here in 1970. The restaurant also added the arched entrance on the south elevation, which was formerly blank and abutted another warehouse that stood where the parking lot is today.

24) SEATTLE ART MUSEUM OLYMPIC SCULPTURE PARK
2006, Weiss/Manfredi (New York); Landscape Architect: Charles Anderson
Broad Street & Western Avenue

This 8.5-acre park was developed by the Seattle Art Museum as a free and public outdoor space for enjoying the natural environment while experiencing a variety of modern and contemporary sculpture. Built on the last undeveloped land parcels of Seattle's Central Waterfront, the park occupies land once contaminated by years of petroleum seepage. Union Oil of California (UNOCAL) operated a storage and transfer facility here from 1910, which by 1950 had expanded to a 6-acre fuel storage complex on both sides of Elliott Avenue. UNOCAL vacated the site by the 1970s but left behind 60 years worth of soil and ground water contamination, as well as their facility, which was torn down in the 1980s. Construction of the Olympic Sculpture Park involved cleanup of the contaminated soil, which had begun in the 1990s, restoration of the bluff, and restoration of a natural beach and shoreline habitat. Three tiers of land, between Western Avenue and Elliott Bay, are linked by a 2,200-foot-long path. The Z-shaped path begins at the angular steel-and-glass pavilion at the Broad Street main entrance and traverses the park three times, terminating at the restored beach located at the edge of the adjacent Myrtle Edwards Park. The design uses walls and vegetation to control views and enhance the sense of expansiveness of this urban open space. The park is divided into four garden zones, called the "Valley," the "Grove," the "Meadow" and the "Shore." The landscape of the Shore garden was designed to aid in restoration of salmon habitat in Elliott Bay. The park includes many significant works by modern sculptors; among the best known are Richard Serra, Alexander Calder, Claes Oldenburg & Coosje van Bruggen, Louise Nevelson and Tony Smith.

*The waterfront streetcar, which served the area since 1982, was housed in a terminal at what is now the western edge of the **Olympic Sculpture Park**. Plans to relocate the terminal to Pioneer Square have met with stumbling blocks, and the future of the waterfront streetcar remains uncertain at the time of this writing. Bus service was initiated along the streetcar route in 2005, when the waterfront terminal was removed.*

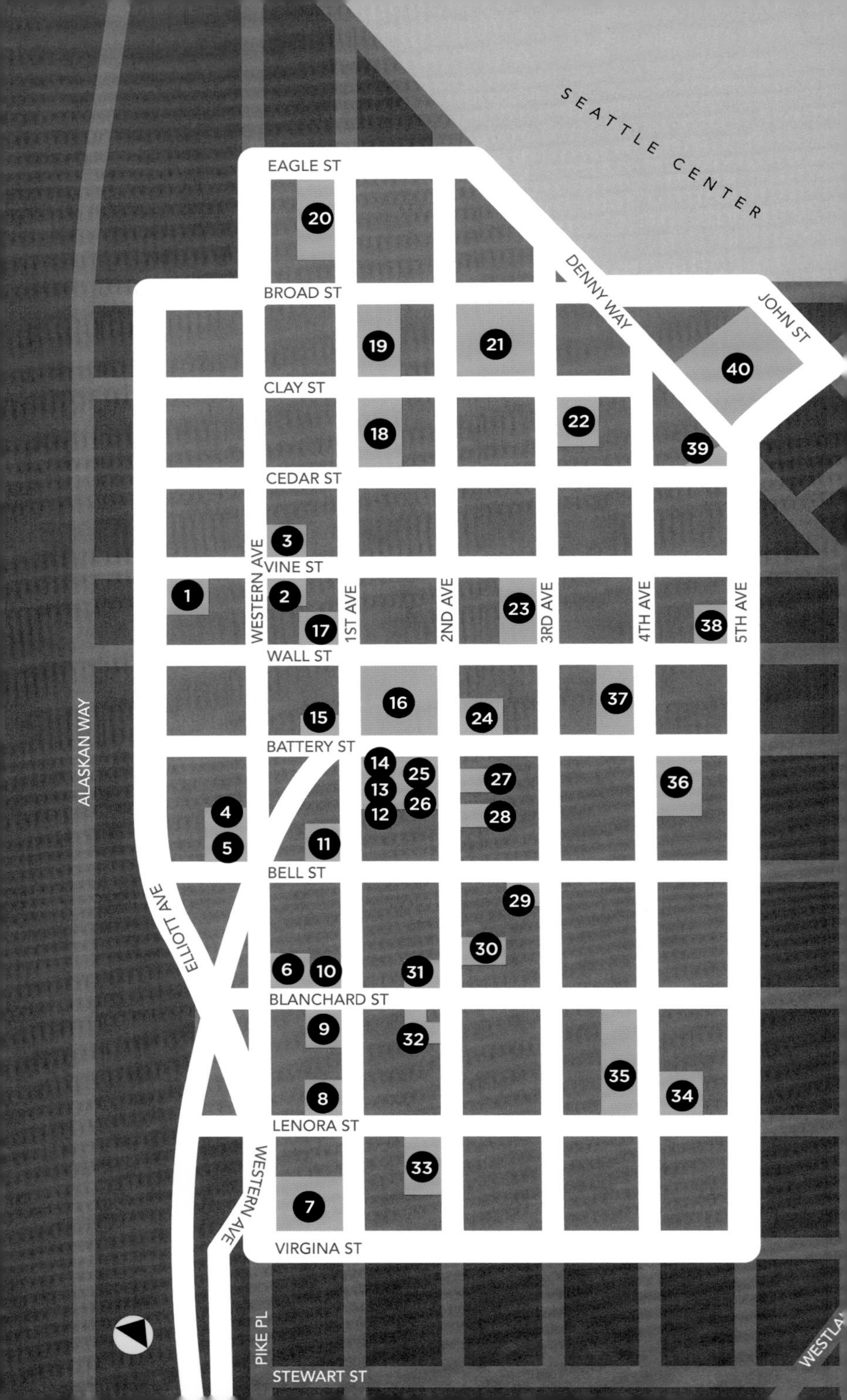
SEATTLE CENTER
EAGLE ST
BROAD ST
CLAY ST
CEDAR ST
VINE ST
WALL ST
BATTERY ST
BELL ST
BLANCHARD ST
LENORA ST
VIRGINA ST
STEWART ST
DENNY WAY
JOHN ST
WESTERN AVE
1ST AVE
2ND AVE
3RD AVE
4TH AVE
5TH AVE
ALASKAN WAY
ELLIOTT AVE
WESTERN AVE
PIKE PL
1
2
3
4
5
6
7
8
9
10
11
12
13
14
15
16
17
18
19
20
21
22
23
24
25
26
27
28
29
30
31
32
33
34
35
36
37
38
39
40

CHAPTER 8
BELLTOWN

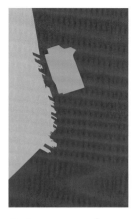

Belltown is one of downtown Seattle's most eclectic neighborhoods. Luxury condominium towers, workingmen's hotels, funky shops, galleries, artists' studios, cafés and nightclubs can all be found within steps of one another. The architecture of Belltown is diverse as well, as the area was developed relatively slowly over the past 100 years. Belltown contains Victorian commercial buildings, turn-of-the-century wood-frame structures, small Art Deco offices, modern high-rises and just about everything in between. The pace of development in Belltown has stepped up considerably in recent decades, however, and the generally low-rise scale and open feeling of the neighborhood is gradually changing. The profile of the towering hill that once stood where Belltown is today may one day be replaced by a horizon of skyscrapers.

Belltown is situated on land claimed by William Bell, who arrived with the first settlers at Alki Point in 1851. Bell left Seattle in 1855 and had little to do with the development of his namesake neighborhood, even after his return to the city in 1870. From the 1850s to the turn of the 20th century, the Belltown neighborhood developed as an isolated community west of Second Avenue, pinched between Elliot Bay and Denny Hill, which had grades so steep that horse-drawn vehicles could not travel them. The only overland access to downtown was along Front Street (now First Avenue); coach service between Belltown and Pioneer Square (the downtown of the 19th century) ran on two-hour intervals.

The neighborhood now commonly known as Belltown incorporates a portion of the Denny Regrade to the east. As the Klondike Gold Rush boom pushed the central business district northward, City Engineer R.H. Thompson saw Denny Hill as an obstacle to the northward expansion of downtown Seattle. He initiated a massive regrading project to level the impeding mound by sluicing it into the bay, employing a hydraulic mining technique he had seen in California. Between 1898 and 1911, the first phase of the Denny Regrade was completed, and 27 blocks from Second to Fifth avenues between Pine and Cedar streets were lowered. The project displaced 6 million cubic yards of earth, making it the largest operation of its type in the world upon completion.

On June 10, 1910 a fire started on the west side of Railroad Avenue (now Alaskan Way) and was blown into Belltown by 40-mile-per-hour winds. The fire destroyed the entire block bordered by Railroad and Elliot avenues and Battery and Wall streets, as well as several buildings north of Wall on Western Avenue, including warehouses, livery stables and other structures. Over a dozen homes and four apartment buildings were lost in the fire.

The opulent Denny Hotel/Washington Hotel, which was perched atop Denny Hill from 1890-1906, was a casualty of the regrade.

The regrading of the hill cleared the way for a grid of flat streets, wide avenues, apartment development and the northern expansion of downtown. The first project proposed for the area was submitted by City Engineer Virgil Bogue. The 1911 Bogue Plan included the development of an architecturally-unified civic center and rail terminal around Fourth Avenue and Blanchard Street, relocating city government to the Regrade area. Land owners in the business district to the south feared financial losses and initiated a bitter campaign to fight the plan. The intense battle and the price tag attached to Bogue's plan, which included a rapid transit tunnel from downtown to Kirkland and the acquisition of Mercer Island for a public park, ultimately led voters to reject it by a wide margin in 1912.

Thompson's vision of the expansion of downtown into the Regrade did not materialize. Buildings such as the Alaska Building, Hoge Building and Smith Tower (see Pioneer Square tour) were concentrating the business district and increasing land value around Second Avenue and Cherry Street. But the Regrade's inexpensive land gradually attracted ancillary businesses such as printing, auto repair, parking, social services, artists and craftspeople—support services that needed to be near downtown but couldn't pay the high rent. Movie studios built film distribution and storage facilities as well as screening rooms, where theater owners from throughout the Pacific Northwest could preview the latest productions.

The Depression halted growth in all of downtown. The land on the still-existing east slope of Denny Hill was worth virtually nothing. The second phase of the Denny Regrade, which leveled 40 blocks east of Fifth Avenue, took place between 1929 and 1930. During World War II, labor unions began constructing offices and meeting halls in the area, as it was close to where many of their members lived and worked.

After World War II, the pattern of vertical expansion continued in a broadening central business district south of Belltown. The lots in the second phase of the Regrade eventually filled with warehouses, auto dealerships and parking lots.

Over the years, much of the Denny Regrade and old Belltown area became run-down or even seedy, making it unattractive for development. The tragic Ozark Hotel fire in 1970 resulted in the loss of many of Belltown's historic single-room-occupancy (workingmen's) hotels because the owners could not afford the upgrades required by the new fire codes.

In 1974, the city passed new land-use zoning for high-rise residential and office development, with requirements for open spaces and landscaped circulation linkages. Developers in Belltown and the Regrade did little, however, other than a series of office buildings constructed by Martin Selig in the late 1970s and a small amount of condominium development in the 1980s. The area's low rents attracted young musicians, artists and restaurateurs and an enclave of art galleries, studios, eateries and nightclubs began to develop, giving the area a hip, bohemian quality.

It was not until the technology boom of the 1990s that Belltown really began to be impacted by the rezoning. A change in the city zoning code in 1990 allowed for the construction of wooden buildings up to six stories if built above a concrete garage. This allowed for higher-density and lower-cost buildings to be erected, making the area more attractive for development. The increase in building activity quickly raised land value in the Belltown neighborhood enough to make steel and concrete construction economically feasible. While these changes were taking place, street improvement projects on First and Second avenues, begun in 1986, and the city-wide Street Tree Master Plan, executed by Seattle landscape architects Worthy & Associates in 1995, improved the pedestrian quality of Belltown.

Many pre-World War II apartment buildings and workingmen's hotels have been acquired by social service agencies and renovated as low income housing. This, along with adaptive re-use projects such as 81 Vine and the Belltown Lofts, has helped preserve remnants of the character of old Belltown. Infill projects that are sensitive to the scale and industrial character of the neighborhood, such as the Banner Building and Belltown Senior Apartments, are bringing high-quality new construction to the area. But as Seattle's population grows and with numerous condominium towers slated to be constructed, demand for land in Belltown will continue to impact its scale and open feel and may threaten to force out its artistic element.

Ironically, the slow growth that disappointed and frustrated the city following the regrades eventually facilitated the development of an area with a unique character that Seattle has come to value. In 1999, the city adopted the Belltown Urban Center Village neighborhood plan. The plan includes "green street" and open space connection strategies, which were initiated in 1995 with the Growing Vine Street Project; and strategies to sustain Belltown's character, including land use code changes and the adoption of Belltown design guidelines. However, with a dense downtown that is hemmed in by water and Interstate 5, striking a balance among density, neighborhood character and diverse affordable housing options is a constant struggle.

1) BELLTOWN P-PATCH & BELLTOWN COTTAGE PARK
1995 & 2004, Friends of Belltown P-Patch, Seattle Parks & Recreation Department, Gaynor Inc. (landscape architect)
2512-2516 Elliot Avenue

These wood-frame cottages are the only three that remain of 11 that were constructed on this site between 1906 and 1916, and are the last single-family homes left in downtown Seattle. This type of housing characterized much of the waterfront and Belltown area up into the 1960s. The developer of these cottages, William Hainsworth, encouraged living close-in; they were advertised in 1916 as "modern cottages," that could "save time and car fare," similar to the appeal of the condominiums being developed in the area today. The buildings were purchased by the city in 1998 and restored by the Friends of Belltown P-Patch; the work on the cottages was completed in 2004. Two of the cottages provide housing for writers-in-residence; the third cottage is used as a community center. The P-patch site, formerly an empty lot, was purchased by the city in 1993 and opened in 1995. It provides 42 gardening patches for use by neighborhood residents. Thousands of hours of community volunteer service went in to creating this historic and open urban green space in an area that once invited crime and vandalism.

2) 81 VINE
1914, Ira S. Harding; renovation and addition, 1995 & 1999, Geise Architects
81 Vine Street

81 Vine Street represents not only adaptive reuse of an early twentieth century factory building, but the potential of grass-roots vision to create a more livable and sustainable urban environment. Architect Carolyn Geise, with a family partnership, purchased and developed the three-story 1914 brick-and-timber building, which was long home to Frayn Printing and Publishing, for renovation into residential lofts and ground-floor

commercial space. The converted units in the main building were completed in 1995. Planned as a two-phase project, a two-story penthouse addition was completed in 1999. The metal-clad penthouse is marked by two barrel vaults, which echo the arched brickwork over the bays on the factory building façades. The penthouse steps back twice from the northern elevation of the old building, creating a wide terrace, balconies and walkways while preserving views down Vine Street. Knowing that Vine Street was designated a "green street" by the city, a concept which had not been clearly defined or initiated, Geise led a community group that founded "Growing Vine Street" to make the green street a reality. The roof of 81 Vine is at the heart of the project, equipped with water-collecting planters and "bow-truss" downspouts that deliver water to the cisterns on Vine Street and eventually will flow down the Cistern Steps.

3) BANNER BUILDING
1994, Weinstein Copeland Architects
2600 Western Avenue

The Banner Building is a mixed-use, concrete post-and-slab structure made up of three components: a commercial and parking base, which includes large studio spaces; fourteen two-story studio lofts, located in the taller building; and six moderate-income studio units in the low-rise part of the complex. The components are linked by an internal community courtyard, terrace and garden space. Developed by Seattle artist and industrial designer Koryn Rolstad, the Banner Building was conceived of as residence for a community of artists and designers who would personalize their own spaces. Each unit was sold as a shell so the owners could tailor them to their own needs and personal style. The modern design of the building utilizes industrial materials such as corrugated metal and concrete, in keeping with the history of the neighborhood. Large walls of glass and angled balconies take advantage of views to Elliott Bay and downtown.

The Vertical Landscape *downspouts on the north façade of the* 81 Vine *building and the large, blue, corrugated aluminum Beckoning Cistern at the northeast corner, were both created by Seattle artist Buster Simpson for the Growing Vine Street project. The cistern's green fingers reach out to collect water runoff from the 81 Vine building. The staggered plantings in the green strip, designed by Geise Architects and Gaynor Inc., serve as bio-filters and provide a barrier between the street and sidewalk, facilitating a cleaner and more pedestrian-oriented environment.*

4) COMPTON BUILDING
(Modelow Company)
1908, unknown
2315 Western Avenue

This 28,800 square-foot, three-story light industry building is one of the oldest wood-clad post-and-beam buildings in downtown Seattle and virtually the only intact remainder of the lumber and woodworking industry that once flourished on the Belltown waterfront. The building was purchased by the Compton Lumber Company, which was founded in Seattle in 1892, in 1950 when construction of the Alaskan Way Viaduct (see Waterfront tour) forced them to relocate. It was Compton's home for the next 36 years. The building is now leased as work and warehouse space.

5) BELLTOWN LOFTS ⊓
(Seattle Empire Laundry)
1914, Ira S. Harding; renovation and addition, 2000, Driscoll Architects and U-Arch Studio
66 Bell Street

This three-story brick masonry building was constructed in 1914 as a commercial laundry, which operated here until 1950. It had many owners and uses over the next 50 years, including use as artists' residence and studio space. The building was renovated to house residential lofts with ground-floor retail and office space on the Western Avenue side in 2000. The project, which is centered on a courtyard, included the addition of a new building to the north containing 33 units. The old building, which includes 25 units, was given light wells to decrease the need for artificial lighting, and rooftop decks for use by residents. Forty percent of the units were reserved for affordable housing.

6) IT'S GOTTA GO
(Union Livery Stable)
1908, unknown
2200 Western Avenue

This four-story brick masonry building was constructed just after the establishment of Pike Place Market and provided stables for the many of the farmers who carted in their goods daily. The building features large arched windows on the upper floors and a gabled parapet on the Western Avenue façade with a handsome terra-cotta medallion of a horse's head. The Union Livery Stable was one of several that once operated in Belltown, but this stable had the distinction of being considered the largest west of the Mississippi when it was built. The building was converted to a garage by the 1930s and now houses a furniture store and warehouse.

7) MARKET PLACE NORTH CONDOMINIUMS
1982, Bumgardner Architects
2001 First Avenue

The distinctive sloping roof of this mixed-use, 154-unit, reinforced concrete condominium building responds to the increasing height limits allowed outside of the Pike Place Market Historic District. The ground-level townhouses along the building's western elevation open up to meandering courtyards, providing outdoor privacy to residents while maintaining an open connection to the activity of the Market. Ground level retail and office space front First Avenue. Developed by Lorig Associates, Market Place North was an early large-scale downtown residential development that helped establish an economically diverse residential population in the Market vicinity and Belltown, and was a forerunner to the many mixed-use residential buildings found in Belltown today.

First Avenue is enlivened by the **First Avenue Linear Park and Urban Arboretum.** *This 1986-1991 Seattle Arts Commission project, meant to distinguish the Belltown portion of First Avenue, was carried out by artists Buster Simpson, Jack Mackie and Paul and Deborah Rinehart. Various elements such as boulders, benches made from sandstone construction remnants, tree supports made from found objects and pavement poems are scattered along the sidewalk. An assortment of trees was planted along the street, including plum trees. The project runs along First Avenue between Virginia Street and Denny Way.*

8) GUIRY HOTEL
1903, attributed to Elliott & West; Schillestad Building, 1907, Andrew McBean; renovation, 1987, Kovalenko Architects
2101-2111 First Avenue

The three-story Guiry Hotel features an arcade of full-height round arches and a corbelled cornice. The Guiry and its neighbor to the south, the three-story Schilles-tad Building, are among the few turn-of-the-century masonry buildings that remain on First Avenue. These former workingmen's hotels with ground-floor storefronts offer a sense of the historic scale and social fabric of the Belltown neighborhood. The Guiry Hotel was jointly renovated into apartments with the Schillestad Building in 1987; the historic buildings now provide low- to middle-income housing.

9) CONTINENTAL PLACE
1981, WJA Design Collaborative
2125 First Avenue

The 34-story Continental Place condominium building features protruding floor-to-ceiling windows and recessions created by deep and shallow balconies, resulting in patterned façades in daylight. The slender concrete framework gives the weighty structure a sense of transparency after dark. The condominium tower steps back from the five-story parking garage at the north side of the building, providing a garden terrace. The parking garage is encased in red brick veneer wall segments with a pattern of rectangular openings, relating it in scale and materials to the historic buildings to the north. Continental Place was an early predecessor of the high-rise condominium towers that are being developed in Belltown and throughout Seattle today.

Continental Place *will hold the distinction of being the tallest residential tower in the Pacific Northwest until the 2008 completion of 1521 Second Avenue. The 38-story building, designed by Weber + Thompson, was the first residential development to take advantage of the 2006 lifting of downtown height restrictions that were imposed by CAP in 1989.*

10) LEWISTON HOTEL
1900, George C. Dietrich (engineer & contractor);
renovation, 2001, Stickney Murphy Romine Architects
2201 First Avenue

This three-story hotel building features a galvanized iron cornice and pebble dash banding with medallions above the top floor windows. An intermediate galvanized iron cornice runs above the glazed storefronts, which are framed in cast iron piers. The Lewiston is among a small group of circa 1900 masonry buildings that remain on First Avenue. This former workingmen's hotel has been managed since 1982 by the Plymouth Housing Group, which purchased it in 1999 and completed renovations in 2001. The Lewiston Hotel provides 48 units of low-income housing and ground-floor retail space.

11) OREGON APARTMENTS
(Oregon Hotel)
1902, Josenhans & Allen; renovation and addition,
1990, John Graham Associates/DLR Group
2305 First Avenue

The three-story Oregon Hotel is among the oldest extant masonry buildings along First Avenue. Built in 1902, the Oregon Hotel reflects the early character of the First Avenue area, which was dominated by workingmen's hotels with storefront businesses. The hotel continued to serve as low-income housing for years but had fallen into disrepair by the 1980s. The Housing Resource Group renovated the building and built the northern addition in 1990 to create the Oregon Apartments, which includes 83 affordable units and 3,628 square feet of retail space.

8 BELLTOWN

12) BARNES BUILDING/BELLTOWN PUB 🍺 🍺
(I.O.O.F Building)
1889, Boone & Meeker
2320 First Avenue

This four-story commercial building displays Victorian design convention with its flat pilasters and various window styles, but is much more restrained in detail than its neighbor, built the following year. Its designer, William Boone, was virtually the only well-established pre-fire architect who continued to practice after the Great Fire of 1889; the Barnes Building is the only one of his pre-fire structures extant today. Construction began in 1888 for the Odd Fellows, but financial problems arose and they sold their interest in the building to Masonic Lodge No. 7. It served as Seattle's first and only Masonic Lodge until 1916 when they constructed a new building on Capitol Hill.

13) AUSTIN A. BELL BUILDING 🍺 🍺
1890, Elmer Fisher (façade only); reconstruction, 1997, Snell Partnership
2324 First Avenue

One of Belltown's most prominent landmarks, this four-story Victorian commercial building was designed by Seattle's most prolific post-fire architect, Elmer Fisher. Like much of Fisher's work, its layered and highly detailed brick façade features elements of Italianate and Gothic Revival design. Its original cornice, which intensified the building's verticality, has been removed. The building was constructed as a memorial to Austin A. Bell, son of the original settler of Belltown, William Bell. Austin's widow carried out his plans to construct the building and had his name and year of death integrated into the design. The building sat largely vacant since 1939 and was damaged by fire in 1981. In 1997, work was completed to reconstruct the building as condominiums. Only the historic façade was saved; the structure behind is entirely new.

14) CATHOLIC SEAMEN'S CLUB
(Paramount Studios)
1937, J. Lister Holmes
2330 First Avenue

The Catholic Seamen's Club was originally built as the northwest regional distribution office for Paramount Pictures, one of approximately twenty film-related buildings in Belltown. Paramount operated out of the Streamline Moderne building until 1951 when it was purchased by the city for the construction of the Battery Street tunnel, which cuts into the basement of the building. Since 1956, the building has housed a clubhouse and small chapel for seamen, and several small businesses.

15) HULL BUILDING ⫟
1889, Elmer Fisher
2401 First Avenue

This three-story, brick masonry Victorian commercial building is one of the oldest in the area, having been constructed in 1889 by Alonzo Hull to house his furniture and upholstery business in hopes that the central business district would expand north into Belltown. The expansion did not occur and Hull had sold the building by 1906. The New Hudson Hotel opened on the upper floors with ground-floor retail below. Its brick façade features narrow, deeply recessed windows and a prominent metal cornice. The Hull Building's ground-floor retail windows are framed with cast-iron columns.

16) BELLTOWN COURT
1992, Hewitt Isley
2414 First Avenue

This full-block building includes ground-floor retail space and 245 residential units centered on a landscaped courtyard. Various façade treatments and the use of brick and bay windows help integrate the large complex with the smaller, historic buildings in the surrounding neighborhood. This complex was among the first to take advantage of a new zoning code that permitted wooden buildings in the downtown area to be up to six stories if built upon a concrete garage, making development more affordable. Belltown Court was built as an apartment building, but its units were sold as condominiums beginning in 1996.

17) EL GAUCHO
(Sailors' Union of the Pacific)
1954, Fred Rogers
2505 First Avenue

This two-story, mid-century building is clad in green terra-cotta tiles, a material which was applied to many early twentieth-century Seattle buildings but was less commonly used after World War II. The building served as headquarters and a hiring hall for the seamen's union and contained 22 hotel rooms and a basement gym for use by merchant marines. Today, the building houses an upscale restaurant with an 18-room Inn on the upper floor. The basement contains a bar and live-jazz venue. The building's current use reflects the changing nature of Belltown from a workingmen's neighborhood with ancillary city services to a trendy residential and night-life hub.

18) CITY CHURCH
(IBEW Union Hall)
1949, Harmon & Detrich; renovation, 2005, Snell Partnership
2700 First Avenue

This two-story, half-block building was constructed as the International Brotherhood of Electrical Workers Local 46 Union Hall, one of several union offices established in the Belltown area. The brick-and-concrete Moderne building combines horizontal lines with a formal, classical composition. A central, glazed entrance pavilion is flanked by two buff-brick wings with light-colored banding running above and below aluminum-frame strip windows. The building is now a satellite campus for the City Church, which uses the building's 500-seat assembly hall to project live services from their Kirkland campus onto three large screens.

19) SEATTLE LABOR TEMPLE
1942, McClelland & Jones; addition, 1955, Harmon Pray Detrich
2800 First Avenue

This half-block building is a fine example of 1940s Modernist design with its clean lines and relative lack of ornamentation. Originally built as a two-story structure in 1942, a third story, compatible with the original building, was added in 1955. Its buff-brick exterior features blue terra-cotta tile trim and tall metal sash windows. The main entrance is trimmed with red granite. A two-story auditorium adjoins the north end. The Seattle Labor Temple was built when the wartime workforce was booming and several unions were establishing offices in the area because of its proximity to waterfront industrial areas. Since its construction, this building has been the hub of union activities.

20) CONCORD CONDOMINIUMS
1999, Driscoll Architects
2929 First Avenue

The Concord Condominiums includes 230 residential units in two 13-story towers connected by a five-story base. Ground-floor retail lines the street frontage. The design features a clearly legible concrete frame and floor-to-ceiling glazing to capture natural light. The absence of corner columns allows the glazing to turn the corner, creating a greater sense of transparency and allowing for unobstructed views. Planned during the technology boom of the 1990s, the Concord Condominiums were among Seattle's first "high-tech" residential developments, catering to technology professionals with a building intranet, multimedia outlets in all units and high-speed Internet access. Developed by a company based in Vancouver, B.C., the design of the Concord echoes new condominium towers in that city.

21) KIRO TV
1968, Fred Bassetti & Co.
2800 Second Avenue

This full-block complex, constructed as KIRO TV's "Broadcast House," features slender, white concrete columns and overhangs encasing a glass-and-steel three-story structure. The building is elevated on columns and straddles a parking garage. Its exterior, appearing somewhat like an exoskeleton, reflects a shift away from the glass box aesthetic of International Style Modernism that had dominated in the post-war era toward an outward expression of materials and architectural elements.

22) MOSLER LOFTS
2007, Mithun
2523 Third Avenue

The 12-story Mosler Lofts is among the first residential developments in Seattle designed to achieve LEED silver certification. Several eco-friendly features were incorporated into the 150-unit, mixed-use project, including a green roof, high-efficiency appliances and mechanical systems, renewable building materials and non-toxic paint. The extensively glazed building was designed to capture maximum daylight using a high-efficiency window wall and glazing system. Landscaping surrounding the building provides a buffer between the street and sidewalk and helps filter storm water runoff. The Mosler lofts include studio, loft, townhome and penthouse units to attract a mixed-income resident community, a desirable consideration in an increasingly upscale downtown. The building features ten-foot-high ceilings in each unit and a shed-roof penthouse level. Brick veneer cladding on the first three floors relates the building to the lower-rise surrounding structures.

23) TRIANON BUILDING
(Trianon Ballroom)
1926, Warren H. Milner & Co.; renovation, 1985,
Anderson Koch Duarte
2505 Third Avenue

This two-story half-block concrete building was originally constructed as a dance hall. In the 1930s and 40s, the Trianon Ballroom was at the heart of Seattle's swing scene. Lionel Hampton and Ray Charles were among many who performed beneath the silver clam shell hood that sheltered the bandstand. The Trianon was the largest dance hall in the Pacific Northwest, able to accommodate over 5,000 dancers on its springy maple dance floor. The dance hall closed in 1955, after which time the building mainly housed retail. The Trianon was renovated 1985 for office space. The original design had a Mediterranean character and

The Trianon Ballroom in its heyday.

featured an open arcade with 16 balconies and a dramatic tower over the Wall Street entrance. The tower was reduced with the renovation and the balconies now serve as terraces for the offices.

The area of **Second Avenue and Wall Street** *is the point at which a bluff on the west side of Denny Hill dropped abruptly to the waterfront, prior to the regrading of the hill.*

24) LEXINGTON CONCORD APARTMENTS
1923, Harry Hudson; renovation, 1991, Stickney & Murphy
2402-2408 Second Avenue

This three-story, brick apartment building has two entries framed by small arched windows with tracery, terra-cotta surrounds and arched bays with terra-cotta balconies. The heavy cornice, brackets and window sills are also terra-cotta. The Lexington Concord Apartments were among several constructed in the 1920s to provide housing for downtown workers. Its architect, Harry Hudson, designed several apartment buildings in the area. The building is owned by the YMCA and provides low-income housing.

The **Second Avenue Urban Design** *street improvement project was completed between 1986 and 1996 by artist Kurt Kiefer. This ten-year project was designed to improve the pedestrian quality of Second Avenue. Sidewalks were widened and curb bulbs were placed at the corners to slow traffic and encourage walking. Concrete planks, recalling Seattle's original wooden sidewalks, were scattered among the concrete pavement. A custom-designed street clock, benches and lamp posts were added and a variety of evergreen and deciduous trees were planted along the street.*

25) MARJORIE
(MGM/Loew's Film Distribution)
1936, Edmund W. Denle (San Francisco)
2331 Second Avenue

This one-story, reinforced concrete building is clad in buff brick with black terra-cotta ornament. The pilasters, window trim and medallions along the stepped parapet were executed in an arrow motif. From 1936 until the 1960s, this small Art Deco building was the northwest regional film distribution office for Metro-Goldwyn-Mayer, and later Loew's films; it was one of approximately twenty such distribution centers that were located in the Belltown area. The building contained seven vaults to store the highly flammable film, which required careful storage and handling. MGM's name was replaced on the building's façade by the insurance company that occupied the building in the 1960s. Today the building is occupied by a restaurant.

26) WILLIAM TELL HOTEL
(Lorraine Hotel)
1924, J. Lister Holmes
2327 Second Avenue

This eclectic three-story hotel building employs Spanish colonial elements, such as its red tile roof, arched entrance and upper-story windows, twisted columns and stucco surfacing; as well as such classical ornament as dentils, egg-and-dart trim, shields and a balustrade, all executed in terra-cotta. The William Tell Hotel was originally an elegant hostelry frequented by celebrities in the golden age of Hollywood. The building was purchased by Plymouth Housing Group in 1986 and contains 52 low-income units.

27) SUYAMA PETERSON DEGUCHI STUDIO/3 X 10
ca. 1890, unknown; renovation, 1998, Suyama Peterson Deguchi
2324-2326 Second Avenue

This former livery stable turned automobile repair shop was renovated in 1998 for use by Seattle-based architects Suyama Peterson Deguchi. The modest, dark grey exterior is punctuated by large storefront windows with deep metal frames flanking a metal garage door. The building's ground level was the second floor prior to the Denny Regrade; the floor had to be lowered several feet along to front of the building to align with the sidewalk. A large open space in the center of the building with a 20-foot-tall ceiling serves as the Suyama Space art gallery, and retains its original plank floors and exposed old-growth timber trusses. The street frontage is shared by the gallery and SPD's retail venture, 3 X 10, fulfilling the city's requirement for storefront space along the street. The 2,000 square-foot architectural office, toward the rear of the building, receives natural light via the addition of an angled roof monitor. Parking spaces and a large wood shop are located in the basement.

28) ROQ LA RUE GALLERY
(RKO Distribution Corporation)
1928, Earl Morrison
2316 Second Avenue

This one-story concrete commercial building was originally constructed as the northwest distribution office for RKO Studio films, one of approximately twenty regional film exchanges that were located in the Belltown area. The tile bulkhead and trim include accents in dragon and ship patterns. The façade's cast-stone pilasters feature Art Deco motifs. The building is now occupied by the Roq la Rue art gallery.

29) BELLTOWN DOG PARK
(Regrade Park)
1976, Landscape Architect: John Ullman; redeveloped, 2004, Seattle Parks & Recreation Department
2551 Third Avenue

This .03-acre site was purchased by the City of Seattle in 1976 for the development of Regrade Park, which opened in 1979. The park, which contained a basketball court, picnic tables and underused play equipment, had become a haven for illegal activity. The site was redeveloped in 2004 as downtown Seattle's first off-leash dog park. It is now fenced and has a variety of surfaces, including grass, bark and concrete. One element retained from Regrade Park was the *Gyro Jack* cast-concrete sculpture by Lloyd Hamrol. The almost constant presence of dogs and their owners has been effective in discouraging the criminal element.

30) BELLTOWN SENIOR APARTMENTS
2002, Weinstein A|U
2208 Second Avenue

This eight-story, concrete frame building was constructed as the new headquarters for Senior Services, a non-profit agency that supports the independence of senior citizens. The project successfully managed tight budget and site constraints. The architects employed a cost-effective, unitized curtain wall and metal panel system to reduce construction time and provide expansive glazing, allowing natural light to penetrate the deep, narrow building. The façade's metal sunscreens allow for controlled natural light. The top five floors include 25 units of low-income senior housing, with three floors of office space below. The building steps back at floors 4-8, creating a landscaped terrace at the fourth floor and further separation of the residential levels from the condominium tower across the alley. A rooftop garden and P-patch were provided for use by the residents.

31) HUMPHREY APARTMENTS
1923, Warren H. Milner & Co.
2205 Second Avenue

The Humphrey Apartment building is a six-story, U-shaped structure that centers on a courtyard along Blanchard Street. The Second Avenue entrance features stained glass and acanthus leaf ornament, and egg-and-dart terra-cotta molding. The development of the courtyard for the street-level restaurant is an uncommon mode of commercial use in an apartment building. The contrasting light-colored brick brightens the interior of the courtyard space, which is entered through an ornate iron and glass canopy. The building is topped with a prominent cornice featuring an acanthus leaf pattern.

32) RIVOLI APARTMENTS
1909, A.H. Albertson and Howells & Stokes
(New York)
2127 Second Avenue

This three-story brick apartment building features an elaborate terra-cotta and marble entry with a stained glass and wrought iron light fixture. The parapet is raised at the center of the façade, marking the entrance. The building retains its original windows, which are topped with flat arches accented with white terra-cotta. Its architect, A.H. Albertson, came to Seattle in 1907 as a representative of the New York firm of Howells & Stokes, who were developing the plan for the Metropolitan Tract (see Retail District tour). He remained in Seattle after completion of the project and became a prominent local architect.

33) CRISTALLA
(Crystal Natatorium)
1916, B. Marcus Priteca; Cristalla, 2002, Weber + Thompson
2030 Second Avenue

This 23-story, 197-unit condominium tower incorporates the façade of the 1916 Crystal Natatorium, designed by B. Marcus Priteca. The arched arcade that runs along the ground floor of Cristalla is all that remains of the ornate Italian Renaissance-style terra-cotta building. The present steel-and-glass dome corner entry mimics the original dome that marked the entrance to the former building. The limestone façade treatment of the first three floors provides a transition from the historic arcade to the fully modern expression of the condominium tower. The building's skin of layered blue glass terminates with a bright yellow band at the penthouse level.

The Crystal Natatorium, Seattle's most popular swimming pool, offered "warm ocean water swimming." Salt water from Elliott Bay was pumped into the building where it was filtered, heated and chlorinated. Arched steel trusses supported a glass roof over the pool. The building's colorful exterior ornamentation included mermaids, dolphins and a statue of Neptune above the domed entrance. By the 1930s, the building had fallen into disrepair along with the Belltown neighborhood. In 1943, the building was converted for use by the Bethel Pentecostal Temple and a floor was built over the pool. The building was eligible for landmark status, but without consent of the church, it could not be approved.

The Crystal Natatorium, B. Marcus Priteca, 1916

34) CINERAMA
(Martin Cinerama Theater)
1963, Raymond H. Peck; renovation, 1999, BOORA
Architects (Portland, OR)
2100 Fourth Avenue

This rather unassuming buff-brick building, with street-level accents of green and blue mosaic tile, is one of only two Super Cinerama theaters remaining in the world, and one of only three venues capable of showing the original Cinerama three-strip films. What interest may be lacking on the exterior is made up for inside the building. The theater was purchased in 1998 by Microsoft co-founder Paul Allen, who had it restored in keeping with its 1960s style and updated with state-of-the-art audio and visual equipment. The shed-ceiling lobby features green and blue mosaic tile, Bertoia Diamond chairs, purple-and-green wallpaper and polka-dot-patterned carpet. Even the concession stand menus are a "throw back" to 1963. The auditorium contains 808 rocking red mohair seats and was designed to provide accessibility for mobility and sensory-impaired patrons. The 90-foot long, 30-foot high, curved screen was restored for special viewings of Cinerama films. The renovation architects developed a second screen for viewing modern 70mm/35mm films, which sits in front of the massive curved screen. The 68-foot-long screen can be broken down in a matter of hours for Cinerama film presentations.

Cinerama *film made its debut with the 1952 movie,* This is Cinerama. *This uniquely American art form involved filming shots with three different cameras at slightly different angles and then projecting the films through three lenses onto a massive, curved screen. The images were coupled with rich sound to provide an entirely new and engulfing cinematic experience. By the mid-1960s, however, the technique had become too expensive and only six more three-strip films were made. 70mm films were shot to be viewed through custom lenses on the Cinerama screens that had been installed in theaters across the United States; however, by the early 1970s, even 70mm Cinerama films had become too costly and almost all Cinerama screens were dismantled.*

The area of **Fourth Avenue and Blanchard Street** *was once the highest peak of Denny Hill. At 240-feet above high tide, the hill was 107 feet above the highest point in the business district; it was lowered 107 feet with the Denny Regrade project.*

35) FOURTH & BLANCHARD BUILDING
(Sedgwick James Building)
1979, Chester L. Lindsey Architects
2101 Fourth Avenue

This 25-story office building is composed of two sharply angled towers linked by a lower-rise, recessed core. The building is clad entirely in black reflective glass. It contains a three-level, below-grade parking garage constructed of concrete but is framed in structural steel from the ground up. The design takes cues from Philip Johnson's Pennzoil Place in Houston; the Fourth and Blanchard Building is locally nicknamed the "Darth Vader building." This is one of a series of medium-rise, half-block office buildings developed by Martin Selig in the Denny Regrade area in the late 1970s.

36) FIRE STATION NO. 2
1920, Daniel Huntington
2334 Fourth Avenue

The concrete frame of this two-story fire station is accentuated by patterned red brick infill. Its regular arched street-level bays and large second-story windows provide a harmonious street frontage. Entrances to the building are marked by raised parapets, treated as pediments. Fire Station No. 2 was one of several stations constructed by the city after the department switched from horse-drawn equipment to motorized trucks. The building included a maintenance shop and auditorium, which served as the main fire department meeting place. This fire station is the oldest in Seattle that is still used for its original purpose. The building was designed by Daniel Huntington during his employment as city architect (1912-1921).

37) FOURTH & BATTERY BUILDING
1977, Chester L. Lindsey Architects
2401 Fourth Avenue

The 14-story, half-block Fourth & Battery Building is a monolithic office development resembling an elongated hexagon outlined in concrete and clad entirely in reflective black glass. This was the first in a series of developments in the late 1970s by Martin Selig after a 1974 land-use zoning plan encouraged the construction of office buildings and in-city residential buildings in the Denny Regrade area. The zoning also stipulated the provision of open green space around the developments. The construction of these buildings was among the earliest signs of downtown spreading north into the Denny Regrade area, which was a primary rationalization for carrying out the regrade projects over 100 years ago.

38) DEVONSHIRE/DAVENPORT
1925, Henry Bittman
420 Wall Street/420 Vine Street

The four-story, U-shaped brick Devonshire Apartment building centers on a second-floor courtyard terrace. The parapet is raised above the fourth-story windows, which are topped with ornate glazed terra-cotta. Henry Bittman was also responsible for its near-twin, the Davenport at 420 Vine Street. These buildings, among the finest that survive from the era, reflect developers' goals for the neighborhood after the first phase of the Denny Regrade. The newly flattened land was touted as "Seattle's Coming Retail and Apartment-House District."

39) TILIKUM PLACE
1912, James Wehn; redevelopment, 1975,
Jones & Jones
Fifth Avenue & Cedar Street & Denny Way

Originally proposed as a fountain and statue of the Roman god Mercury, Seattle sculptor James Wehn proposed Chief Seattle (Chief Sealth) as a more appropriate subject. He worked from the only surviving photograph of Chief Seattle, which had been taken by Seattle's first-known photographer, E.M. Sammis, in 1864. The cast bronze statue with spouting bear heads and watering basin for horses was unveiled by the chief's great-great-granddaughter, Myrtle Loughery, on Founder's day, November 13, 1912, a day commemorating the landing of the Denny party at Alki Point. The chief stands with a welcoming gesture toward Alki, four miles across Elliot Bay. "Tilikum" is Chinook trade jargon meaning greeting or welcome. A 1975 restoration of the statue, which is a city historic landmark, and redevelopment of the park included enlargement of the triangle, replacement of the basin with the present pond and the addition of trees and benches.

40) FISHER PLAZA/KOMO TV
2000 & 2003, Lance Mueller & Associates Architects,
Landscape Architects: Berger Partnership
100 Fourth Avenue N.

This two-building, multi-use complex was developed by Seattle-based Fisher Communications to house their local ABC affiliate, KOMO 4 TV, their local radio stations and as speculative office and retail space designed to cater to the needs of high-tech companies. The exterior is clad in prefabricated rain screen aluminum panels with a granite base and features extensive areas of curved, green glazing, including two full-height corner towers. Fisher Plaza was the region's first full-building use of under-floor HVAC and electrical and communication wiring, which is accessible beneath 18-inch elevated floors. The first phase of the 330,000 square-foot facility, the five-story, L-shaped Fisher Plaza East, home to KOMO TV, was built on the site of the parking lot of KOMO's former building and was completed in 2000. The second phase, the six-story Fisher Plaza West, built on the site of KOMO's former building, was completed in 2003. The complex includes a heliport and centers on a 30,000 square-foot plaza, which is located above a 700-space parking garage.

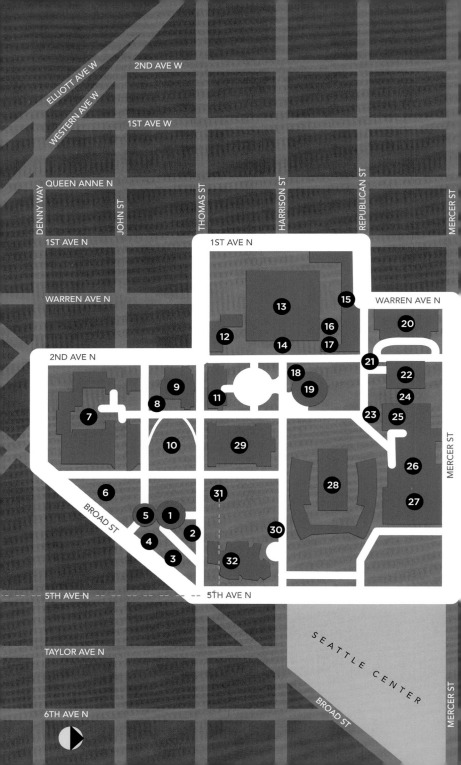

CHAPTER 9
SEATTLE CENTER

Seattle Center's 74-acre campus, a cultural center and community "back yard," offers an opportunity to enjoy a variety of art installations and architecture away from automobile traffic and crowded sidewalks. People of all ages gather here for numerous events held throughout the year, including the Bumbershoot, Northwest Folklife and ethnic heritage festivals. It is home to three major theater companies, the Pacific Northwest Ballet and the Seattle Opera. Seattle Center is best known as the location of the 1962 Century 21 World's Fair, but the site has a long history as a social and entertainment center.

The Duwamish people wore a path across the flat meadow that stretched from Denny Hill to Queen Anne Hill traveling between their villages on Lake Union and Elliott Bay. They created the meadow by burning off the brush in order to hunt duck and waterfowl with nets stretched between poles. A Duwamish legend told of an underground stream running below the meadow, allowing orcas to pass between the lake and the bay.

In the 1850s, David and Louisa Boren Denny homesteaded on this land, which settlers called "the Prairie." They built their cabin near the present location of the Northwest Rooms. Louisa's flower garden was known for the Sweetbriar roses that she brought with her on the journey west.

Given the shortage of large areas of flat land in Seattle, the Prairie was used for events needing level expanses of ground, including traveling circuses and religious revivals. Army mules grazed here while awaiting shipment to the Philippines during the Spanish-American War.

The seeds for the development of a civic center were planted in 1881 when saloon owner James Osborne bequeathed $20,000 to the city for the construction of a civic hall whenever matching funds were available ($20,000 was equal to Seattle's annual budget in 1881). Eight years later, David and Louisa Boren Denny donated 28 acres of their land to the city with the stipulation that it be reserved for "public use forever." Finally, in 1927, Seattle citizens voted to fund a civic entertainment center. Osborn's gift, which had been gaining interest for over 40 years, had grown to $109,000. The city "matched" it with an additional $900,000 and began constructing the Civic Auditorium (now McCaw Hall), Civic Ice Arena (now Mercer Arts Arena) and Civic Ballfield (on the site of Memorial Stadium). The site was a logical one given the Denny gift, its relatively flat land and proximity to downtown. Although the auditorium acoustics were criticized, Seattle at last had a cultural and entertainment center befitting a city whose population had grown to over 315,000.

During the Great Depression, the Civic Ice Arena was a popular gathering place for children and teens who could skate all day for just a nickel. The Civic Ballfield was home to Seattle's Pacific Coast Baseball League team, the Seattle

Indians, from 1932 until 1938 when they moved to Sick Stadium (on Rainier Avenue) as the Seattle Rainiers.

The National Guard Armory (now Center House) was built in 1939. The full-block Moderne-style building was used for military purposes but also for entertainment such as dances and big-band performances after the war. In 1948, the Armory was the location of the Washington State Legislature's anti-Communist fact-finding hearings, chaired by Senator Albert Canwell.

Memorial Stadium, dedicated to Seattle high school students killed in World War II, was built by the Seattle School District to replace the Civic Ballfield in 1947. On Thanksgiving Day 1948, the state championship high school football game between Wenatchee and West Seattle, played on this field, was the first live sports event telecast in Seattle.

In 1955, Seattle City Councilman Al Rochester, who as a boy had attended nearly every day of the 1909 Alaska-Yukon-Pacific Exposition, proposed the idea of hosting a World's Fair to commemorate its 50th anniversary. The World's Fair Commission held their first meeting in autumn, 1955. It soon became clear that they would not be able to pull the event together by 1959, but they were undeterred.

The Commission considered several sites for the fair, including Duwamish Head, Sand Point Naval Air Station, the Civic Auditorium site and First Hill, among others. The Civic Auditorium site was considerably smaller at just 74 acres. Sand Point, for instance, could provide 350 acres.

While the World's Fair Commission searched for a site, the Civic Center Advisory committee had put on the ballot a $7.5 million bond issue for the construction of a sports arena, convention Center and opera house; this passed in 1956. The World's Fair Commission recommended that the fair be tied in with the upgrade of the Civic Auditorium site, so that the build-

1939 aerial photograph of future fair grounds with the newly completed National Guard Armory.

ings that remained after the fair could be used for a larger civic center complex. Although the site was smaller than what they had originally envisioned, their confidence in its workability was bolstered by the success of London's 1951 Festival of Britain, which was held on a mere 28 acres.

Many also felt the choice of the civic center site would provide an opportunity for urban renewal. The neighborhood around the civic center had a high incidence of crime, run-down rental housing, parking lots and warehouses. The city soon began acquiring property and clearing it for the fair.

The Century 21 theme with its emphasis on science was inspired by an event thousands of miles from Seattle. The successful launch of Sputnik on October 4, 1957, by the Soviet Union amplified Cold War anxiety and fear of falling behind the Soviets in military technology and science. A World's Fair showcasing a prosperous and scientifically-advanced free world would be an ideal way to renew faith in the strength and ultimate triumph of democracy and capitalism.

With the theme firmly established, Fair Commission President Eddie Carlson proposed the idea for a lofty restaurant overlooking the fair and the entire city. He was inspired by a recent trip to Stuttgart where he had dined at a restaurant atop a 400-foot tower. The John Graham & Co. architecture firm proposed that the restaurant revolve; they had recently built the world's first revolving restaurant in Hawaii. University of Washington architecture professor Victor Steinbrueck was hired as a design consultant and after many schemes, the team arrived at the tripod structure that came to be called the Space Needle.

Paul Thiry, one of the architects who had introduced International Style architecture to Seattle in the late 1930s, was selected as the fair's principal architect. Thiry designed several permanent structures, including the

1962 World's Fair NASA exhibit showing space capsule poster.

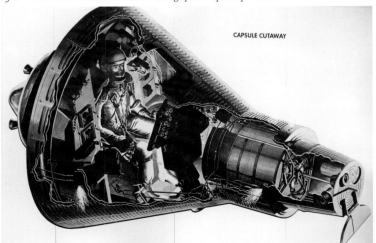

CAPSULE CUTAWAY

Washington State Coliseum (now Key Arena), as well as the overall plan and project oversight. Design competitions were held for the International Fountain and the United States Science Pavilion. Kazuyuki Matsushita and Hideki Shimizu won the commission for the fountain, and University of Washington-educated Minoru Yamasaki would work with Seattle firm, Naramore Bain Brady & Johanson to construct his winning design for the Science Pavilion (now the Pacific Science Center). Renowned San Francisco landscape architect Lawrence Halprin was chosen to design the grounds.

Buildings constructed for the fair faced inward to the center of the site and away from the streets, as the complex was enclosed with admission booths at several gates. Construction continued until the very last minute. On April 21, 1962, President Kennedy launched the fair by pressing the same gold-nugget-encrusted telegraph key that President Taft had used to open the Alaska-Yukon-Pacific Exposition 53 years earlier; however, this time the message was transmitted via satellite.

The Century 21 World's Fair was a huge success. ten million visitors had come through the gates by closing day on October 21, 1962. President Kennedy was scheduled to visit the fair on its final day, but was forced to cancel due to illness. The ironic truth, of course, was that he could not close the fair that was designed to quell fears of domination and nuclear annihilation by the Soviets because he was in the midst of the Cuban Missile Crisis, the event that brought the Cold War closest to nuclear conflict.

After the removal of many temporary buildings, the site became Seattle Center. There were many differing opinions on what the character of the expanded civic center should be. Some wanted it to be preserved for high art and culture, while others felt it should be a place of amusement and recreation. The resulting complex reflects a compromise. The Seattle Center Advisory Commission was established in February 1963 to serve as a citizens' oversight committee and to assess operations, plans and policies regarding the management and development of the Center.

The fair site and remaining buildings were converted or altered immediately after the fair. The grounds were redesigned by Seattle landscape architect Richard Haag in 1964. The Science Pavilion was taken over by the non-profit organization, Pacific Science Center Foundation. The city purchased the Washington State Coliseum and began the conversion into a sports arena. The amusement park, called the "Gayway" during the fair, was sold to a private party, renovated and renamed the "Fun Forest." Preexisting buildings were also converted, or reverted back, to other uses (see individual entries). The Monorail was originally to be torn down but was instead given to the City of Seattle as a gift from the Alweg Company (which had also financed its construction) to avoid demolition costs and leave a demonstration system for potential customers. The system has run, with few interruptions, for over 45 years.

The Bumbershoot Arts Festival began its annual run at the Center as the "Seattle Arts Festival" in 1971. The following year, the Northwest Folklife Festival joined the lineup of annual events held at Seattle Center.

The Seattle Center Foundation, a public non-profit organization dedicated to encouraging and managing monetary donations and grants to the Center, was established in 1977 to help the Center face its ongoing financial challenges.

Disney Imagineering was hired by the city in 1987 to make a study and development plan to revitalize the struggling Center. Their plan called for the demolition of several structures and replacing Memorial Stadium with a "Memorial Meadow." The plan was also accompanied by an astronomical price tag and was scrapped.

The "Seattle Center 2000" plan was adopted by City Council in 1990 for improvements to the grounds and existing facilities and the addition of new ones. Significant improvements have been made under this plan, including the development of the sculpture garden on the south side, and opening up the campus to the surrounding streets. Generous donations from corporations and individuals have resulted in major new buildings such as the Experience Music Project, Fisher Pavilion, and the Children's Theatre and renovations and additions to the Pacific Science Center and Marion Oliver McCaw Hall.

Future development plans for Seattle Center are currently (2007) being considered, including the controversial proposal to demolish Memorial Stadium for green space with parking below. However, the facility is still owned and used by the Seattle School District and efforts have begun to preserve it as an historic landmark. Continued community support and involvement will guide the future of this unique place, which has for decades provided Seattleites and millions of tourists with recreation, education and culture.

1) SPACE NEEDLE

1962, John Graham & Co., Victor Steinbrueck (consulting); addition, 1982, John Graham & Co.; renovation, 2000, Callison Architecture
400 Broad Street

The 605-foot Space Needle was designed as the centerpiece of the 1962 Seattle World's Fair. It became the tallest structure in Seattle upon its completion, the first to surpass the Smith Tower (see Pioneer Square tour). The 3,700-ton steel tower is attached to its 30-foot-deep by 120-foot-diameter foundation with 32-foot-long bolts. The Space Needle was engineered to withstand winds of over 150 miles per hour, doubling the requirements of the 1962 building code. It features an observation deck at 520 feet and the SkyCity restaurant at 500 feet. A 14-foot ring along the windows of the restaurant interior revolves one full turn every 47 minutes, allowing diners to experience the 360-degree view. The "SkyLine" level, at 100 feet, was a controversial addition, completed in 1982. The original plans had included a lower level, so the platforms on which it was built were already in place. A 2000 renovation involved the addition of the transparent, nautilus-shaped Pavilion level, remodeling of the revolving restaurant and the SkyLine banquet facility, exterior lighting additions and renovation of the observation deck. At $20 million, the renovation cost was nearly five times that of the original construction. In 1999, at 37 years old, the Space Needle became Seattle's youngest historic landmark. The Space Needle's tapered tripod and flying saucer form have become an internationally recognized symbol of Seattle.

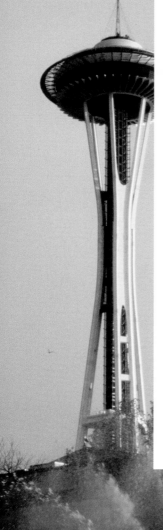

Sculpture Garden
Grounds northeast and southwest of Space Needle.
The sculpture garden is located on the Broad Street
Green, the former site of Building 50, which contained
the World's Fair Fashion and Commerce Pavilion. After
serving as a storage facility for city departments, the
building was demolished in 1991 to create a public sculp-
ture park and a more open Fifth Avenue & Broad Street
entrance to Seattle Center.

2) MOSES
1975
Tony Smith

Moses is an abstract geometric sculpture weighing 5,500 pounds. It is made up of painted black steel components and is 15 feet long by 11 feet high. *Moses* was the first major art piece acquired under the 1% for art program, which requires one percent of the cost of city-funded construction to go toward public art.

3) BLACK LIGHTNING
1981, Ronald Bladen

This painted steel sculpture, resembling a lightning bolt, is 24 feet high and 60 feet long. It was originally installed at the Seattle Center Flag Pavilion in 1981 and moved here as part of the development of the sculpture park.

4) MOON GATES
1999, Doris Chase

Moon Gates is a four-piece bronze sculpture with simple geometric forms cut into columns and slabs ranging in size from 9 feet to 17 feet in height. The work invites movement through and around its components and various visual and physical experiences of space.

5) HOWARD S. WRIGHT MEMORIAL FOUNTAIN
2000
Broad Street turnaround

The fountain and turnaround were added as part of the 2000 renovation of the Space Needle. The fountain is named for the founder of the Howard S. Wright Construction Company, established in 1885. Howard S. Wright Construction built the Space Needle, the monorail system, and the Washington State Coliseum (now Key Arena) among other Seattle Center facilities. Howard S. Wright Construction was one of the original financiers of the Space Needle and today the Howard S. Wright family is the major stock holder of the Space Needle Corporation.

6) OLYMPIC ILIAD
1984, Alexander Liberman

Forty-one steel cylinders ranging in size from 48 to 64 inches in diameter were cut, piled and painted bright red to create *Olympic Iliad*. The sculpture is 45 feet high, 60 feet wide and 30 feet deep. *Olympic Iliad* was shipped from the artist's Connecticut studio to Seattle on eight 40-foot flat-bed trucks.

7) PACIFIC SCIENCE CENTER/IMAX
(U.S. Science Pavilion)
1962, Minoru Yamasaki (Detroit), Naramore Bain
Brady & Johanson; south entrance addition, 1993,
The Callison Partnership; addition, 1998, Denis
Laming (Paris)
200 Second Avenue N.

Built as the U.S. Science Pavilion for the 1962 World's Fair, the Pacific Science Center is composed of six interconnected white concrete buildings surrounding a courtyard with five white 110-foot aluminum arches standing above reflecting pools. The building was assembled on site of pre-cast concrete. Yamasaki's interest in Venetian Gothic architecture is evident in the narrow, pointed arch facades of the building and most obviously in the five towering arches. With a modern, geometric take on Gothic tracery, they appear to be free-standing ribs of a medieval cathedral vault. The 1998 addition of the IMAX Theater and Ackerley Family Exhibit Gallery marked the first U.S. commission for French architect Denis Laming. Laming's geometric design consists of a monumental fiberglass oval engaged with a glass-and-steel rectangle. The resulting complex provokes consideration of the changing ideas about the future of architecture over the course of 36 years.

8) BABY WHALE'S TAIL/NEOTOTEM II
2002, Gloria Bornstein

Baby Whale's Tail, or *Neototem II*, is a bronze companion sculpture to *Neototems*, located by the International Fountain, which depicts breeching whale backs. The whale tail is four feet high and 13 feet wide. Water sprays out of the tail mimicking the splash made when whales surface.

9 SEATTLE CENTER

9) CHARLOTTE MARTIN THEATER/SEATTLE CHILDREN'S THEATRE
1993, Mahlum & Nordfors McKinley Gordon; addition, 2000, LMN
Second Avenue & Thomas Street

The Charlotte Martin Theater, home to the Seattle's Children's Theatre and drama school, presents a lively street presence with its various forms, volumes and decorative exterior tiles. The series of undulating vaults was adapted from the roofline of the adjoining 1956 Shrine temple designed by Samuel G. Morrison & Associates, which is now part of the theatre complex. Public areas are glazed floor to ceiling, providing views of both the outdoors and the activity within. Local artist Garth Edwards created the entrance murals, which depict whimsical characters that are also carried into the lobby details, such as the handrail panels, auditorium entry arches and ventilation grills. The Allen Family Technical Pavilion was added in 2000. The design features compatible colors, materials and volumes; however, the addition is more rectilinear, striking a balance between the existing theatre buildings and the neighboring Pacific Science Center. The technical pavilion houses scene, prop and costume shops, production offices, rehearsal and classroom spaces and new loading dock facilities. Founded in 1975, the Seattle Children's Theatre is one of the largest theaters for young audiences in North America.

10) THE SEATTLE MURAL ₸
1962, Paul Horiuchi
Mural Amphitheatre, east of Charlotte Martin Theatre

Seattle Mural was commissioned for the 1962 World's Fair. The 17-by-60-foot mural was considered the largest work of art in the Pacific Northwest upon its completion. The mural is composed of 160 shades of glass tile on 54 concrete slabs. Horiuchi's design for the mural was transferred to glass by Venetian artisan, Olivo Santagostino. The mural reflects the artist's abstract collage style, which is said to have been inspired by the layers of paper on the bulletin board in Seattle's International District (see International District tour). The mural was originally installed on a curving concrete wall, designed by World's Fair principal architect Paul Thiry, and stood over a pool of water, which is now the location of the Mural Amphitheatre stage. Today this site serves as a venue for summer events such as the Northwest Folklife Festival and Bumbershoot.

11) FISHER PAVILION
2002, The Miller/Hull Partnership

Fisher Pavilion is built on the former site of the Flag Pavilion, a temporary structure built to last six months that served the center for 39 years. The deteriorating Flag Pavilion stood atop the hillside, blocking views of the International Fountain from the Seattle Children's Theatre. In response, the site was excavated 22 feet and the Fisher Pavilion was built into the hillside, opening up the view and creating a 19,000-square-foot roof top plaza. The cast-in-place concrete structure features a fully glazed north façade with roll-up garage doors that open up the exhibition and event space to the two-acre South Fountain Lawn in front. At the rooftop plaza level, two concrete pylons with steel-and-glass canopies mark the entrance to the building and contain the elevators and mechanical equipment. Pavers on the plaza simulate the look of raindrops on the surface of water when viewed from the Space Needle. Fisher Pavilion serves as an important community gathering space and the location of several festival and performance activities. The 50 flagpoles that once stood on this site were moved to Warren G. Magnuson Park, seven miles northeast of Seattle Center.

12) SEATTLE CENTER PAVILION
(Great Britain Pavilion)
1962, Paul Thiry
West of Fisher Pavilion

The eastern portion of the two-story Seattle Center Pavilion was designed by World's Fair principal architect Paul Thiry as part of the International Commerce and Industry buildings surrounding the Washington State Coliseum (now Key Arena) and was meant as a permanent structure. Like the other buildings in the complex, it features rectilinear forms opening to a courtyard, glazed façades and patterned concrete exterior walls. During the fair, the pavilion housed the Great Britain exhibit. Starting in 1965, the pavilion was used by the Seattle Art Museum for modern art and traveling exhibits until 1991 when the museum moved from Volunteer Park into their downtown building (see West Edge tour). Subsequently, the pavilion was used for conference and rental space. Seattle Center Pavilion closed in 2002; its future use is yet to be determined.

13) KEY ARENA
(Washington State Coliseum/Seattle Center Coliseum)
1962, Paul Thiry; renovation, 1964, Paul Thiry; renovation, 1995, NBBJ
305 Harrison Street

Seattle World's Fair principal architect Paul Thiry applied his interest in innovative structures to the design of the Washington State Coliseum, now Key Arena. At the time of its construction, the Coliseum was among the largest clear-span structures in the world, covering nearly four acres of unobstructed space. The hyperbolic paraboloid aluminum roof was cable-net suspended from the framework of concrete beams. The innovative roof structure was problematic, however, as it swayed in high winds and sometimes leaked. After the World's Fair, Thiry oversaw the conversion of the exhibition space into a sports arena and concert venue. By 1991 the building was in need of updating and expanding to accommodate its use by professional

During the 1962 World's Fair, the Washington State Coliseum was the location of the popular "World of Century 21" exhibits that offered a glimpse of what life would be like in the year 2000. Visitors explored the tri-level exhibition space in the "Bubbleator," a 150-person plexiglass elevator shaped like a giant bubble. After the fair, the Bubbleator was moved to the Center House, where it remained until 1980. It is now privately owned and used as an outdoor greenhouse.

The Bubbleator transported fairgoers to the "World of Century 21."

sports teams and as a concert venue. The structure was renovated and the roof replaced. The roof structure was augmented with rigid diagonal trusses, which eliminated the wind and leak problems while allowing the designers to retain the distinctive shape of the original roof. The renovation also involved lowering the arena floor 35 feet and replacement of the seating bowl. The resulting facility includes 17,000 seats, 58 luxury suites and improved sight lines.

14) ACROBAT CONSTELLATION
1995, Timothy Siciliano
East entrance to Key Arena

These sheet-metal acrobats with fiber optic lights celebrate the history of Seattle Center as a place of entertainment, referring not only to the current activities and the World's Fair, but also to the traveling circuses that performed here on the original homestead of David and Louisa Boren Denny.

15) NORTHWEST ROOMS
1962, Paul Thiry; renovation, 1992, Buffalo Design Inc.
North of Key Arena

This concrete and steel framed complex was built for the 1962 World's Fair as part of the International Commerce and Industry Buildings surrounding the Washington State Coliseum. It was built as a permanent structure for use after the fair. The L-shaped complex is covered by a continuous overhanging flat roof with exposed steel trusses. It is arranged around a courtyard with upper and lower plaza levels. The east façade windows (facing the International Fountain) feature *Pool*, an oil-on-plywood painting by Randy Haye. The panels were installed in 1985 to replace a concrete wall. The Northwest Rooms were renovated into classroom, commercial and conference space in 1992.

16) DUPEN FOUNTAIN
(Fountain of Creation)
1962, Everett DuPen; redesigned, 1992, Nakano Dennis Landscape Architects, Everett DuPen
Lower courtyard of the Northwest Rooms

DuPen Fountain is made up of three bronze sculptures in a concrete pool. Originally titled *Fountain of Creation*, the sculptures represent life forms in the sea, air and on land. The central element is the "tree of life," which shows the development of life from protozoa to fish, mammals and humans. The sculptures and spray heads were relocated in 1992. DuPen Fountain is a popular summer attraction for young children, who use it as a wading pool.

17) NORTHWEST CRAFT CENTER
(Sweden Pavilion)
1962, Paul Thiry
East of Northwest Rooms

This one-story concrete and steel frame building was constructed as a temporary structure, not intended for use after the 1962 World's Fair. Like the neighboring Northwest Rooms, it was part of the International Commerce and Industry complex and housed the Sweden Pavilion. The Northwest Craft Center, one of Seattle's oldest galleries, opened here immediately after the fair.

18) NEOTOTEMS
1995, Gloria Bornstein
Southwest side of International Fountain

These two sand-cast bronze sculptures of breeching whale backs refer to the Duwamish legend about an underground stream running under this area that allowed orcas to pass between Elliot Bay and Lake Union.

19) THE INTERNATIONAL FOUNTAIN
1962, Kazuyuki Matsushita, Hideki Shimizu; reconstruction, 1995, Kenichi Nakano & Associates (landscape architects), WET Design (mechanical designer)

The International Fountain was constructed for the World's Fair and is the centerpiece of the open space known as the Fountain Lawn. The original fountain show featured water shoots controlled in different patterns with colored lights. The original hard iron "sea urchin" style nozzles, steep grade and surrounding sharp rocks made it hazardous to children, forcing the Center to rope off the fountain during festivals. The fountain was replaced and expanded in 1995. It was made safer and more accessible with the design of a 4 percent-grade ramp, which allows people to access the floor of the fountain by foot or wheelchair. The water and sound features were updated with computerized water, sound and lighting control. 283 water shooters propel 66 gallons of water up to 120 feet in the air. The water shows are synchronized with various music selections.

The International Fountain *was the site of an impromptu memorial to the fallen after the September 11, 2001, terrorist attacks. Thousands of mourners brought flowers and notes to what became known as the million-flower vigil. The flowers were gathered by volunteers from the Interbay P-Patch and the Seattle Parks and Recreation Department and turned into compost. The compost was used to nourish the Liberty Community Garden in lower Manhattan, which was destroyed in the attack, and the flower garden in front of the Fisher Pavilion.*

20) BAGLEY WRIGHT THEATRE
(Seattle Repertory Theatre)
1983, NBBJ; addition, 1996, Callison Architecture
155 Mercer Street

The 856-seat Bagley Wright Theatre was the first major new construction at Seattle Center after the 1962 World's Fair. The sprawling green building features curving forms and horizontal bands vaguely recalling art deco design. The east-facing façade features an 8-foot by 50-foot neon art installation by Stephen Antonakos. The 286-seat Leo Kreilsheimer Theatre was added to the south end of the complex in 1996. It features an expanded lobby with a 45-foot glazed rotunda that overlooks the Fountain Lawn. Founded in 1963, the Seattle Repertory Theatre performed in what is now the Intiman Theatre until the construction of the Bagley Wright Theatre complex.

21) FOUNTAIN OF SESERAGI
2000, Gerard Tsutakawa
East of Bagley Wright Theatre, south side of Intiman Theatre

This welded fabricated bronze fountain is 12 feet long and five feet six inches high. The name *Seseragi* means "the sound of a murmuring mountain stream" in Japanese, which is represented by the two streams traveling down each side of the Y-shaped fountain and swirling together.

22) INTIMAN THEATRE
(The Playhouse)
1962, Kirk Wallace McKinley & Associates; renovation, 1987, Bumgardner Architects
201 Mercer Street

Intiman Theater was built as The Playhouse for the 1962 World's Fair. The building was constructed in just 34 days using innovative pre-cast concrete construction. The building is faced in beige brick and features a 30-foot-high portico supported by simple, slender columns. The theater is built around a courtyard, the centerpiece of which is the *Fountain of the Northwest,* by James Fitzgerald. The 20-foot high bronze sculpture, which was installed for the fair, has the appearance of being naturally eroded by the falling water. The Playhouse building was renovated to upgrade the facility and tailor it to the needs of the Intiman Theatre Company. The renovation involved removing nearly half the seats of the 800-seat Playhouse to achieve its present 425-seat configuration. The Intiman Theatre Company, founded in 1972, moved into the renovated building in 1987.

23) KOBE BELL ⛩
(Friendship Bell)
1962, Dr. Shusa Noji, Hatsune Nakagawa (Kobe, Japan) (LL)
South of Intiman Playhouse

The Kobe Bell was given to Seattle by its Japanese sister city, Kobe, in honor of the 1962 World's Fair and as a symbol of ongoing friendship between the United States and Japan. The one-ton "Friendship Bell" is housed in a 15-foot-high cypress wood Japanese temple pagoda set on a concrete slab. The temple was rededicated with a Shinto purification ceremony after structural repair in 2002. Seattle established its sister-city relationship with Kobe in 1957.

24) FOUNDER'S COURT
1962 Lawrence Halprin; redesigned, 1995, Atelier Landscape Architects
Between Intiman Theatre and Pacific Northwest Ballet

The Founder's Court was created to honor the 1962 World's Fair founders and redesigned in 1995. The space features paving by Horace Washington, which includes a bronze medallion set in granite paving. The central medallion was designed by George Tsutakawa in 1962 for the fair. The *Julius C. Lang Memorial Fountain*, by Francois Stahly, which was originally conceived as a sculpture, was installed in the center of the courtyard on a concrete aggregate base and turned into a fountain for the fair. The stone column was relocated to the side of the courtyard in 1995 and its base removed, returning it to being a sculpture rather than a fountain. *Encircled Stream* or *Vortex Fountain*, by Ned Kahn, was installed with the 1995 redesign. The swirling water suggests the currents of time, nature and culture that have passed through the site.

25) PHELPS CENTER
(Exhibition Hall)
Kirk Wallace McKinley & Associates, 1962; renovation, 1993, Gordon Walker Architecture
301 Mercer Street

The Exhibition Hall was designed as part of the complex of beige brick-veneered buildings along Mercer Street, which included the Playhouse (Intiman Theatre) and the Mercer Arts Arena and Opera House (McCaw Hall). Unlike the others, however, the Exhibition Hall features a zigzag roofline, which is visible on the eastern and western elevations.

Prior to the construction of Marion Oliver McCaw Hall, the buildings were all connected visually and physically by the 30-foot-high portico that runs along the Mercer Street façade. During the fair, this building housed the fine arts exhibit. Built as a permanent structure, it was used for a variety of purposes until the Pacific Northwest Ballet began renovations in 1990. The building's three stories originally enclosed a one-story volume of space with a mezzanine around all sides. The renovation involved building in the unused airspace between the ground floor and the roof.

26) MARION OLIVER MCCAW HALL
(Civic Auditorium)
1928, Schack Young & Myers; renovation to Opera House, 1962, James Chiarelli and Marcus B. Priteca; renovation and expansion, 2003, LMN Architects; Landscape Architect: Gustafson Guthrie Nichol Ltd.
321 Mercer Street

Today's Marion Oliver McCaw Hall was originally constructed as the 6,000-seat Civic Auditorium in 1928. The building, which had always been criticized for its draftiness and poor acoustics, was renovated for the 1962 World's fair

*At the 2000 groundbreaking ceremony for **Marion Oliver McCaw Hall**, the contents of a time capsule, first sealed upon the completion of the Civic Auditorium in 1928, were displayed. The capsule had been opened and resealed with additional items during the 1962 renovation. Among the items inside were Sweetbriar roses from Louisa Boren Denny's flower garden and one World's Fair Trade Dollar.*

into a 2,800-seat opera house and given the same beige brick veneer as the other buildings along Mercer Street. By the 1990s, the facility had become too small and outdated. Rather than replacing the building, the Seattle Center, Pacific Northwest Ballet and Seattle Opera chose to renovate, upgrade and expand the existing structure. The new 2,890-seat facility is clad in dark blue-gray steel and features a lobby enclosed by a 100-foot-long, five-story serpentine glass curtain wall. The lobby looks out onto a new 17,800-square-foot plaza, formerly an enclosed ticket area. The Plaza, called Kreilsheimer Promenade, has an unusual water feature with three shallow pools underfoot. 12 feet overhead, nine 30-foot tall metal scrims, spaced 20-feet apart, span the width of the plaza on tensioned cables supported by columns in both the lobby and outdoors. The scrims were designed by New York artist Leni Schwendinger and are illuminated at night by multi-color light projection.

The Civic Auditorium, Schack Young & Myers, 1928.

27) MERCER ARTS ARENA
(Civic Arena)
1928, Schack Young & Myers; renovation, 1962, Kirk Wallace McKinley & Associates
East of Marion Oliver McCaw Hall

The Civic Arena was originally constructed in 1928 as part of the civic center complex, which included the Civic Auditorium (McCaw Hall) and the Civic Ballfield (Memorial Stadium). The building housed an ice arena, which was home to several hockey teams. The arena served as performance space for the 1962 World's Fair and was given the same beige brick veneer treatment as the other buildings along Mercer Street. Mercer Arts Arena became the temporary home of the Seattle Opera and Pacific Northwest Ballet during the Opera House renovation. The arena closed in 2003; its future use is yet to be determined.

28) SEATTLE HIGH SCHOOL MEMORIAL STADIUM
1947, George W. Stoddard
South of Mercer Arts Arena

Memorial Stadium was constructed on the site of the Civic Ballfield. The 12,000-seat stadium, though owned by the Seattle School District and not a part of the Seattle Center complex, was the site of opening ceremonies for the 1962 World's Fair and a water-skiing performance. The Stadium was named Memorial Stadium to honor Seattle high school students who died in World War II. On the east side of the stadium, a concrete memorial wall designed by Garfield High School student Marianne Hanson bears the names of the fallen. The memorial wall was dedicated in 1950.

29) CENTER HOUSE
(National Guard Armory/Food Circus)
1939, Floyd Naramore and A.M. Young; renovation, 1962, Durham Anderson & Freed; renovation, 1994, The Callison Partnership and Van Horne & Van Horne
Southwest of Memorial Stadium

This four-story reinforced concrete and brick infill structure was built as a National Guard Armory in 1939. The Streamline Moderne design includes rounded corners, a horizontal emphasis with banded aluminum windows and entrances flanked by curved walls. On the primary northern façade, the projecting entrance features two brick towers and monumental concrete eagles framing double glass doors with aluminum trim. The north lobby and staircase still reflect the original Moderne style. During the 1962 World's Fair, the building was converted to house the Food Circus. It was later renamed Center House. The 1994 renovation included expansion of the Seattle Children's Museum, located in the atrium space of the Center House.

30) THE REEDS
2002, John Fleming
Northeast of Center House

The Reeds, designed by local architect and artist John Fleming, consists of 110 30-foot high laminated steel reeds. Meant to suggest the motion of blades of grass, the reeds are thicker at the bottom so that they sway gently in the breeze. The art installation lines the pedestrian corridor and separates it from the Memorial Stadium parking lot.

31) SEATTLE MONORAIL
1962, Alweg (Cologne, Germany)
South of The Reeds

Built for the 1962 World's Fair as a vision of the future of urban mass transit, the Seattle Monorail was the first full-scale commercial Alweg monorail system. The two trains travel their 1.2-mile line between Seattle Center and Westlake Center (see Retail tour) on pre-stressed concrete beam ways built on T-pylons spaced 85-feet apart. A futuristic terminal and modern office building (now Fun Forest offices) were designed by Adrian Wilson & Associates, but have undergone several alterations.

32) EXPERIENCE MUSIC PROJECT
2000, Frank O. Gehry Associates (Santa Monica, CA)
and LMN Architects; renovation, 2004, Miller/Hull
Partnership
325 Fifth Avenue N.

Financed by Microsoft co-founder Paul Allen to honor the Pacific Northwest rock-and-roll legacy, the vibrant colors and free forms of the Experience Music Project (EMP) were inspired conceptually by the distorted sounds of the music of Seattle rock legend Jimi Hendrix, and formally by the arrangement of pieces of cut-up electric guitars. The exterior skin is made up of stainless steel and painted aluminum shingles. Each shingle was cut and bent into its unique shape and placed onto a larger panel. Over 3,000 panels containing a total of 21,000 shingles were precisely fitted to the design using CATIA, a three-dimensional computer program developed for the design of Mirage fighter jets. The EMP contains rock-and-roll memorabilia and interactive displays that allow visitors to create music and experience the studio environment. The building was renovated in 2004 to replace the "Artist's Journey" attraction with the Science Fiction Museum and Hall of Fame.

GLOSSARY
OF ARCHITECTURAL TERMS

Abacus: The flat slab forming the top of a column capital.

Acanthus: A common plant of the Mediterranean, the large-toothed leaves of which form the characteristic decoration on Corinthian and Composite capitals; also appears on friezes, panels, and modillions

Apse: A semicircular or polygonal projection of a building, esp. used at the sanctuary end of a church.

Arcade: A series of arches supported by pillars or columns; also, a roofed passageway or lane, especially one with shops on one or both sides.

Arch: A curved or pointed structural member which is supported at the sides or ends. Arches vary in shape from the horizontal flat arch to pointed arches. An arch sometimes consists of wedge-shaped blocks called voussoirs.

Architrave: The lowest division of an entablature, resting directly on the column capitals and supporting the frieze.

Art Deco: The term Art Deco comes from the 1925 Paris Exposition Internationale des Arts Décoratifs Industriels et Modernes, which celebrated life in the modern world. Art Deco ornamentation consists largely of low relief geometrical designs, often in the form of parallel straight lines, zigzags, chevrons and stylized floral motifs. Art Deco was essentially a style of decoration and was applied to jewelry, clothing, furniture and buildings. Industrial designers created Art Deco motifs for their streamlined cars, trains and kitchen appliances. Practitioners of the style attempted to describe the sleekness they thought expressive of the machine age. In the 1920s, setback ordinances were passed in many major cities (1923 in Seattle): upper stories of a tall building were to be stepped back from the lower stories to allow more light to reach the street. Art Deco buildings applied the setback ordinance, making it a common feature of their form.

Art Moderne: An architectural style found principally in buildings constructed in the 1930s following the earlier Art Deco. The Art Moderne style has a distinctive streamlined look. The streamlined effect is often emphasized by the use of curved window glass that wraps around corners. Sometimes Art Moderne is identified with Art Deco. Although somewhat different in overall appearance, both styles share stripped-down forms and geometric ornamentation. The streamlined industrial design of ships, airplanes, and automobiles influenced the Art Moderne style. The smooth surfaces, curved corners, and horizontal emphasis of the Art Moderne style give the feeling of aerodynamics. Also called *Streamline Moderne*.

Balconette: A pseudo-balcony; a small window balcony.

Balcony: An elevated platform, typically enclosed by a railing or parapet, projecting from a wall of a building.

Baluster: A pillar or column supporting a handrail or coping, a series of such being called a balustrade.

Balustrade: A railing with supporting balusters, popular from the Renaissance onward. Found in derivatives of Classical Greek and Roman architecture.

Banding: Horizontal subdivisions of a column or wall often using a change in profile or change in materials.

Barrel vault: A straight, continuous arched vault or ceiling, either semicircular or semi-elliptical in profile.

Base: The lowest part of a structure.

Basilica: The form of the early Christian church; a central high nave with clerestory, lower aisles along the sides only, with a semicircular apse at the end, often preceded by a vestibule (narthex) and atrium.

Bay: A part of a building marked off by vertical elements, such as columns or pilasters; sometimes relating to the structural frame, i.e. structural bays.

Beaux Arts style: Generally, the term "Beaux Arts" refers to a very rich, lavish and heavily ornamented classical style. Beaux Arts style was influential in the US as many of the leading late nineteenth-century architects had been trained at the Ecole des Beaux Arts in Paris. Beaux Arts encompasses the American Renaissance period from about 1890 to 1920 and the French Renaissance, Italian Renaissance, and Neoclassical Revivals.

Bell: The underlying part of a foliated column capital, as in the Corinthian and Composite orders.

Belt course: A molding or projecting course running horizontally along the face of a building; also called a *stringcourse*.

Blindstory: A level of a building having no exterior windows.

Bracket: A projection from a vertical surface providing structural support or decoration under cornices, balconies, or any other overhanging element; prior to 1940, often in the shape of scrolls or modillions. In Northwest regional Modernism, brackets are sometimes used to support roof overhangs or balconies.

Brutalism: A later movement in modern architecture (1950s-1970s), reflecting the influence of the work of Le Corbusier after 1945, and emphasizing massive forms and raw surfaces, particularly of concrete.

Byzantine architecture: The architecture of the later Roman Empire, centered in Constantinople (now Istanbul), which influenced church architecture for centuries. Byzantine churches were characterized by shallow domes, round arches and masonry construction. Byzantine church interiors featured elaborate glass mosaics, frescos and marble facing.

Caisson: In engineering, a chamber used in the construction of foundations in or near a body of water or on unstable ground. The caisson is typically a cylinder or box, open at the top and bottom, of size and shape to suit the projected foundation and with a cutting edge around the bottom. It is sunk by its own weight and by excavation, and then filled with concrete.

Capital: The head or crowning feature of a column or pilaster.

Cartouche: A panel or tablet, often round or oval in shape, usually for an inscription of a coat of arms, date or initial but sometimes purely decorative.

Chicago window: A tripartite window composed of a wide fixed pane flanked by narrow, double hung, operable windows.

Cladding: The protective covering on the exterior of a building, typically distinct from structure. Buildings with structural frames have some kind of cladding providing enclosure and weather protection.

Classical Revival: An early twentieth-century architectural movement based on the use of Roman and Greek forms.

Clerestory: An upper portion of a wall having a row of windows, which admit daylight to the interior below.

Clustered column: A number of columns grouped together and physically connected so they act as a single structural or decorative element.

Colonnade: A series of regularly-spaced columns supporting arches or an entablature and often one side of a roof.

Column: A supporting pillar; in classical architecture, typically consists of a base, a shaft and a capital; in modern architecture, columns are usually found without decorative features—for example, the steel columns in a high-rise building.

Composite: The order of classical architecture characterized by columns on which the Corinthian order capital is modified by the Ionic order, having the larger Ionic volutes set diagonally on a bell decorated with acanthus leaves. The order originated in Roman antiquity.

Coping: A protective or finishing cap or course that is applied to an exterior wall of a building to shed water.

Corbel: An arrangement of bricks or stones in which each course extends farther out from the wall than the course below, often supporting a cornice or overhanging element.

Corbel table: A portion of projecting wall or masonry strip (stringcourse) supported by a range of corbels.

Corinthian: The most ornate order of classical architecture characterized by slender fluted columns having bell-shaped capitals ornamented with acanthus leaves, thin volutes and an abacus with concave sides. One of the three orders of Greek architecture.

Cornerstone: A stone prominently situated near the base of a corner in a building, displaying information recording the dedicatory ceremonies; in some instances containing a vault in which contemporary memorabilia are preserved.

Cornice: Any crowning projection.

Course: A continuous row or layer of stone, tile, brick, etc., in a wall.

Cupola: A small dome on a circular or polygonal base, crowning a roof or turret.

Curtain wall: An exterior wall, often of limited strength, supported by the structural frame of a building typically supporting only its own weight and wind resistance.

Dentil: A small rectangular block (a tooth-like cube) used in a series forming a molding, often under a cornice.

Dome: A convex roof. Domes are categorized according of the shape of both the base and the section through the center of the dome. The base may be circular, square or polygonal depending on the plan of the drum (the walls on which the dome rests). The section of a dome may be the same shape as any arch.

Doric: The oldest and simplest order of classical Greek architecture characterized by fluted columns and capitals having a cushion-like echinus surmounted by a thin square abacus.

Dormer: A projection from a sloping roof, most often for a window; dormer tops include hipped, gabled, arched and similar forms.

Echinus: The prominent rounded molding supporting the abacus of a Doric or Tuscan capital.

Ecole des Beaux Arts: A School of arts founded in Paris in 1648 for developed studies in architecture, drawing, painting, sculpture, engraving, modeling, and gem cutting. The Ecole curriculum focused on classical arts – Greek and Roman architecture and studying and imitating the Great Masters.

Egg-and-dart: A decorative molding carved with a series of alternating rounded ovals and arrowheads.

Engaged: Partially attached to a wall, having the appearance of being bonded to the wall (e.g., a tower or column).

Entablature: The horizontal section of a classical structure that rests on columns, typically made up of a cornice, frieze and architrave.

Façade: The exterior face of a building that is the architectural front; the primary façade is usually street-facing.

Finial: An ornament, usually pointed, on top of the peak of an arch or arched structure, roofline or gable.

Flat arch: An arch with a horizontal intrados and radiating voussoirs.

Fluting: Shallow vertical grooves on the shaft of a column or pilaster.

Foundation: The lowest structural division of a building, usually of concrete or stone and partly or wholly below the surface of the ground.

Foil: A lobe or leaf-shaped curve formed between cusps inside an arch or circle.

Fret: A decorative design consisting of a repeated geometric pattern and contained within a border or band. See also *meander*.

Frieze: A panel below the upper molding or cornice of a wall or entablature, often decorated.

Gable: The portion of an exterior wall immediately under the end of a pitched roof, generally of a triangular shape matching the slope of the roof.

Gabled roof: A pitched roof having a gable at one or both ends.

Garland: A string of ribbons, flowers, fruit or foliage draped between two supports; also called a *swag*.

Georgian/Georgian Revival: Named after the reigns of the three King

Georges (1714-1820), the Georgian style was dominant in England and the American colonies from 1714-1776. The Georgian Revival style was popular in the United States from 1900-1940. The features of Georgian/ Georgian Revival may be generally described as symmetrical composition enriched with classical detail. Georgian buildings have hipped or gabled roofs, sometimes with a cupola, and dormers are a common feature. Ornamentation occurs around the door and at the cornice.

Glazed: Fitted or covered with glass.

Gothic/Gothic Revival: Gothic architecture was dominant in France and the western half of Europe in the twelfth through the middle of the sixteenth centuries. The Gothic Revival style was popular in the United States from 1830-1860. Characteristics may include a progressive lightening and heightening of structure, flying buttresses and pointed arches.

High-rise: A building with a relatively large number of stories (10-15), equipped with a passenger elevator.

Hipped roof: A roof with four sloped sides on a rectangular building, and six sloped sides on a hexagonal building.

International Style: A broad term often applied to Modern architecture of the 1920s to the 1950s, and reflecting the "International" (i.e. non-regional) character then thought to be typical of Modernism. International Style buildings often emphasize thin, planar elements, minimal detail, functional planning and modern materials. Many early International Style buildings were white.

Intrados: The inner curve of an arch.

Ionic: An order of classical Greek architecture characterized by fluted columns and prominent volutes on the capitals.

Jacobean/Jacobean Revival: Jacobean style is an early phase of English Renaissance architecture and decoration; refers to architecture during the reign of James I (1603-25) in Britain. In the early twentieth century, there was a revival of Jacobean style architecture, which was characterized by masonry or stone walls and stone trim, restrained Classical ornamentation, rooflines consisting of peaked or stepped gables and dormers, tall chimney stacks and bay windows.

Keystone: The central stone in the curve of an arch or vault; the central voussoir of an arch.

LEED: The Leadership in Energy and Environmental Design (LEED) Green Building Rating System™ is the nationally accepted benchmark for the design, construction, and operation of high performance green buildings. The rating system was launched in 1995. LEED promotes a whole-building approach to sustainability by recognizing performance in five key areas of human and environmental health: sustainable site development, water savings, energy efficiency, materials selection, and indoor environmental quality *(source: The United States Green Building Council. www.usgbc.org).*

Loft: A large, unpartitioned upper floor of a warehouse or factory building. Lofts are sometimes converted for use as living quarters or artist's studio and exhibition space.

Loggia: A colonnaded or arcaded space built into a building but open to the outdoors on one side, often at an upper story, sometimes overlooking a courtyard.

Low-rise: A building having 1-3 stories, often without a passenger elevator.

Mansard roof: A roof with two slopes, the lower almost vertical to allow extra space for the attic rooms. The lower roof can have a straight, convex or concave shape. The form is named for French Renaissance architect François Mansart (1598-1666).

Masonry: Includes all stone products, all brick products and all concrete block units.

Meander: a running ornament consisting of a fret with many involved turnings and an intricate variety of designs.

Medallion: An ornamental plaque on which an object in relief is represented.

Mezzanine: A low or partial story between two main stories of a building that projects as a balcony, esp. when the low story and the one beneath it form part of one composition.

Mid-rise: A building having a moderate number of stories (usually 4-9), equipped with one or more passenger elevators.

Modernism: A twentieth-century architectural style having a conscious lack of ornamentation and an emphasis on function and often structural expression. Modern architecture is frequently characterized by use of new technology such as expansive glazing or glass curtain walls.

Modillion: An ornamental bracket used in series to support the underside of a cornice.

Module: Standardized, often interchangeable components used in assembling units of various size or function.

Modular design: Planning and design using prefabricated modules and correlating the dimensions of the structure and the unit size of its components for ease of construction, flexible spatial arrangement and flexible use.

Molding: A decorative strip used for ornamentation or finishing.

Mosaic: A pattern, design or representational picture consisting of small pieces of stone, tile, glass or enamel inlaid into a cement or plaster matrix.

Mullion: A vertical or horizontal member between the lights of a window or door.

Multifoil: Having more than five foils, lobes or articulated divisions.

Nave: The central or principal part of a church interior, typically flanked by aisles.

Neoclassical: An architectural movement based on the use of Roman and Greek forms popular during the late eighteenth-century and early nineteenth-century. Neoclassical buildings typically have porticos of white classical columns, pediments and dormer windows.

Ogee arch: An arch consisting of two opposed ogee curves (made up of a convex and concave curve) meeting in a point at the top.

Palladian: Of or characteristic of the architectural style or principles of Italian Renaissance architect Andrea Palladio (1508-1580), most commonly related to rural Italian villas characterized by symmetry and central pavilions flanked by lower, horizontal wings.

Parapet: A low, protective wall that rises from the edge of a balcony, terrace or roof.

Pavilion: A prominent portion of a façade, usually central or terminal, identified by projection, height, and special roof forms.

Pebble dash: Flat stucco embedded with pebbles for a textured effect.

Pediment: A wide, low-pitched gable surmounting a portico, colonnade door or window; sometimes arched or divided at the peak, as in a broken pediment.

Pergola: A structure of parallel colonnades supporting an open roof of beams and crossing rafters; usually a garden structure with trellises for training plants and vines.

Pilaster: A shallow engaged column, often rectangular, projecting slightly from a wall, often treated as a column having a capital and base, sometimes used to frame bays or doorways.

Portico: A roofed porch supported on at least one side by columns, typically leading to the entrance of a building.

Postmodernism: A movement in architecture that emerged in 1970s and dominated the field through the 1980s. Postmodernism rejected the stripped-down aesthetic and functionalism of the Modern movement in favor of applied decoration and symbolism.

Quoin: The dressed stones at the corners of buildings, often laid so their faces are alternately large and small.

Renaissance/Renaissance Revival: A style characterized by a formalism found in the French or Italian Renaissance style (fifteenth-century to seventeenth-century), initially characterized by the use of classical orders, round arches, and symmetrical composition. Renaissance Revival style occurred from 1840-1890 in the United States and Europe, which was characterized by a studied formalism found in the Renaissance style. A later revival of Renaissance-inspired design in the United States occurred from about 1890-1930.

Rib: A curved structural member supporting any curved shape or panel; a molding which projects from the surface and separates roof or ceiling panels.

Rib vault: A vault supported by or decorated with arched diagonal ribs.

Romanesque: The name given Western European architecture of the later eleventh-century to the twelfth-century because certain architectural elements, particularly the round arch, resembled those of ancient Roman architecture; the term serves to distinguish Romanesque from Gothic buildings. Characteristics of Romanesque architecture include heavy articulated masonry construction with narrow openings, the use of the round arch and barrel vault, wall arcade or buttress, cylindrical apse and chapels and the introduction of central and western square, round or polygonal towers.

Richardsonian Romanesque: The Romanesque style as interpreted by American architect Henry Hobson Richardson (1838-1886) in the 1870s and 1880s, which became a uniquely American style. Stylistic features include heavy masonry, deep window reveals, cavernous door openings and short, often clustered, robust columns.

Rose window: The round window with tracery, often resembling a flower, frequently found on the facades of Gothic churches.

Rosette: Any rose-shaped ornament, usually round and sometimes divided into petals.

Rotunda: A round, domed building; or a large circular space in a round building or round portion of a building.

Round arch: A semicircular arch having a continuously curved intrados.

Roundel: A small circular window or panel.

Rustication: Masonry cut in large blocks and having rough, irregular surfaces and deep or beveled mortar joints; used to give a bold, heavy appearance often to the lower part of an exterior wall, or to frame doors or windows.

Scrim: Coarse fiberglass or metal mesh.

Scroll: An ornament consisting of a spirally wound band.

Segmental arch: A circular arch in which the intrados is less than a semicircle.

Shed roof/Shed ceiling: A roof or ceiling shape having only one sloping plane.

Skeleton construction: A construction system using a framework of columns and beams to transfer building loads to the foundation.

Skyscraper: An exceptionally tall building (typically over 15 stories), supported by a concrete or steel frame, from which walls are suspended.

Spandrel: In a multistory building, the space between the top of the window in one story and the sill of the window in the story above; in classical architecture, the triangular-shaped area above two adjoining arches.

Spandrel panel: In a multistory building, a wall panel filling the space between the top of the window in one story and the sill of the window in the story above.

Streamline Moderne: see *Art Moderne*.

Stringcourse: A molding or projecting course running horizontally along the face of a building; also called a belt course.

Sullivanesque: Architecture of or characteristic of the work of American architect Louis Sullivan (1856-1924). Sullivan designed with the principle of reconciling the world of nature with science and technology. "Form ever follows function" was his famous dictum. His buildings were detailed with lush, yet subdued organic ornamentation that was contained within the architectural elements; the idea being that ornamentation be integral to the building itself, rather than merely applied. Decorative characteristics include an intricate weaving of linear and geometric forms with stylized foliage in a symmetrical pattern.

Swag: A string of ribbons, flowers, fruit or foliage draped between two supports; also called a *garland*.

Terrace: An open area connected to a building that may serve as an outdoor living area.

Terra-cotta: Literally, "baked earth"; a hard, fired clay used for cladding and ornamenting buildings that can be molded into any number of shapes. It may be used unglazed or glazed in multiple colors.

Tourelle: A small round tower, often decorative and corbelling out from the corner of a building.

Tracery: An arrangement of intersecting rib work, usually in the upper part of a Gothic window, forming a pierced pattern.

Trefoil: A three-lobed circle or arch formed by cusping; windows or arches having three foils, lobes or articulated divisions.

Trompe l'oeil: A finely detailed image, usually a drawing or painting, meant to create the illusion of a three-dimensional spatial quality.

Truss: A rigid framework, as of wooden or steel beams, designed to support a structure such as a roof or floor.

Turret: An engaged tower, usually round or faceted, that is part of a larger building.

Tuscan: The order of classical Roman architecture characterized by unfluted columns, a plain base and capital, and no decoration other than moldings.

Urn: A vase, which may be of varying size and shape, usually having a footed base or pedestal.

Vault: An arch forming the supporting structure of a roof or ceiling.

Veneer: A nonstructural facing attached to an exterior or interior wall as finish or insulation.

Victorian: "Victorian" refers to the period of the reign of England's Queen Victoria (1837-1901); in American architecture it generally refers to American architecture of the last half of the nineteenth century, which was characterized by a high degree of inventiveness. The term as applied to architecture does not refer to a particular style, but may instead be said to embody an approach to architectural design which was often freely inventive, combining elements of different styles in the period—Second Empire, Gothic Revival, Italianate and the like. Victorian compositional strategies for Seattle's urban buildings often included façades divided by pilasters and stringcourses. Irregularity was frequently present, although some buildings in the period display symmetry as well.

Volute: A scroll-like ornament found on the column capitals of the Ionic, Corinthian and Composite orders.

Voussoirs: The wedge-shaped blocks forming the curved parts of an arch or vault.

X-bracing: A pair of transverse braces used for stabilizing a structural frame against lateral forces such as earthquakes and wind.

SOURCES
AND SUGGESTED READINGS

Aldredge et al. *Impressions of Imagination: Terra Cotta Seattle*. Seattle: Allied Arts of Seattle, 1986

Andrews, Mildred Tanner, ed. *Pioneer Square: Seattle's Oldest Neighborhood*. Seattle: Pioneer Square Community Association/University of Washington Press, 2005.

---------- *Woman's Place: A Guide to Seattle and King County History*. Seattle: Gemil Press, 1994.

Bagley, Clarence B. *History of Seattle from the Earliest Settlement to the Present Time.*   Chicago: S.J. Clarke Publishing Co., 1916.

---------- *History of King County, Washington* Vol. 1. Chicago: S.J. Clarke Publishing Co., 1929.

Bass, Sophie Frye. *When Seattle was a Village*. Seattle: Lowman & Hanford Co., 1947.

Berman, Richard C. *Seattle in the Twentieth Century*, Vols. 1 and 2. Seattle: Charles Press, 1991, 1992.

Buerge, David. *Seattle in the 1880s*. Seattle: Historical Society of Seattle and King County, 1986.

Burke, Edward and Elizabeth. *Seattle's Other History: Our Asian-American Heritage.*   Seattle: Profanity Hill Press, 1979.

Chew, Ron ed. *Reflections of Seattle's Chinese Americans: The First 100 Years*. Seattle: University of Washington Press and Wing Luke Asian Museum, 1994.

Crowley, Walt. *National Trust Guide Seattle*. New York: John Wiley & Sons, 1998.

---------- *Rites of Passage: A Memoir of Seattle in the Sixties*. Seattle: University of Washington Press, 1995.

de Barrows, Paul. *Jackson Street After Hours: The Roots of Jazz in Seattle*. Seattle: Sasquatch Books, 1994.

Dorpat, Paul. *Seattle Now & Then* Vols. 1, 2 and 3. Seattle: Tartu Press, 1984, 1988, 1989.

Duncan, Don. *Meet Me at the Center: The Story of Seattle Center from the Beginnings to the 1962 Seattle World's Fair to the 21st Century*. Seattle: Seattle Center Foundation, 1992.

Findlay, John M. *Magic Lands: Western Cityscapes and American Culture After 1940.* Los Angeles: University of California Press, 1992.

Hines, Neal O. *Denny's Knoll: A History of the Metropolitan Tract of the University of   Washington.* Seattle: University of Washington Press, 1980.

Kirk, Ruth and Alexander, Carmela. *Exploring Washington's Past: A Road Guide to History.* Seattle: University of Washington Press, 1990, 1995.

Kreisman, Lawrence. *Made to Last: Historic Preservation in Seattle and King County.* Seattle: Historic Seattle Preservation Foundation/University of Washington Press, 1999.

----------- *Art Deco Seattle.* Seattle: Allied Arts of Seattle, 1979.

----------- *The Stimson Legacy: Architecture in the Urban West.* Seattle: Willows Press/University of Washington Press, 1992.

Mighetto, Lisa and Montgomery, Marcia Babcock. *Hard Drive to the Klondike: Promoting Seattle During the Gold Rush.* Seattle: University of Washington Press, 2002

Morgan, Murray and Shorett, Alice. *The Pike Place Market: People, Politics and Produce.* Seattle: Pacific Search Press, 1982.

Morgan, Murray. *Skid Road.* New York: Viking, 1951, 1962, 1982.

Nesbit, Robert C. *He Built Seattle: A Biography of Judge Thomas Burke.* Seattle: University of Washington Press, 1961.

Ochsner, Jeffrey Karl, ed. *Shaping Seattle Architecture: A Historical Guide to the Architects.* Seattle: University of Washington Press, 1994, 1998.

----------- and Andersen, Dennis. *Distant Corner: Seattle Architects and the Legacy of H.H. Richardson.* Seattle: University of Washington Press, 2003.

Pierce, J. Kingston. *Eccentric Seattle: Pillars and Pariahs Who Made the City Not Such a Boring Place After All.* Pullman, Washington: Washington State University Press, 2003.

Phelps, Myra. *Public Works in Seattle: A Narrative History of the Engineering Department 1875-1975.* Seattle: City of Seattle, 1978.

Rupp, James and Randlett, Mary. *Art in Seattle's Public Places: An Illustrated Guide.* Seattle: University of Washington Press, 1992.

Sale, Roger. *Seattle Past to Present: An Interpretive History of the Foremost City of the Pacific Northwest.* Seattle: University of Washington Press, 1976, 1982, 1989.

----------- *Seeing Seattle.* Seattle: University of Washington Press, 1994.

Schwantes, Carlos. *Railroad Signatures Across the Pacific Northwest.* Seattle: University of Washington Press, 1993.

Seattle Department of Community Development. *A Detailed History of the Corner Market Building & Environs.* Seattle: Department of Community Development, 1975.

Shamash, Diane and Huss, Steven, ed. *A Field Guide to Seattle's Public Art.* Seattle: Seattle Arts Commission, 1991.

Speidel, Bill. *Sons of the Profits: The Seattle Story, 1851-1901.* Seattle: Nettle Creek Publishing, 1967.

Stein, Alan J. *The Olympic: The Story of Seattle's Landmark Hotel since 1924.* Seattle: History Link/University of Washington Press, 2005.

Steinbrueck, Victor. *Seattle Architecture, 1850-1953.* New York: Reinhold Press, 1953.

------------ *Seattle Cityscape.* Seattle: University of Washington Press, 1962.

------------ *Seattle Cityscape #2.* Seattle: University of Washington Press, 1973.

------------ *Market Sketchbook.* Seattle: University of Washington Press, 1968, 1997.

Tobin, Caroline. *Downtown Seattle Walking Tours.* Seattle: City of Seattle, 1985.

------------ et al. *Seattle's Waterfront: the Walker's Guide to the History of Elliott Bay.* Seattle: Waterfront Awareness, 1981.

Warren, James. *The Day Seattle Burned, June 6, 1889.* Seattle: Museum of History and Industry, 1989.

------------ *The War Years: A Chronicle of Washington State in World War II.* Seattle: History Link/University of Washington Press, 2000.

Woodbridge, Sally and Montgomery, Roger. *A Guide to Architecture in Washington State.* Seattle: University of Washington Press, 1980.

INTERNET SOURCES:

ARCADE:
www.arcadejournal.com

Belltown:
www.belltown.org

DoCoMoMo WeWa (Documentation and Conservation of the Modern Movement in Western Washington):
www.docomomo-wewa.org

Growing Vine Street:
www.growingvinestreet.org

History Link:
www.historylink.org

Historic Seattle:
www.historicseattle.org

Pike Place Market:
www.pikeplacemarket.org

Pioneer Square:
www.pioneersquare.org

Port of Seattle:
www.portseattle.org

Puget Sound Business Journal:
www.bizjournals.com/seattle

Seattle Architecture Foundation:
www.seattlearchitecture.org

Seattle Center:
www.seattlecenter.com

Seattle Chinatown-International District:
www.internationaldistrict.org

Seattle Daily Journal of Commerce:
www.djc.com

Seattle Department of Neighborhoods:
www.seattle.gov/neighborhoods/preservation/historicresources.htm

Seattle Parks and Recreation:
www.seattle.gov/parks/

Seattle Post Intelligencer
www.seattlepi.nwsource.com

Seattle Times:
www.seattletimes.nwsource.com

Washington State Department of Archaeology and Historic Preservation:
www.dahp.wa.gov

EXPANDED BIBLIOGRAPHY

GENERAL SOURCES:

Aldredge et al. *Impressions of Imagination: Terra Cotta Seattle.* Seattle: Allied Arts of Seattle, 1986

Andrews, Mildred Tanner, ed. *Pioneer Square: Seattle's Oldest Neighborhood.* Seattle: Pioneer Square Community Association/University of Washington Press, 2005.

---------- *Woman's Place: A Guide to Seattle and King County History.* Seattle: Gemil Press, 1994.

Bagley, Clarence B. *History of Seattle from the Earliest Settlement to the Present Time.* Chicago: S.J. Clarke Publishing Co., 1916.

---------- *History of King County, Washington* Vol. 1. Chicago: S.J. Clarke Publishing Co., 1929.

Bass, Sophie Frye. *When Seattle was a Village.* Seattle: Lowman & Hanford Co., 1947.

Berman, Richard C. *Seattle in the Twentieth Century,* Vols. 1 and 2. Seattle: Charles Press, 1991, 1992.

Buerge, David. *Seattle in the 1880s.* Seattle: Historical Society of Seattle and King County, 1986.

Chew, Ron ed. *Reflections of Seattle's Chinese Americans: The First 100 Years.* Seattle: University of Washington Press and Wing Luke Asian Museum, 1994.

City of Seattle. *Decennial Population, City of Seattle 1900-2000.* <www.seattle.gov/dpd/stellent/groups/pan/@pan/documents/web_informational/dpds_006755.pdf>

Crowley, Walt. *National Trust Guide Seattle.* New York: John Wiley & Sons, 1998.

---------- *Rites of Passage: A Memoir of Seattle in the Sixties.* Seattle: University of Washington Press, 1995.

---------- and McRoberts, Patrick. *Seattle Neighborhoods: Downtown Seattle Thumbnail History.* 1999. History Link Essay # 1041 <www.historylink.org>

de Barrows, Paul. *Jackson Street After Hours: The Roots of Jazz in Seattle.* Seattle: Sasquatch Books, 1994.

Dorpat, Paul. *Seattle Now & Then* Vols. 1, 2 and 3. Seattle: Tartu Press, 1984, 1988, 1989.

Duncan, Don. *Meet Me at the Center: The Story of Seattle Center from the Beginnings to the 1962 Seattle World's Fair to the 21st Century.* Seattle: Seattle Center Foundation, 1992.

Enlow, Clair. "Lofty Ambitions: Seattle's High-rise Builders." *Seattle Daily Journal of Commerce.* April 24, 1997. <www.djc.com/special/const97>

Erickson, Steve. *Viewpoints: Modern to Postmodern.* Unpublished tour script. Seattle Architecture Foundation, 2001.

---------- and Elaine Gagnon. *Modernism.* Unpublished tour script. Seattle Architecture Foundation, 2003.

Everett, Randy et al. *Concrete, Glass, Steel and Egos: Skyscrapers.* Unpublished tour script. Seattle Architecture Foundation, 2005.

Findlay, John M. *Magic Lands: Western Cityscapes and American Culture After 1940.* Los Angeles: University of California Press, 1992.

Fuller, Gary and Jost, Richard. *Ornamentation: More than Just a Pretty Face.* Unpublished tour script. Seattle Architecture Foundation, 2005.

Gantenbein, Douglas. "Seattle CAPs Downtown Growth." *Architectural Record.* July 1989, Vol. 177, Iss. 8. p. 51.

Hines, Neal O. *Denny's Knoll: A History of the Metropolitan Tract of the University of Washington.* Seattle: University of Washington Press, 1980.

Kirk, Ruth and Alexander, Carmela. *Exploring Washington's Past: A Road Guide to History.* Seattle: University of Washington Press, 1990, 1995.

Kreisman, Lawrence. *Made to Last: Historic Preservation in Seattle and King County.* Seattle: Historic Seattle Preservation Foundation/University of Washington Press, 1999.

----------- *Art Deco Seattle.* Seattle: Allied Arts of Seattle, 1979.

----------- *The Stimson Legacy: Architecture in the Urban West.* Seattle: Willows Press/University of Washington Press, 1992.

----------- *The Roaring 20s, Northwest Style: Art Deco.* Unpublished tour script. Seattle Architecture Foundation, 2001.
----------- and Jost, Richard. *Historic Theaters.* Unpublished tour script. Seattle Architecture Foundation, 1998.

----------- and Erickson, Steve. *Houses of Worship Tour.* Unpublished tour script. Seattle Architecture Foundation, 1996.

Kueter, Vince. "150 Years: Seattle By and By." *The Seattle Times.* September 16, 2001. p. B2.

Lamm, Greg. "Growth Management Act Tames Sprawl: Growth Law Steers

Housing." *Puget Sound Business Journal.* March 24, 2006. <www.seattle.bizjournals.com/seattle/stories>

Lange, Greg. *Arsonist Kills 20 and injures 10 at the Ozark Hotel Fire in Seattle on March 20, 1970.* 1999. History Link Essay # 698. <www.historylink.org>

----------- *Northern Pacific's Orphan Road.* 2000. History Link Essay # 2286. <www.historylink.org>

Mighetto, Lisa and Montgomery, Marcia Babcock. *Hard Drive to the Klondike: Promoting Seattle During the Gold Rush.* Seattle: University of Washington Press, 2002

Morgan, Murray. *Skid Road.* New York: Viking, 1951, 1962, 1982.

Morse, Jason and Michaelsen, Guy. *Outside the Box: Urban Open Spaces in Downtown Seattle.* Unpublished tour script. Seattle Architecture Foundation, 2004.

Nesbit, Robert C. *He Built Seattle: A Biography of Judge Thomas Burke.* Seattle: University of Washington Press, 1961.

Ochsner, Jeffrey Karl, ed. *Shaping Seattle Architecture: A Historical Guide to the Architects.* Seattle: University of Washington Press, 1994, 1998.

----------- and Andersen, Dennis. *Distant Corner: Seattle Architects and the Legacy of H.H. Richardson.* Seattle: University of Washington Press, 2003.

Pierce, J. Kingston. *Eccentric Seattle: Pillars and Pariahs Who Made the City Not Such a Boring Place After All.* Pullman, Washington: Washington State University Press, 2003.

Phelps, Myra. *Public Works in Seattle: A Narrative History of the Engineering Department 1875-1975.* Seattle: City of Seattle, 1978.

Purser, Robert S. *Graham, Gould, Bittman Tour.* Unpublished tour script. Seattle Architecture Foundation, 2002.
Raymond, Aaron and Montgomery, Julie. *Form Follows Function: Evolving Styles-Contemporary Architecture in Downtown Seattle.* Unpublished tour script. Seattle Architecture Foundation, 2005.

Rupp, James and Randlett, Mary. *Art in Seattle's Public Places: An Illustrated Guide.* Seattle: University of Washington Press, 1992.

Sale, Roger. *Seattle Past to Present: An Interpretive History of the Foremost City of the Pacific Northwest.* Seattle: University of Washington Press, 1976, 1982, 1989.

----------- *Seeing Seattle.* Seattle: University of Washington Press, 1994.

Schwantes, Carlos. *Railroad Signatures Across the Pacific Northwest.* Seattle: University of Washington Press, 1993.

Seattle Daily Journal of Commerce staff reporter. "What Else is Going On? A List of Major Renovation Projects Under Way in the Seattle Area." *Seattle Daily Journal of Commerce*. September 30, 1999.

Shamash, Diane and Huss, Steven, ed. *A Field Guide to Seattle's Public Art*. Seattle: Seattle Arts Commission, 1991.

Speidel, Bill. *Sons of the Profits: The Seattle Story, 1851-1901*. Seattle: Nettle Creek Publishing, 1967.

Stein, Alan J. *The Olympic: The Story of Seattle's Landmark Hotel since 1924*. Seattle: History Link/University of Washington Press, 2005.

Steinbrueck, Victor. *Seattle Cityscape*. Seattle: University of Washington Press, 1962.

------------ *Market Sketchbook*. Seattle: University of Washington Press, 1968, 1997.

Tobin, Caroline. *Downtown Seattle Walking Tours*. Seattle: City of Seattle, 1985.

Walsh, Wendi. *Dynamic Downtown*. Unpublished tour script. Seattle Architecture Foundation, 2004.

Warren, James. *The War Years: A Chronicle of Washington State in World War II*. Seattle: History Link/University of Washington Press, 2000.

Whyte, William H. *The Social Life of Small Urban Spaces*. Washington, D.C.: Conservation Foundation, 1980.

Wilma, David and Crowley, Walt. *Citizen's Alternative Plan wins ant the polls on May 16, 1989*. 2001. History Link Essay #3539 <www.historylink.org>

------------ *Native Americans Attack Seattle on January 26, 1856*. 2003. History Link Essay # 5208. <www.historylink.org>

 Woodbridge, Sally and Montgomery, Roger. *A Guide to Architecture in Washington State*. Seattle: University of Washington Press, 1980.

Young, Bob. "Taller Skyscrapers on the Horizon." *The Seattle Times*. March 22, 2006. p. A1.

------------ "High-rise Boom Coming to Seattle? Council Votes to Allow Taller Buildings. Developers Have Plans in Hand, Including 2 Condo Towers Near Pike Place Market." *The Seattle Times*. April 4, 2006. p. B1.

ADDITIONAL SOURCES BY CHAPTER:

PIONEER SQUARE

Crowley, Walt. *Downtown Seattle: Pioneer Square Thumbnail History*. 2004, History Link Essay # 3392. <www.historylink.org>

Flom, Eric L. *Fire Burns Seattle's Grand Opera House on November 24, 1906.* 2000, History Link Essay # 2651. <www.historylink.org>

Hadley, Jane. "Restoring Seattle's Grand Ol' Lady: King Street Station on Track to Return to One-time Splendor." *Seattle Post-Intelligencer.* June 20, 2005. p. B1

Historic Seattle, *Cadillac Hotel.* 2003. <www.historicseattle.org/projects/cadillachotel.aspx>

Jago, Jill. "Renovations Bring Boom Times Back to Pioneer Square." *Seattle Daily Journal of Commerce.* October 12, 2000. <www.djc.com/news>

Lane, Polly. "81-year-old Hotel Remains a Pioneer: Renovation Gives Historic District its First Luxury Inn." *The Seattle Times.* July 15, 1995. p. D1

Nabbefeld, Joe. "New County Office Building to Rise Near King St. Station: Nonprofit Corporation Will Develop Parking Lot Site," *Puget Sound Business Journal.* August 1, 1997. Vol. 18, Iss. 12; p. 3.

Porter, Lynn. "Alaska Building to be a Hotel/Condo Combo." *Seattle Daily Journal of Commerce.* April 5, 2006. <www.djc.com/news>

Spanger, Pat. *Creating Public Art in the Puget Sound Area.* 2004 Eastern Washington University. <www.ewu.edu>
Seattle Department of Neighborhoods. Parcel ID 0939000080, Alaska Building. <www.seattle.gov/neighborhoods/preservation/historicresources.htm>

Seattle Department of Neighborhoods. Parcel ID 0939000130, Broderick Building. <www.seattle.gov/neighborhoods/preservation/historicresources.htm>

Seattle Department of Neighborhoods. Parcel ID 5247800695, Burke-State Building.<www.seattle.gov/neighborhoods/preservation/historicresources.htm>

Seattle Department of Neighborhoods. Parcel ID 0939000155, Butler Garage.<www.seattle.gov/neighborhoods/preservation/historicresources.htm>

Seattle Department of Neighborhoods. Parcel ID 5247800715, Cadillac Hotel.<www.seattle.gov/neighborhoods/preservation/historicresources.htm>

Seattle Department of Neighborhoods. Parcel ID 5247800980, Chin Gee Hee Building.<www.seattle.gov/neighborhoods/preservation/historicresources.htm>

Seattle Department of Neighborhoods. Parcel ID 0939000025, Collins Building.<www.seattle.gov/neighborhoods/preservation/historicresources.htm>

Seattle Department of Neighborhoods. Parcel ID 0939000100, Corona Building.<www.seattle.gov/neighborhoods/preservation/historicresources.htm>

Seattle Department of Neighborhoods. Parcel ID 5247800481, Delmar Building and State Hotel.<www.seattle.gov/neighborhoods/preservation/historicresources.htm>

Seattle Department of Neighborhoods. Parcel ID 5247800725, Fire Station # 10.<www.seattle.gov/neighborhoods/preservation/historicresources.htm>

Seattle Department of Neighborhoods. Parcel ID 5247801000, Frye Hotel. <www.seattle.gov/neighborhoods/preservation/historicresources.htm>

Seattle Department of Neighborhoods. Parcel ID 5247800320, Globe Building. <www.seattle.gov/neighborhoods/preservation/historicresources.htm>

Seattle Department of Neighborhoods. Parcel ID 5247800390, Grand Central on the Park. <www.seattle.gov/neighborhoods/preservation/historicresources.htm>

Seattle Department of Neighborhoods. Parcel ID 52478005555, Interurban Building. <www.seattle.gov/neighborhoods/preservation/historicresources.htm>

Seattle Department of Neighborhoods. Parcel ID 5247800130, J & M Hotel. <www.seattle.gov/neighborhoods/preservation/historicresources.htm>

Seattle Department of Neighborhoods. Parcel ID 5247800345, Jackson Building. <www.seattle.gov/neighborhoods/preservation/historicresources.htm>

Seattle Department of Neighborhoods. Parcel ID 7666202580, Journal Building. <www.seattle.gov/neighborhoods/preservation/historicresources.htm>

Seattle Department of Neighborhoods. Parcel ID 5247801160, King Street Station. <www.seattle.gov/neighborhoods/preservation/historicresources.htm>

Seattle Department of Neighborhoods. Parcel ID 5427800880, Longshore Union Hall. <www.seattle.gov/neighborhoods/preservation/historicresources.htm>

Seattle Department of Neighborhoods. Parcel ID 0939000120, Lowman Building. <www.seattle.gov/neighborhoods/preservation/historicresources.htm>

Seattle Department of Neighborhoods. Parcel ID 5247800180, Maud Building. <www.seattle.gov/neighborhoods/preservation/historicresources.htm>

Seattle Department of Neighborhoods. Parcel ID 5427800035, Maynard Building. <www.seattle.gov/neighborhoods/preservation/historicresources.htm>

Seattle Department of Neighborhoods. Parcel ID 5427800550, Merchant's Café. <www.seattle.gov/neighborhoods/preservation/historicresources.htm>

Seattle Department of Neighborhoods. Parcel ID 5479600000, Merrill Place Building. <www.seattle.gov/neighborhoods/preservation/historicresources.htm>

Seattle Department of Neighborhoods. Parcel ID 5247800595, Metropole Building. <www.seattle.gov/neighborhoods/preservation/historicresources.htm>

Seattle Department of Neighborhoods. Parcel ID 8591400075, Mutual Life Building. <www.seattle.gov/neighborhoods/preservation/historicresources.htm>

Seattle Department of Neighborhoods. Parcel ID 5427800695, Occidental Mall. <www.seattle.gov/neighborhoods/preservation/historicresources.htm>

Seattle Department of Neighborhoods. Parcel ID 5427800405, Occidental Park. <www.seattle.gov/neighborhoods/preservation/historicresources.htm>

Seattle Department of Neighborhoods. Parcel ID 0939000150, Pioneer Building. <www.seattle.gov/neighborhoods/preservation/historicresources.htm>

Seattle Department of Neighborhoods. Parcel ID 039000160, Pioneer Park Pergola. <www.seattle.gov/neighborhoods/preservation/historicresources.htm>

Seattle Department of Neighborhoods. Parcel ID 093900160, Pioneer Park Chief Seattle Fountain. <www.seattle.gov/neighborhoods/preservation/historicresources.htm>

Seattle Department of Neighborhoods. Parcel ID 0939000160, Pioneer Park Totem Pole. <www.seattle.gov/neighborhoods/preservation/historicresources.htm>

Seattle Department of Neighborhoods. Parcel ID 5247800005, Pioneer Square Hotel. <www.seattle.gov/neighborhoods/preservation/historicresources.htm>

Seattle Department of Neighborhoods. Parcel ID 7666202565, Polson Building. <www.seattle.gov/neighborhoods/preservation/historicresources.htm>

Seattle Department of Neighborhoods. Parcel ID 5247800046, Schwabacher Building. <www.seattle.gov/neighborhoods/preservation/historicresources.htm>

Seattle Department of Neighborhoods. Parcel ID 8591400100, Seattle Steam/Old Post Station. <www.seattle.gov/neighborhoods/preservation/historicresources.htm>
Seattle Department of Neighborhoods. Parcel ID 0939000060, Smith Tower. <www.seattle.gov/neighborhoods/preservation/historicresources.htm>

Seattle Department of Neighborhoods. Parcel ID 5247800695, State Building. <www.seattle.gov/neighborhoods/preservation/historicresources.htm>

Seattle Department of Neighborhoods. Parcel ID 5247800041, Terry Denny Building. <www.seattle.gov/neighborhoods/preservation/historicresources.htm>

Seattle Department of Neighborhoods. Parcel ID 8670450000, Traveler's/Post Mews. <www.seattle.gov/neighborhoods/preservation/historicresources.htm>

Seattle Department of Neighborhoods. Parcel ID 5247800930, Union Gospel Mission. <www.seattle.gov/neighborhoods/preservation/historicresources.htm>

Seattle Department of Neighborhoods. Parcel ID 5247800360, Union Trust Building. <www.seattle.gov/neighborhoods/preservation/historicresources.htm>

Seattle Department of Neighborhoods. Parcel ID 5247800735, Washington Shoe Building. <www.seattle.gov/neighborhoods/preservation/historicresources.htm>

Seattle Department of Neighborhoods. Parcel ID 524780055, Yesler Building. <www.seattle.gov/neighborhoods/preservation/historicresources.htm>

Seattle Parks and Recreation. *Pioneer Square Area Park Improvements: Pioneer Square Park, Occidental Park and Occidental Corridor.* 2005. <www.ci.seattle. wa.us/parks/proparks/pioneersquare.htm>

Washington State Department of Archaeology & Historic Preservation. *National Register of Historic Places Inventory Nomination Form.* DAHP ID KI00238, Hoge Building. <www.dahp.wa.gov>

Washington State Department of Archaeology & Historic Preservation. *National Register of Historic Places Inventory Nomination Form.* DAHP ID KI00625, Lyon Building. <www.dahp.wa.gov>

Washington State Department of Archaeology & Historic Preservation. *National Register of Historic Places Inventory Nomination Form.* DAHP ID KI00666, Rector Hotel. <www.dahp.wa.gov>

INTERNATIONAL DISTRICT

Asian Reporter staff. "Wing Luke Asian Museum Plans Move to Historic Building." *The Asian Reporter.* August 16, 2005. Vol.15, Iss.33; p. 12.

Burke, Edward and Elizabeth. *Seattle's Other History: Our Asian-American Heritage.*   Seattle: Profanity Hill Press, 1979.

Chansanchai, Athima. "Historic Building Getting a New Lease on Life: Once a Chinatown Anchor, Structure to House Museum." *Seattle Post-Intelligencer.* September 9, 2005. p. B1.

City of Seattle. Board of Public Works Building Permit # 8120. May 14, 1901.

Crowley, Walt. *Seattle Neighborhoods: Chinatown-International District Thumbnail History.* 1999. History Link Essay # 1058. <www.historylink.org>

-------------- *Seattle's Union Station Re-opens as Sound Transit Headquarters on October 16, 1999.* 2006. History Link Essay # 7751. <www.historylink.org>

-------------- *Anti-Chinese Activism, Seattle.* 1999. History Link Essay # 1057. <www. historylink.org>

Davila, Florangela and Mayo, Justin. "The Struggle for the Soul of the International District." *The Seattle Times.* October 14, 2000. p. A1.

Ducey, Karen. "Building Offers City History Lesson: Kong Yick Yields Treasures as it is Renovated for Asian Museum." *Seattle Post-Intelligencer.* June 21, 2006. p. B2.

Eskenazi, Stuart. "Hotel is Reminder of City's Japanese-American Past." *The Seattle Times.* June 11, 2001. p. B1.

Hai-Jew, Shalin. "Ray Chin and the Wa Sang Association Revives Rex Apartments with $2,100,000 Renovation." *Northwest Asian Weekly.* January 5, 1996. Vol. 14, Iss. 52; p. 11.

Historic Seattle. *Main Street School.* 2000. <www.historicseattle.org/projects/projectdetail>

Ho, Vanessa. "A Drive to Recapture the Spirit of Historic Japantown: Reviving a Neighborhood of the Past." *Seattle Post-Intelligencer.* February 28, 2005. p. B1.

Inter*Im. *Affordable Housing Projects.* 2006. <www.interimicda.org/affhouprojs.htm>
International Examiner staff reporter, "The Culmination of a Dream: Wing Luke Asian Museum and Northwest Asian American Theatre Open at New Site." *International Examiner.* January 21, 1987. Vol. 14, Iss. 2; p. 4.

Jago, Jill. "Seattle's Biggest Jigsaw Puzzle: Fifteen Years, a Host of Players and an Elusive Final Picture Made Opus Center." *Seattle Daily Journal of Commerce.* November 9, 2000. <www.djc.com/news>

------------- "More Than Meets the Eye at 505 Union Station." *Seattle Daily Journal of Commerce.* August 10, 2000. <www.djc.com/news>

Kang, Cecilia. "Seattle Loses Icon of Japanese Heritage: Landmark Nippon Kan Theater Now a Messenger Office." *Seattle Post-Intelligencer.* November 26, 2005. p. A1.

Kuo, Fidelius. "Kong Yick Buildings are Rich Source of History." *Northwest Asian Weekly.* August 18, 1995. Vol. 14, Iss. 32; p. 1.

Leff, Marni. "Time for a New I.D.?" *Seattle Post-Intelligencer.* July 9, 2001. p. E 1.

McIntosh, Heather. *Construction on Seattle's Oregon and Washington Station Begins in January 1910.* 1999. History Link Essay # 936. <www.historylink.org>

Mizuki, Andy. *A Brief History of the Eastern Hotel.* 2006. <www.bulosan.org/html/eastern_hotel.html>

Mulady, Kathy. "Uwajimaya's Treasures: Historic Store Anchors Area." *Seattle Post-Intelligencer.* July 19, 2001.

Nguyen, Nhien. "New Museum Design Presented to Community." *International Examiner.* December 15, 2004. Vol. 31, Iss. 24; p. 4.

Panama Hotel. *Historic Panama Hotel.* <www.panamahotel.net/history/htm>

Sasaki, Shihou. "Panama Hotel Receives National Historic Landmark Status." *North American Post.* April 26, 2006. Vol. 61, Iss. 34; p. 1.

Seattle Chinatown-International District. *Celebrating the Diverse Cultures of Asia.* <www.internationaldistrict.org/history.asp>

Seattle DCLU. Restoring a Sense of Place in Seattle's Nihonmachi: Plans for Future Development. 2004. <www.cityofseattle.net/DCLU/CityDesign/Design-Leadership/Nihonmachi/4_plans_nihonmachi.pdf>

Seattle Parks and Recreation. *Kobe Terrace.* 2006. <www.seattle.gov/parks/parkspaces/kobeterrace.htm>

Silver, Jon. "From Coal Plant to Depot to Office Complex." *Seattle Daily Journal of Commerce.* November 9, 2000. <www.djc.com/news>

Steinbrueck, Victor and Nyberg, Folke. *International District: An Inventory of Buildings and Urban Design Resources.* Seattle: Historic Seattle Preservation and Development Authority, 1975.

Tabafunda, James. "New Homes Open in Old Japantown." *Northwest Asian Weekly.* April 15, 2006. <www.nwasianweekly.com>

Tsutakawa, Mayumi. *George Tsutakawa (1910-1997).* 2001. History Link Essay # 3088. <www.historylink.org>

Vu, Carol N. "Full Speed Ahead as Uwajimaya Counts Down to Grand Opening." *Northwest Asian Weekly.* June 30, 2000. Vol. 19, Iss. 26; p. 1.

Wilma, David. *U.S. President Franklin D. Roosevelt Approves Loan for Yesler Terrace Public Housing on December 2, 1939.* 1999. History Link Essay # 2105. <www.historylink.org>

CIVIC/FINANCIAL DISTRICT

Athens, Lucia. "Seattle LEEDs the Nation in Sustainable Building: 11 City Projects Now Registered Under the System." *Seattle Daily Journal of Commerce.* July 25, 2002. <www.djc.com/news>

Barber, Mike. "Walrus Repairs on the Way: Bids are in For Restoring Bandaged Heads." *Seattle Post-Intelligencer.* October 12, 1996. p. A1

Bishop, Todd and Shukovsky, Paul. "Seattle Was an Early 9/11 Target, But Plans Were Overruled by Bin Laden, Panel Says." *Seattle Post-Intelligencer.* June 17, 2004. p. A1.

Buildings.com. *New Construction Awards 2003: Seattle Justice Center, Seattle, WA.* 2003. < www.buildings.com/articles/detail.asp?articleID=1583>

Carter, Mike. "Alleged 9-11 Plotter Had Eye On Seattle." *The Seattle Times.* June 17, 2204. p. A1.

City of Seattle. Civic Center Master Plan. 1999. <www.seattle.gov/fleetsfacilities/civiccenter/masterplan/default.htm>

------------ *Seattle Municipal Archives: City Hall Exhibit.* 2000. <www.cityofseattle.net/cityarchives/resources/cityhall/proposed.htm>

Crowley, Walt. "Towering Inferno." *The Seattle Times: Pacific Northwest Magazine.* April 24, 2005. <www.seattletimes.nwsource.com/pacificnw/2005/0424/nowthen.html>

Dickie, Lance. "Demolishing a Sanctuary, Preserving a Church." *The Seattle Times.* May 10, 2002. p. B6.

Dietrich, William. "Meet Your New Central Library." *The Seattle Times: Pacific Northwest Magazine.* April 23, 2004. <www.seattletimes.nwsource.com/paficicnw/2004/0425/cover.html>

Eskenazi, Stuart. "Final Talks Underway: Church's Days Numbered." *The Seattle Times.* March 4, 2006. p. B1.

-------------- "City Hall Cultivates Downtown Housing Boom." *Knight Ridder Tribune Business News.* October 1, 2006. p. 1

Gilmore, Susan. "Methodist Church Can Be Torn Down, Appeals Court Rules." *The Seattle Times.* November 23, 2005. p. B1.

Hise, Sarah. Interview by Maureen Elenga. 2006.

Kossen, Bill. "View of Work Changes Not Far Off the Ground." *The Seattle Times.* April 19, 2001. p. C1.

Lindblom, Mike. "Developer with plans to demolish church backs out ; 1910 sanctuary Church leaders focus on offer that would save building." The Seattle Times. Aug 27, 2006. p. B 5

Long, Pricilla. *William Kenzo Nakamura Receives Medal of Honor for World War II Heroism in a Ceremony on June 21, 2000.* History Link Essay # 2767. 2000. <www.historylink.org>

Metro King County. *King County Courthouse History.* 1998. <www.metrokc.gov/history.html>

Morden, Mark R. Interview by Maureen Elenga. 2006.

Mott, Erik. Interview by Maureen Elenga. 2007.

Mulady, Kathy. "Members Back Deal to Demolish Downtown Church." *Seattle Post-Intelligencer.* June 5, 2006. p. B1.

Nabbefeld, Joe. "$2.2M Refit on 4th Avenue." *Puget Sound Business Journal.* February 19-February 25, 1999. Vol. 19, Iss. 42, p. 3.

Seattle Department of Neighborhoods. Parcel ID 0942001150, 400 Yesler Building. <www.seattle.gov/neighborhoods/preservation/historicresources.htm>

Seattle Times staff reporter. "Remodel to Woo High Tech." *The Seattle Times.* February 18, 2000. p. D8.

Tate, Cassandra. *Young Men's Christian Association (YMCA) of Greater Seattle.* History Link Essay # 3090. 2001. <www.historylink.org>

Tu, Janet I. "Church will "seriously consider" alternate offer: First United Methodist Developer Nitze-Stagen would save sanctuary, provide Belltown site." The Seattle Times. Jul 4, 2006. p. B1

United States Green Building Council. "Seattle Justice Center Team & Process." LEED Certified Project Case Study. 2003. <www.leedcasestudies.usgbc.org>

Washington State Department of Archaeology & Historic Preservation. National Register of Historic Places Inventory Nomination Form. DAHP ID KI00108. Rainier Club. <www.dahp.wa.gov>

Whitely, Peyton. "Walrus Heads Due for Face Lift: Historic Tusked Terra Cottas are Decaying." The Seattle Times. August 10, 1996. p. A1.

RETAIL DISTRICT

Bain, Bill and Tully, Jim. Interview by Maureen Elenga. 2006.

------------ et al. "Rethinking the Courthouse from Inside Out: Designers Seek to Shine Light on the Judicial Process- With Windows." Seattle Daily Journal of Commerce. September 23, 2004. <www.djc.com/news>

Boyer, Tom. "Converting the Cobb: Downtown Office Building Being Turned into Living Spaces." The Seattle Times. September 3, 2005. p. E1.

Brunner, Jim. "City Puts Lid on More Skybridges-For Now." The Seattle Times. May 22, 2001. p. B3.

Cafazzo, Debbie. "Nordstrom Wins a Vote to Reopen Pine Street." The News Tribune. Tacoma, WA. December 20, 1994. p. D1.

Clever, Dick. "Will Neighbors Dwarf Tower? Critics Fear the Effect of 55-Story Building." The Seattle Times. August 20, 1985. p. C1.

Crowley, Walt. Metro Transit Begins Excavating Downtown Seattle Transit Tunnel on March 6, 1987. History Link Essay # 2700. 2006. <www.historylink.org>

Eskenazi, Stuart. "Landmark Hotel to Close: The Camiln Hotel and its Cloud Room Lounge Bought by Redmond-based Trendwest Resorts, Will Reopen as a 100-room Private Vacation Club." The Seattle Times. June 5, 2003. p. B1.

Faget, Paul. "Restructuring a Proud Building." Seattle Daily Journal of Commerce. November 7, 1996. <www.djc.com/special/design96>

Goldsmith, Steven. "Big Convention Center Project Moves a Step Closer to Start." Seattle Post-Intelligencer. August 11, 1998. p. B1.

------------ "Convention Center Gets Green Light: City Council Approves Glass Arch, Expansion." Seattle Post-Intelligencer. April 6, 1999. p. B1.

Gorlick, Arthur. "Jay Jacobs Bankrupt, Closing its 114 Stores: 'All Options Exhausted', Firm's Finance Chief Says." Seattle Post-Intelligencer. September 4, 1999. p. B3.

Higgins, Mark. "One With Development, Voters Say." Seattle Post Intelligencer. March 15, 1995. p. A1.

Hines, Neal O. Denny's Knoll: A History of the Metropolitan Tract of the University of Washington. Seattle: University of Washington Press, 1980.

Kreisman, Lawrence. Metropolitan Tract: a Viewpoints Discovery Tour. Unpublished tour script. Seattle Architecture Foundation, 2004.

McOmber, Martin J. "Council to Decide on Trade Center: Design Worries Fade, OK Likely." The Seattle Times. April 5, 1999. p. B1.

Moriwaki, Lee. "Beam by Beam, Pacific Place Complex Takes Shape; Massive Steel Framework Should be Done in 3 Weeks." The Seattle Times. November 4, 1997. p. F1.

Paramount Theatre. History of the Paramount Theatre. <www.theparamount.com/about.paramount-history.asp>

Rice, Norm and Drago, Jan. "Public Funding for Garage is a Wise City Investment." The Seattle Times. December 25, 1997. p. B5.

Richman, Dan. "Seattle's Sheraton to Expand: Addition Will Make it the City's Largest Hotel, with 1,260 Rooms." Seattle Post-Intelligencer. May 14, 2004. p. C1.

Seattle Times staff reporter. "Elusive Dream: A History of Westlake Plans." The Seattle Times. May 3, 1987. p. B2.

Schaefer, David. "Westlake Mall 'Off and Running': Quarter-century Struggle Apparently Near End." The Seattle Times. June 4, 1986. p. A1.

UNICO Properties. About UNICO: Company Profile. <www.unicoprop.com/about/profile.aspx>

Virgin, Bill. "Things are Looking Up at Convention Center." Seattle Post-Intelligencer. October 18, 1997. p. B3.

Washington State Department of Archaeology & Historic Preservation. National Register of Historic Places Inventory Nomination Form. DAHP ID KI00599. 1411 Fourth Avenue Building. <www.dahp.wa.gov>

Washington State Department of Archaeology & Historic Preservation. National Register of Historic Places Inventory Nomination Form. DAHP ID KI00638. Camlin Hotel. <www.dahp.wa.gov>

Washington State Department of Archaeology & Historic Preservation. National Register of Historic Places Inventory Nomination Form. DAHP ID KI00575. Cobb Building. <www.dahp.wa.gov>

Washington State Department of Archaeology & Historic Preservation. *National Register of Historic Places Inventory Nomination Form*. DAHP ID KI00091. Coliseum Theater. <www.dahp.wa.gov>

Washington State Department of Archaeology & Historic Preservation. *National Register of Historic Places Inventory Nomination Form*. DAHP ID KI00080. Eagles Auditorium Building. <www.dahp.wa.gov>

Washington State Department of Archaeology & Historic Preservation. *National Register of Historic Places Inventory Nomination Form*. DAHP ID KI00735. Medical Dental Building. <www.dahp.wa.gov>

Washington State Department of Archaeology & Historic Preservation. *National Register of Historic Places Inventory Nomination Form*. DAHP ID KI00090. Northern Life Tower. <www.dahp.wa.gov>

Washington State Department of Archaeology & Historic Preservation. *National Register of Historic Places Inventory Nomination Form*. DAHP ID KI00109. Olympic Hotel. <www.dahp.wa.gov>

Washington State Department of Archaeology & Historic Preservation. *National Register of Historic Places Inventory Nomination Form*. DAHP ID KI00242. Paramount Theatre. <www.dahp.wa.gov>

Washington State Department of Archaeology & Historic Preservation. *National Register of Historic Places Inventory Nomination Form*. DAHP ID KI00677. Seabord Building. <www.dahp.wa.gov>

Washington State Department of Archaeology & Historic Preservation. *National Register of Historic Places Inventory Nomination Form*. DAHP ID KI00102. Skinner Building. <www.dahp.wa.gov>

Washington State Department of Archaeology & Historic Preservation. *National Register of Historic Places Inventory Nomination Form*. DAHP ID KI00077. Times Square Building. <www.dahp.wa.gov>

Wilma, David. *Washington State Trade and Convention Center Officially Opens in Seattle on June 23, 1988*. History Link Essay # 2646. 2000. <www.historylink.org>

Wong, Brad. "Sheraton Hopes Bigger Will be Better for All: Expansion Work is to Start Next Month and End by the Spring of 2007." *Seattle Post-Intelligencer*. July 30, 2005. p. D1.

WEST EDGE

Anderson, Rick. "The Ex-Mayor's Booby Prize: The Lusty Lady's Not For Sale, So He and Some Developer Friends Bought the Sky Above." *Seattle Weekly*. March 29, 2006. <www.seattleweekly.com>

Bacon, Sheila. "Where Cash Meets Culture: A Marriage of a Seattle Bank and the

City's Art Museum in One Building Tests the Creativity of a Large Project Team." *Constructor Magazine*. November-December, 2005. <www.constructor.construction.com>

Bolt, Kristen Millares. "Downtown Goes Upscale: Building on Rise, So Are Prices." *Seattle Post-Intelligencer*. January 25, 2006. p. F1.

Craig, Jerry. "Wild Ginger Restaurant Will Spice Up Third Avenue Project." *Seattle Daily Journal of Commerce*. November 10, 1998. <www.djc.com/news>

Bain, Bill and Tulley, Jim. Interviewed by Maureen Elenga. 2006.

Flores, Michele Matassa. "Harbor Steps Project Appealed." *The Seattle Times*. July 14, 1990. p. B6.

------------ "Downtown Harbor Steps Development Moves Ahead." *The Seattle Times*. March 4, 1993. p. C5.

Glackin, William. "Seattle's New Jewel: A Superb Concert Hall." *The Sacramento Bee*. September 16, 1998. p. H1.

Godden, Jean. "The Steps: A Cool Place to Hang Out." *The Seattle Times*. September 11, 1994. p. B1.

King, Marsha. "The Best Designs for a Livable City." *The Seattle Times*. August 4, 1988. p. D1.

Leotta, Kathy and Wolcott, John. "Seattle Art Museum Partners With Washington Mutual." *Northwest Construction*. March 2005. Vol. 8, Iss. 3, p. 25.

Lentz, Florence K. "The Grand Pacific Hotel: In-Again, Out-Again Style." *The Seattle Times*. June 18, 1989. p. B4.

Mahoney, Sally Gene. "55-Story Tower Due Amid Downtown Space Glut." *The Seattle Times*. July 25, 1985. p. A1.

McDaniel, Sylvia. "DSA Puts a Downtown Neighborhood on the 'Edge': An Area between Belltown and Pioneer Square is Being Marketed by the Downtown Seattle Association as the West Edge." *Seattle Daily Journal of Commerce*. August 9, 2001. <www.djc.com/news>

McIntyre, Sean. *The Moore Theatre History*. <www.themore.com/about/moore/asp>

Olson, Sheri. "Seattle Art Museum Unveils Allied Works' Expansion Design." *Architectural Record*. January 1, 2004. Vol. 192, Iss. 1, p. 32.

------------ "Seattle Art Museum Unveils Expansion Design." *Seattle Post-Intelligencer*. November 13, 2003. p. C1.

Paynter, Susan. "Harbor Steps to Build Over a Ribald Past." *Seattle Post-Intelligencer*. March 22, 1993. p. B1.

staff reporter. "Seattle Hotel Group Unveils New Four Seasons Design: An Elegant Downtown High-Rise." *Business Wire*. November 18, 2004. p.1.

Updike, Robin. "An Artist's Symphony of Images: Robert Rauschenberg Leaves a Visual 'Echo' in Benaroya Hall's Lobby." *The Seattle Times*. September 15, 1998. p. F1.

------------- "Urbane Development: At Waterfront Place, Downtown's at Your Door." *The Seattle Times*. September 1, 1985. p. E1.

Virgin, Bill. "Four Seasons Hotel-Condos Combination set for Seattle." *Seattle Post-Intelligencer*. October 23, 2004. p. C1.

Washington State Department of Archaeology & Historic Preservation. *National Register of Historic Places Inventory Nomination Form*. DAHP ID KI00632. Agen Warehouse. <www.dahp.wa.gov>

Washington State Department of Archaeology & Historic Preservation. *National Register of Historic Places Inventory Nomination Form*. DAHP ID KI00248. Colman Building. <www.dahp.wa.gov>

Washington State Department of Archaeology & Historic Preservation. *National Register of Historic Places Inventory Nomination Form*. DAHP ID KI00592. Doyle Building. <www.dahp.wa.gov>

Washington State Department of Archaeology & Historic Preservation. *National Register of Historic Places Inventory Nomination Form*. DAHP ID KI00088. Globe Building, Beebe Building, Hotel Cecil. <www.dahp.wa.gov>

Washington State Department of Archaeology & Historic Preservation. *National Register of Historic Places Inventory Nomination Form*. DAHP ID KI00089. Grand Pacific Hotel. <www.dahp.wa.gov>

Washington State Department of Archaeology & Historic Preservation. *National Register of Historic Places Inventory Nomination Form*. DAHP ID KI00094. Holyoke Building. <www.dahp.wa.gov>

Washington State Department of Archaeology & Historic Preservation. *National Register of Historic Places Inventory Nomination Form*. DAHP ID KI00591. Josephinum Hotel. <www.dahp.wa.gov>

Washington State Department of Archaeology & Historic Preservation. *National Register of Historic Places Inventory Nomination Form*. DAHP ID KI00093. Moore Theater & Hotel. <www.dahp.wa.gov>

Washington State Department of Archaeology & Historic Preservation. *National Register of Historic Places Inventory Nomination Form*. DAHP ID KI00086. National Building. <www.dahp.wa.gov>

Washington State Department of Archaeology & Historic Preservation. *National Register of Historic Places Inventory Nomination Form*. DAHP ID KI00672. Old Federal Office Building. <www.dahp.wa.gov>

Washington State Department of Archaeology & Historic Preservation. *National Register of Historic Places Inventory Nomination Form*. DAHP ID KI00077. Times Square Building. <www.dahp.wa.gov>

Washington State Department of Archaeology & Historic Preservation. *National Register of Historic Places Inventory Nomination Form*. DAHP ID KI00098. United Shopping Tower. <www.dahp.wa.gov>

Washington State Department of Archaeology & Historic Preservation. *National Register of Historic Places Inventory Nomination Form*. DAHP ID KI00086. Western Building. <www.dahp.wa.gov>

Watson, Emmett. "Schell Feels He's Ready For a New Challenge, Once Again." *The Seattle Times*. December 31, 1987. p. E1.

Whalen, Christine. "A Step Up Downtown: Park Opens Tomorrow." *The Seattle Times*. August 17, 1994. p. A1.

Wilma, David. *Benaroya Hall Opens as New Home of Seattle Symphony on September 12, 1998*. 2001. History Link Essay # 3531. <www.historylink.org>

------------ *Seattle Art Museum Opens Downtown on December 5, 1991*. 2001. History Link Essay # 3540. <www.historylink.org>

PIKE PLACE MARKET

Crowley, Walt. *Pike Place Market Thumbnail History*. 2000. History Link Essay # 1602. <www.historylink.org>

Heyamoto, Lisa. "Celebrating Market Heritage: UW Grads Design Pike Place Museum." *The Daily*. University of Washington Student Newspaper. August 18, 1999. <www.archives.thedaily.washington.edu>

Mahoney, Sally Gene. "Condo By the Market Comes With Views of the City and Bay." *The Seattle Times*. May 18, 1986. p. E13.

Morgan, Murray and Shorett, Alice. *The Pike Place Market: People, Politics and Produce*. Seattle: Pacific Search Press, 1982.

Pike Place Market. <www.pikeplacemarket.org>

Seattle Department of Community Development. *A Detailed History of the Corner Market Building & Environs*. Seattle: Department of Community Development, 1975.

Simpson, Mark. "Retirement Housing: Design for a Moving Target." *Seattle Daily Journal of Commerce*. Special, Design '95. <www.djc.com/special/design95>

Snell, Alan. "Market's History Finds a Home at Center." *Seattle Post-Intelligencer*. August 18, 1999. p. B1.

staff reporter. "Pike Place Market." *The Seattle Times*. February 14, 1907. p.3.

staff reporter. "Pike Place Buys First & Pine Building." *Puget Sound Business Journal*. December 9, 2005. <www.bizjournals.com/seattle>

Washington State Department of Archaeology & Historic Preservation. *National Register of Historic Places Inventory Nomination Form*. DAHP ID KI00243. Alaska Trade Building. <www.dahp.wa.gov>

Washington State Department of Archaeology & Historic Preservation. *National Register of Historic Places Inventory Nomination Form*. DAHP ID KI00246. Butterworth Building. <www.dahp.wa.gov>

Washington State Department of Archaeology & Historic Preservation. *National Register of Historic Places Inventory Nomination Form*. DAHP ID DT00054. Pike Place Public Market Historical District. <www.dahp.wa.gov>

Washington State Department of Archaeology & Historic Preservation. *National Register of Historic Places Inventory Nomination Form*. DAHP ID KI00571. US Immigration Building. <www.dahp.wa.gov>

WATERFRONT

Anderson, Rick. "Sea Monster? Activists Angry Over Plans for New Aquarium that Will Block Waterfront Views, Eat Up Open Space, and Cost $200 Million." *Seattle Weekly*. March 8, 2000. <www.seattleweekly.com>

Anderson, Ross. "Dutiful Servant, Brutal Barrier: The Viaduct at a Crossroads." *The Seattle Times Pacific Northwest Magazine*. April 7, 2002. p.1.

Batsell, Jake. "Pier 66 to be Home Base for Cruises to Alaska." *The Seattle Times*. September 15, 1998. p. B1.

Burrows, Alyssa. *William Adair Bugge Assumes Duties as Director of Highways on July 1, 1949*. History Link Essay # 7256. <www.historylink.org>

Dorpat, Paul. *Seattle Central Waterfront Tour*. 2001. History Link Essay # 2481. <www.historylink.org>

------------ *Now & Then: Seattle Waterfront at Northern Pacific Railroad Piers*. 1999. History Link Essay # 2578. <www.historylink.org>

------------ and Wilma, David. *Ivar Haglund Buys Pier 54 on Seattle Waterfront on June 7, 1966*. 2000. History Link Essay # 2509. <www.historylink.org>

Dunn, Paul, et al. "Graceless Waterfront Hotel a Bad Idea." *The Seattle Times*. June 1, 1999. p. B5.

editorial. "View Damage Done: Let Waterfront Hotel Go Ahead." *Seattle Post-Intelligencer*. June 14, 1999. p. A9.

Epes, James. "Central Waterfront Condo Project Inches Closer." *Puget Sound Business Journal*. October 27, 1995. Vol. 16, Iss. 24, Sec. 1. p. 18.

Eskenazi, Stuart. "Park Hailed as Beautiful Future for Site Once Polluted, Neglected: Olympic Sculpture Park, Scheduled to Open Summer 2006." *The Seattle Times*. June 7, 2005. p. B1.

Finneran, Frank, et al. "New Hotel an Attractive Waterfront Asset." *The Seattle Times*. June 11, 1999. p. B5.

Gagnon, Elaine and Michaelsen, Guy. *Viewpoints: The Seattle Waterfront Transformed*. Unpublished tour script. Seattle Architecture Foundation. 2000.

Gangnes, Drew A. "Sculpting a Park Out of a Brown Field: Olympic Sculpture Park Showcases Restorative Engineering" *Seattle Daily Journal of Commerce*. July 17, 2003. <www.djc.com/news>

Hewitt, David. "Designing the Jewel of the Waterfront: Architects Strive to Create a Framework For Economic Success." *Seattle Daily Journal of Commerce*. Special, Bell Street Pier. <www.djc.com/special/maritime>

Jago, Jill. "Perfecting Pier 56: Such Unique Engineering Challenges are Only to be Found in Seattle." *Seattle Daily Journal of Commerce*. November 16, 2000. <www.djc.com/news>

Langston, Jennifer. "Viaduct's Demise Could Turn Waterfront into Urban Oasis: But Vision of Parks and Promenades Comes with a Price." *Seattle Post-Intelligencer*. January 10, 2006. p. A1.

Lilly, Dick. "Waterfront Projects Moving Ahead." *The Seattle Times*. May 4, 1989. p. D3.

Maritime Heritage Network. <www.maritimeheritage.net>

McClary, Daryl C. *Great Northern Tunnel*. 2002. History Link Essay # 4029. <www.historylink.org>

McRoberts, Patrick. *Seattle Aquarium*. 2000. History Link Essay # 2203. <www.historylink.org>

Mulady, Kathy. "Waterfront's Past Can Inspire Plan for Future: Historian Hired by City Shares Discoveries." *Seattle Post-Intelligencer*. April 11, 2005. p. B3.

Nelson, Robert T. "City Announces Its Plans to Buy Waterfront Piers 62 and 63 for $3.8 Million." *The Seattle Times*. February 15, 1989. p. B2.

Peters, Sue. "Sculpting Controversy: SAM's Sculpture Park is on Schedule Despite a Few Bumpy Months." *Seattle Weekly*. January 18, 2006. <www.seattle-weekly.com>

Pope, Charles. "House Ok's $284 Billion Transportation Bill: It Would Repair Seattle Seawall and Unclog Bremerton Ferry Area." *Seattle Post-Intelligencer*. March 11, 2005. p. A3.

Port of Seattle. <www.portseattle.org>

Ramsey, Bruce. "Port Will Sell Acre for New Waterfront Hotel: Marriott Expected to be Completed in August 1998." *Seattle Post-Intelligencer*. October 9, 1996. p. A1.

Robertson, Ian. "Cultivating the Waterfront." *Seattle Post-Intelligencer*. December 24, 2006. p. E1.

Rhodes, Elizabeth. "The Central Seattle Waterfront's First Condominium Project Won't Break Ground." *The Seattle Times*. November 5, 1995. p. G1.

Seattle Art Museum. *Olympic Sculpture Park*. <www.iamsamcampaign.org>

Seattle Aquarium. *New Currents Project Information*. <www.seattleaquarium.org>

Seattle Department of Neighborhoods. Parcel ID 7666202500. Fire Station No. 5. <www.seattle.gov/neighborhoods/preservation/historicresources.htm>

Seattle Parks and Recreation. *Pier 62-63 Piling Replacement and Central Waterfront Park Planning Process*. <www.seattle.gov/parks/maintenance/pier62-63/default.htm>

Shaw, Liz. "Footbridges Make Good Neighbors: Bell Street Project Helps Connect Waterfront to Belltown, Pike Place Market." *Seattle Daily Journal of Commerce*. Special, Bell Street Pier. <www.djc.com/special/maritime>

Solomon, Christopher. "Living on the Edge: Seattle Banks on Residential Development to Reclaim Waterfront." *Chicago Tribune*. May 26, 1996. p. F4.

staff reporter. "If This Trolley Could Talk." *The Seattle Times*. November 10, 2005. p. A1.

Talerico, Teresa. "On the Waterfront Once a No-Man's Land, Seattle Piers Sprout New Life." *Seattle Post-Intelligencer*. May 13, 1998. p.22.

Tobin, Caroline, et al. *Seattle's Waterfront: the Walker's Guide to the History of Elliott Bay*. Seattle: Waterfront Awareness, 1981.

Virgin, Bill. "Pier 70 Developer Sets Sights on Skyway." *Seattle Post-Intelligencer*. November 25, 1999. p. C1.

Washington State Department of Archaeology & Historic Preservation. *National Register of Historic Places Inventory Nomination Form*. DAHP ID KI00129. Washington Street Public Boat Landing Facility. <www.dahp.wa.gov>

Whatcom Museum. *The Moran Brothers*. <www.whatcommuseum.org/pages/archives/moran.htm>

BELLTOWN

Anglin, Bob. "Unrealized Dreams: A Story of the Denny Regrade." *Arcade*. Vol. 2, No. 3 (August-September), 1982. pp. 3-9.

City of Seattle. Board of Public Works Building Permit # 20390. May 8, 1903.

------------ Department of Buildings Permit # 128588. December 10, 1913.

------------ Department of Buildings Building Use Permit # 497653. June 20, 1962.

Compton, Steve. *Compton Lumber Company History.* 2005. Compton Lumber Company. <www.comptonlbr.com/clchist.html>

Dimock, Arthur A. "Preparing the Groundwork for a City: The Regrading of Seattle, Washington." *Transactions of the American Society of Civil Engineers.* Paper No. 1669; 1926. pp. 717-734.

Dorpat, Paul. *Seattle's Belltown Fire of 1910.* 1999. History Link Essay # 4180 <www.historylink.org>

Ellison, Jake. "Belltown Park Goes to the Dogs." *Seattle Post-Intelligencer.* March 8, 2004. p. A1.

Enlow, Clair. "A Watershed Moment on a Belltown Street: Growing Vine Street is Taking Root as Local Artists and Developers Collaborate on a Watershed in a Dense Downtown Neighborhood." *Seattle Daily Journal of Commerce.* February 19, 2003. <www.djc.com/news>

------------- "Growing Vine Street Takes Root at 81 Vine: Seattle's Homegrown Vision of an Urban Future." *Seattle Daily Journal of Commerce.* September 5, 2001. <www.djc.com/news>

Geise, Carolyn. Interviewed by Maureen Elenga, 2006.

Lee, Megan. "H-wood in B-town: Belltown's Historic Film Row." *Belltown Messenger.* July 2005. <www.belltownmessenger.com>

Lorig, Bruce. "Infill Problems? Get Creative: Building Urban Infill Takes Patience and Creativity." *Seattle Daily Journal of Commerce.* August 9, 2001. <www.djc.com/news>

Madsen, Jana J. "New Construction Awards 2003. Specialty Spaces Winner: Fisher Plaza, Seattle, Washington." *Buildings Magazine.* October, 2003. <www.buildings.com>

Olson, Sheri. "Belltown Architecture: The Good, the Bad and the Ugly." *Seattle Post-Intelligencer.* March 19, 2002. p. B1.

------------- "More Closely Resembling a Gallery, These Offices Help the Architects Convey a Refreshing Artistic Sentiment." *Architectural Record.* December 2002. Vol. 190, Iss. 12. p. 136.

Seattle Cinerama Theater. <www.seattlecinerama.com/theater>

Seattle Department of Neighborhoods. *Belltown Neighborhood Plan.* <www.se-attle.gov/neighborhoods/npi/plans/belltown>

Sheridan, Mimi. *Belltown: A Community of Change.* Unpublished tour script. Se-attle Architecture Foundation, 2001.

staff reporter. "Seattle Tower First to Meet City's New Zoning Laws." *Building Design & Construction.* June 2006. Vol. 47, Iss. 7, p. 14.

staff reporter. "Renovated Hotel to House the Poor." *The Seattle Times.* March 7, 1989. p. E3.

staff reporter. "Fisher Plaza's Built-in Technology Features and Timeless Design Recognized with Two Industry Awards." *Business Wire.* December 15, 2003. p.1.

staff reporter. "A Look at the Belltown Lofts." *Seattle Daily Journal of Commerce.* October 2, 2000. <www.djc.com/const>

Steinbrueck, Victor and Nyberg, Folke. *Denny Regrade: An Inventory of Buildings and Urban Design Resources.* Historic Seattle Preservation and Development Au-thority, 1975.

Tarbill, V.V. "Mountain-moving in Seattle." *Harvard Business Review.* July 1930. pp. 482-489.

Trivedi, Kruti. "Tenants Get What they Want, But Lose." *Seattle Post-Intelligencer.* July 14, 1998. p. C1.

Virgin, Bill. "Build More Than Structures North of Downtown." *Seattle Post-Intel-ligencer.* March 12, 1999. p. D1.

Washington State Department of Archaeology & Historic Preservation. *National Register of Historic Places Inventory Nomination Form.* DAHP ID KI00579. Guiry and Schillestad Buildings <www.dahp.wa.gov>

Washington State Department of Archaeology & Historic Preservation. *National Register of Historic Places Inventory Nomination Form.* DAHP ID KI00073. Hull Building. <www.dahp.wa.gov>

SEATTLE CENTER

Adcock, Joe. "Leo K. Does Wrap on Rest of the Rep." *Seattle Post-Intelligencer.* December 10, 1996. p. C1.

Alweg Archives. <www.alweg.com>

Bacon, Sheila. "Marion Oliver McCaw Hall: Multi-faceted Project Transforming Opera Hall into World-Class Facility." *Northwest Construction.* July 20, 2002. Vol. 5, Iss. 7, p. 22.

Bennett, Sam. "Snapshots: A Look at Local Designers and What Makes Them

Tick: Kenichi Nakano, Nakano Associates, LLC" *Seattle Daily Journal of Commerce.* July 14, 1999. <www.djc.com/ae/sn>

Bock, Bill and Feldman, Rich. "The Heart of the Center: It's Time to Renew Our Investment in Seattle's Premier Gathering Place." *The Seattle Times.* June 11, 2006. p. D 1.

Burton, Howard. "Key Arena: Recycling on a Grand Scale." *Seattle Daily Journal of Commerce.* 1995. Special: Design '95. <www.djc.com/special/design95>

Canty, Don. "Mixing Whimsy and Substance, Children's Theatre Building Livens Seattle Center Grounds." *Seattle Post-Intelligencer.* September 23, 1993. p. C1.

Connelly, Joel. "Century 21 Introduced Seattle to Its Future." *Seattle Post-Intelligencer.* April 16, 2002. p. A1.

Crowley, Walt. *Seattle Center Opens Historic Civic Center and Opera House Time Capsule on January 17, 2002.* 2002. History Link Essay # 3673. <www.historylink. org>

Doss, Lori. "Space Needle Renovations Propel Foodservice to New Heights." *Nation's Restaurant News.* February 25, 2002. Vol. 36, Iss. 8. p. 22.

Eskenazi, Stuart. "Former State Rep. Albert Canwell, 95; Knight of the Red Scare Dies, Controversial to the Very End." *The Seattle Times.* April 6, 2002. p. A1.

Experience Music Project. <www.emplive.org/aboutemp>

Hackett, Regina. "City's Art History Began a New Chapter in '62." *Seattle Post-Intelligencer.* April 29, 2002. p. D1.

Howard S. Wright Construction Company. <www.howardswright.com>

Intiman Theatre. *Intiman Theatre History.* <www.intiman.org/about/history>

Lange, Gregg. *Seattle Holds Groundbreaking Ceremony for the Space Needle on April 17, 1961.* 1999. History Link Essay # 722. <www.historylink.org>

Mulady, Kathy. "Saving Memorial Stadium: 2 Take on Challenge to get WWII Tribute Declared a Landmark." *Seattle Post-Intelligencer.* October 30, 2006. p. B1.

----------- "Everett DuPen, 1912-2005: Sculptor's Work Found Around the World. UW Professor Influenced Generations." *Seattle Post-Intelligencer.* June 13, 2005. p. B2.

Nodell, Bobbi. "Pavilion Gets Salutes Where Flags Once Flew: $11.2 Million Fisher Projects Opens at Seattle Center." *The Seattle Times.* September 15, 2002. p. B1.

Olson, Sheri. "Built to Last: Many Century 21 Structures Assumed Public Duties." *Seattle Post-Intelligencer.* P. E1.

------------ "McCaw Hall is a Real Star at Night With Its 30-foot-tall Mesh Scrims Bathed in Colored Light." *Seattle Post-Intelligencer.* June 19, 2003. p. E 12.

Phinney, Susan. "A Fair to Remember: Century 21 Remnants Found New Homes, Where Are They Now?" *Seattle Post-Intelligencer.* April 16, 2002. p. E1.

Ramirez, Marc. "Seattle Center: Forty Years After the World's Fair Spun Dreams of a Grandiose Future, Its Most Enduring Legacy is a Low-key 74-acre Plot of Land That Has Become Our Community Front Porch." *The Seattle Times.* April 14, 2002. p. A1.

Rhodes, Elizabeth. "Amazing Space: Miller/Hull's Woodsy, Stylized Designs Define the Region and Win National Acclaim." *The Seattle Times.* December 15, 2002. p. D1.

Richards, Sarah E. "A 'New' Needle Already Has Ayes: $20 Million Renovation of Landmark Completed." *The Seattle Times.* June 1, 2000. p. B2.

Seattle Center. <www.seattlecenter.org>

Seattle Department of Neighborhoods. Parcel ID 1988200700. Civic Arena/Mercer Arts Arena. <www.seattle.gov/neighborhoods/preservation/historicresources.htm>

Seattle Department of Neighborhoods. Parcel ID 1988200440. Fine Arts Pavilion/Phelps Center. <www.seattle.gov/neighborhoods/preservation/historicresources.htm>

Seattle Department of Neighborhoods. Parcel ID 1988200440. Intiman Playhouse. <www.seattle.gov/neighborhoods/preservation/historicresources.htm>

Seattle Department of Neighborhoods. Parcel ID 1988200440. Kobe Bell. <www.seattle.gov/neighborhoods/preservation/historicresources.htm>

Seattle Department of Neighborhoods. Parcel ID 1985200550. Monorail Office. <www.seattle.gov/neighborhoods/preservation/historicresources.htm>

Seattle Department of Neighborhoods. Parcel ID 1985200185. Nile Temple Building/Seattle Children's Theatre. <www.seattle.gov/neighborhoods/preservation/historicresources.htm>

Seattle Department of Neighborhoods. Parcel ID 1985200003. Northwest Rooms. <www.seattle.gov/neighborhoods/preservation/historicresources.htm>

Seattle Department of Neighborhoods. Parcel ID 1985200003. Seattle Center Pavilion. <www.seattle.gov/neighborhoods/preservation/historicresources.htm>

Seattle Department of Neighborhoods. Parcel ID 1985200130.The Seattle Mural/Mural Amphitheatre. <www.seattle.gov/neighborhoods/preservation/historicresources.htm>

Seattle Department of Neighborhoods. Parcel ID 1985200305. Washington

National Guard Armory. <www.seattle.gov/neighborhoods/preservation/historicresources.htm>

Sheridan, Mimi. *Seattle Center: Change and Continuity in a Community Gathering Place*. Unpublished tour script. The Seattle Architecture Foundation, 1996.

Smith, Cary. "Review: Public Gets Time to Enjoy Seattle Rep's New Theater." *The News Tribune*. December 15, 1996. p. G7.

staff reporter. "Two Kings (Elvis and Tut), A Cycle of Rings: Forty Years of Culture in the Heart of Seattle." *The Seattle Times*. April 14, 2002. p. I 1.

staff reporter. "Allen Gives $4 Million to Seattle Center Projects." *Seattle Post-Intelligencer*. December 24, 1996. p. C3.

staff reporter. "The Debut of Murmuring Mountain Stream." *The Seattle Times*. October 3, 2000. p. B5.

Stein, Alan J. *Century 21: The 1962 Seattle World's Fair, parts 1 &2*. 2000. History Link Essays # 2290 & 2291 <www.historylink.org>

Stripling, Sherry. "Lions and Sonics and Ballerinas, Oh My!" *The Seattle Times*. April 14, 2002. p. J3.

Thorness, Bill. "9/11 Flower Vigil Compost Enriches New York Garden." *Seattle Post-Intelligencer*. October 1, 2002. p. E1.

Wingate, Marty. "Seattle Center's 9/11 Memorial Garden is Rooted in Compassion." *Seattle Post-Intelligencer*. September 5, 2002. p. E 6.

PHOTO CREDITS

All the maps in this book were designed by Sarah Kirk.

FRONTMATTER
p. xii, *Keith Pegorsch,* Courtesy of Cary Stitt
p. 1, *Space Needle,* Roger Williams FAIA

HISTORICAL OVERVIEW
p. xxii, *Yesler's Cookhouse,* University of Washington Libraries, Special Collections Division, UW5695
p. xxv, *Seattle Fire,* University of Washington Libraries, Special Collections, UW34156
p. xxv, *Ruins of Fire,* University of Washington Libraries, Special Collections, UW5951
p. xxvi, *Cooper & Levy Outfitters,* University of Washington Libraries, Special Collections, A. Curtis 26368
p. xxvi, *AYP Fair Grounds,* University of Washington Libraries, Special Collections, UW96
p. xxvii, *Tideflats,* 1898 PEMCO Webster & Stevens Collection, MOHAI, 1983.10.6049.4
p. xxvii, *Smith Tower,* University of Washington Libraries, Special Collections, UW388
p. xxix, *Fair Grounds,* University of Washington Libraries, Special Collections, UW924

PIONEER SQUARE
All photos in this chapter not listed below are by Roger Williams FAIA.
p. 5, *Yesler-Leary,* University of Washington Libraries, Special Collections, UW6229
p. 5, *Reconstruction,* University of Washington Libraries, Special Collections, A. Curtis 26442
p. 8, *Earthquake Damage, 1949,* Seattle Post-Intelligencer Collection, MOHAI, 1986.5.2353
p. 11, *Opera House,* University of Washington Libraries, Special Collections, Warner 66x
p. 12, #4, Courtesy of MITHUN
p. 18, *Occidental Hotel, 1909,* PEMCO Webster & Stevens Collection, MOHAI, 1983.10.8235
p. 19, #15, Courtesy of HEWITT
p. 19, *Butler Block,* University of Washington Libraries, Special Collections, Butler Boyd and Braas 53
p. 19, #16, Dennis Haskell FAIA
p. 19, *Broderick Building Rendering,* Courtesy of Jones & Jones Architects and Landscape Architects LTD
p. 20, #18, Courtesy of Zimmer Gunsul Frasca Architects LLP
p. 21, #19, Dennis Haskell FAIA
p. 24, #23, Dennis Haskell FAIA
p. 25, #25, Dennis Haskell FAIA

p. 25, #26, Dennis Haskell FAIA

p. 26, #28, Dennis Haskell FAIA

p. 27, #29, Dennis Haskell FAIA

p. 30, #35, Courtesy of Jones & Jones Architects and Landscape Architects LTD

p. 30, *Earl Layman Clock,* Dennis Haskell FAIA

p. 32, *Fire Station Rendering,* Courtesy of Weinstein A|U

p. 36, #46, Dennis Haskell FAIA

INTERNATIONAL DISTRICT
All photos in this chapter not listed below are by Dennis Haskell FAIA.

p. 39, *Illustration,* University of Washington Libraries, Special Collections, UW546

p. 41, *Bailey Gatzert School, 1942,* Seattle Post-Intelligencer Collection, MOHAI, PI25525

p. 42, *Anti-Kingdom Demonstration, 1972,* Courtesy of Wing Luke Asian Museum, 1995.044

p. 44, #2, Courtesy of NBBJ

p. 45, #4, Roger Williams FAIA

p. 46, #5, Roger Williams FAIA

p. 48, *Yesler Terrace,* University of Washington Libraries, Special Collections, UW8301

p. 49, #11, Roger Williams FAIA

p. 50, #12, Roger Williams FAIA

p. 51, #14, Courtesy of Les Tonkin, Tonkin/Hoyne/Lokan Architecture & Urban Design

p. 53, #20, Courtesy of Olson Sundberg Kundig Allen Architects

p. 59, #33, Courtesy of NBBJ

FINANCIAL/CIVIC
All photos in this chapter not listed below are by Roger Williams FAIA.

p. 61, *City Hall, ca. 1900,* MOHAI, 2002.3.1493

p. 62, *Public Safety Building, ca. 1951,* Seattle Post-Intelligencer Collection, MOHAI, PI20965

p. 64, #2, Courtesy of Weaver Architects

p. 65, *Arctic Building Detail,* Courtesy Benjamin Benschneider

p. 66, #4, Courtesy of Zimmer Gunsul Frasca Architects LLP

p. 66, #5, Courtesy of The Seattle Public Library

p. 67, *Yesler Mansion, ca. 1900,* MOHAI, 88.33.1

p. 68, #6, Courtesy of NBBJ

p. 69, #7, Courtesy of Kennedy Wilson Properties NW

p. 70, *YMCA Detail,* Photo by Sydney W. Dobson

p. 73, #13, Nic Lehoux, Courtesy of Bassetti | Bohlin Cywinski Jackson

p. 75, #16, Courtesy of NBBJ

p. 75, *Sidebar,* Courtesy of NBBJ

p. 76, #17, Courtesy of Bassetti Architects

RETAIL DISTRICT
All photos in this chapter not listed below are by Roger Williams FAIA.

p. 81, *Territorial University,* University of Washington Libraries, Special Collections, A. Curtis 08317

p. 82, *Fourth & University,* University of Washington Libraries, Special Collections, UW26761z

p. 89, #6, *Monorail & Space Needle, Seattle World's Fair, 1962,* MOHAI, 1994.40.1

p. 90, #8, Courtesy of NBBJ

p. 92, #13, Michelle Mills, Zimmer Gunsul Frasca Architects LLP

p. 93, #14, Courtesy of Harbor Properties, Inc.

p. 93, #15, Courtesy of Unico Properties, LLC

p. 93, *Cobb Building Detail,* Larry Gill Photography

p. 94, #16, Courtesy of Unico Properties, LLC

p. 95, #18, Courtesy of Unico Properties, LLC

p. 96, #19, Courtesy of NBBJ

p. 96, *Metropolitan Theatre, 1956,* Seattle Post-Intelligencer Collection, MOHAI, 1986.5.12648.1

p. 97, #20, Courtesy of Unico Properties, LLC

p. 97, *IBM Building Detail,* Larry Gill Photography

p. 98, #21, Courtesy of Unico Properties, LLC

p. 98, #22, Courtesy of Unico Properties, LLC

p. 99, #24, Courtesy of Callison

p. 100, #25, Courtesy of NBBJ

p. 101, #27, Courtesy of Callison

p. 102, #29, Courtesy of The Westin Hotel

p. 102, *Orpheum Theater,* University of Washington Libraries, Special Collections, Todd 17939

p. 103, #31, Courtesy of NBBJ

p. 104, #32, Courtesy of Callison

p. 104, #33, Courtesy of NBBJ

p. 105, #35, Courtesy of BOORA

p. 106, *Sheraton Hotel Detail,* Courtesy of Sheraton Seattle

p. 106, #36, Courtesy of Sheraton Seattle

p. 107, #38, Courtesy of Union Square LLC

p. 107, #39, Courtesy of NBBJ

p. 109, #41, Larry Gill Photography

p. 109, #42, Dennis Haskell FAIA

p. 109, *Convention Center detail,* Courtesy of Seattle's Convention and Visitors Bureau

p. 110, #43, Courtesy of Callison

p. 110, #44, Courtesy of Callison

p. 112, #46, Courtesy of NBBJ

WEST EDGE

All photos in this chapter not listed below are by Roger Williams FAIA.

p. 115, *Burke Building,* University of Washington Libraries, Special Collections, A. Curtis00093

p. 119, *Postcard Montage,* University of Washington Libraries, Special Collections, UW26756z

p. 122, #8, Dennis Haskell FAIA

p. 123, #10, Photo by Eduardo Calderon, Courtesy of NBBJ

p. 123, #11, © Eduard Hueber / archphoto.com

p. 124, #12, © Jeff Goldberg/Esto

p. 126, #15, Zimmer Gunsul Frasca Architects LLP

p. 127, #17, Courtesy of Weinstein A|U

p. 130, *Colman Building,* University of Washington Libraries, Special Collections, UW5230

p. 130, #23, Bassetti Architects
P. 133, #28, Courtesy of HEWITT
p. 134, #29, Courtesy of HEWITT
p. 134, #30, Dennis Haskell FAIA
p. 135, #31, Courtesy of Bumgardner Architecture + Interiors + Planning
p. 136, #33, Courtesy of Bumgardner Architecture + Interiors + Planning
p. 137, #34, Courtesy of Bumgardner Architecture + Interiors + Planning
p. 138, #36, Courtesy of Seattle Art Museum
p. 139, #37, Courtesy of Seattle Art Museum
p. 141, #40, Courtesy of NBBJ

PIKE PLACE MARKET
All photos in this chapter not listed below are by Roger Williams FAIA.
p. 144, *Pike Place Market,* University of Washington Libraries, Special Collections, UW11161
p. 145, *Pike Place Market,* University of Washington Libraries, Special Collections, UW443
p. 146, *Victor Steinbrueck, 1971,* Seattle Post-Intelligencer Collection, MOHAI, 1986.5.54096.1
p. 154, #11, Courtesy of Bassetti Architects
p. 157, #18, Photo by Dick Busher
p. 159, #23, Courtesy of Bassetti Architects
p. 161, #28, Photo by Jared Polesky
p. 162, #32, Photo by Victor Gardaya

WATERFRONT
All photos in this chapter not listed below are by Roger Williams FAIA.
p. 167, *Prospectors Departing,* University of Washington Libraries, Special Collections, UW7807
p. 167, *Steamer Construction, 1898,* MOHAI, 88.33.217
p. 168, *Railroad Avenue,* University of Washington Libraries, Special Collections, SEA2149
p. 169, *Seawall Construction, 1934,* Seattle Post-Intelligencer Collection, MOHAI, 1986.5.12202.3
p. 172, *SS Idaho, ca. 1900,* MOHAI, SHS229
p. 176, #10, Courtesy of the Seattle Aquarium Society
p. 177, *Tunnel Construction,* University of Washington Libraries, Special Collections, A.Curtis 04387
p. 178, #14, Courtesy of Jensen / Fey Architecture and Planning
p. 179, #16, Courtesy of HEWITT
p. 179, #17, Courtesy of HEWITT
p. 181, #21, Courtesy of HEWITT
p. 182, #22, Photo by Daniel M. Ramas
p. 183, #24, Courtesy of Seattle Art Museum

BELLTOWN
All photos in this chapter not listed below are by Roger Williams FAIA.
p. 185, *Belltown Fire, 1910,* PEMCO Webster & Stevens Collection, MOHAI, 1983.10.8649.1
p. 186, *Denny Hotel,* University of Washington Libraries, Special Collections, Warner 190
p. 189, #3, Michael Shopenn Photography, Courtesy of Weinstein A|U

p. 191, #7, Courtesy of Bumgardner Architecture + Interiors + Planning

p. 192, #9, Courtesy of WJA Design Collaborative / Joel Rogers, joelrogers.com

p. 193, #10, Photo by Maureen R. Elenga

p. 196, #16, Courtesy of HEWITT

p. 198, #20, Courtesy of Driscoll Architects

p. 199, #22, Photo by Benjamin Benschneider

p. 199, *Trianon Ballroom*, MOHAI, 95.6.172

p. 201, #27, Courtesy of Suyama Peterson Deguchi

p. 201, *Suyama Space Interior*, Courtesy of Suyama Peterson Deguchi

p. 204, #33, Courtesy of Weber + Thompson Architects

p. 204, *Crystal Natatorium, ca. 1920*, PEMCO Webster & Stevens Collection, MOHAI, 83.10.769; ca.

p. 205, *Denny Regrade*, University of Washington Libraries, Special Collections, UW4812

p. 208, #39, Courtesy of Jones & Jones Architects & Landscape Architects LTD

p. 208, #40, John Edwards Photography

SEATTLE CENTER
All photos in this chapter not listed below are by Dennis Haskell FAIA._

p. 212, *Future Fair Grounds, 1939*, PEMCO Webster & Stevens Collection, MOHAI, 1983.10.17888

p. 213, *NASA Exhibit*, University of Washington Libraries, Special Collections, UW26766z

p. 221, #11, Photo by Steve Keating Photography

p. 222, *Bubbleator, 1962*, MOHAI, 65.3598.15.35

p. 225, #20, Courtesy of NBBJ

p. 226, #22, Roger Williams FAIA

p. 228, #26, ©Eduard Hueber/archphoto.com, Courtesy of LMN Architects

p. 229, *Civic Auditorium*, University of Washington Libraries, Special Collections, UW14600

INSIDE BACK COVER
Seattle Skyline from Alki Point, Roger Williams FAIA

INDEX

The following is primarily an index of names. The index covers the main text of the book, pages 3-232; places generally are not indexed as the book is arranged by neighborhood. Bold print indicates page number of main entry.

9-1 SPACE NEEDLE

8-20 CONCORD

8-36 FOURTH & BATTERY

7-24 OLYMPIC SCULPTURE PARK

7-22 PIER 70

7-22 PORT OF SEATTLE

7-20 SEATTLE INT'L TRADE CENTER

7-19 THE EDGEWATER

7-16 PIER 66